Praise for *Gen BuY*

"A telling look at how to truly understand and reach a demographic of those that won't be fooled."

—**Andrea Learned, coauthor, *Don't Think Pink***

"Technically savvy (with the world at their keyboards!) and more privileged than previous generations, today's teens and twenty-somethings are the driving force behind our consumer culture. *Gen BuY* is an insightful and fascinating look at how this generation is transforming the retail landscape."

—**Meredith Barnett, founder and CEO, StoreAdore.com**

"An insightful trip into the heart of consumption. I read the book with fascinated horror."

—**Paco Underhill, author, *Why We Buy: The Science of Shopping***

"Technology, research, and psychographics combine to give us an excellent primer on the honesty and transparency needed to motivate and reach the Millennials. Yarrow and O'Donnell merge two streams of thinking to effectively build the case that Gen Yers are savvy to every tactic in the marketing equation. To bring them into our customer base, we must respect them every step of the way."

—**Peter Stringham, chairman and chief executive officer, Young & Rubicam Brands**

"Thanks to extensive research, including one-on-one interviews, focus groups, and a national online survey, the authors offer an astute look at the motivations and influence of these powerful consumers. This enlightening book is a must-read for all who hope to keep their companies relevant and viable."

—***Publishers Weekly***

"Compelling and important reading, especially in today's economy. The headlines tell you the numbers. This book tells you how to make them better."

—Ben Stein, economist, actor, and *New York Times* columnist

"This book is a must-read for anyone who wants to appeal to the most powerful consumers of all time. Yarrow and O'Donnell capture the essence of a generation that, fortunately for retailers, really loves to shop!"

—Tracy Mullin, president and CEO, National Retail Federation

"*Gen BuY* unlocks the secrets of learning about and understanding the youth of America and their purchasing patterns. It's time well spent."

—Keith Crain, chairman, Crain Communications

Gen BuY

Gen BuY

How Tweens, Teens, and Twenty-Somethings Are Revolutionizing Retail

Kit Yarrow

Jayne O'Donnell

JOSSEY-BASS
A Wiley Imprint
www.josseybass.com

Published by Jossey-Bass
A Wiley Imprint
989 Market Street, San Francisco, CA 94103-1741—www.josseybass.com

Readers should be aware that Internet Web sites offered as citations and/or sources for further information may
have changed or disappeared between the time this was written and when it is read.

Jossey-Bass books and products are available through most bookstores. To contact Jossey-Bass directly call our
Customer Care Department within the U.S. at 800-956-7739, outside the U.S. at 317-572-3986, or fax
317-572-4002.

Jossey-Bass also publishes its books in a variety of electronic formats. Some content that appears in print may
not be available in electronic books.

Library of Congress Cataloging-in-Publication Data
Yarrow, Kit, 1958–
    Gen buY : how tweens, teens, and twenty-somethings are revolutionizing retail / Kit Yarrow,
Jayne O'Donnell.—1st ed.
        p. cm.
    Includes bibliographical references and index.
    ISBN 978-0-470-40091-3 (cloth)
    1. Young adult consumers—Attitudes. 2. Generation Y—Attitudes. 3. Marketing. I. O'Donnell, Jayne.
II. Title.
    HF5415.332.Y66Y37 2009
    658.8'340835—dc22
                                                                                    2009017419

Printed in the United States of America

FIRST EDITION

HB Printing   10 9 8 7 6 5 4 3 2 1

Contents

For Russ, my husband and hero
—Kit

For Richard and Cate, with love
—Jayne

Introduction

Generation Y, those born between 1978 and 2000, has overtaken baby boomers in sheer numbers and is poised to do the same with its incomes by 2017. Often called Millennials, these tween, teen, and twenty-somethings have become the nation's tastemakers, holding unprecedented sway over almost every aspect of shopping. From their own—and their parents'—clothing styles, to the design of everything from cars to fitting rooms, and the way we learn about products and evaluate options, Gen Y's stamp is everywhere.

The economic downturn that began in earnest in 2008 has resulted in nothing short of a new American consumer, and Gen Y, always on the forefront, has already mastered the mentality and expertise that other generations will mimic—notably the confidence to demand that retailers bow to their needs, and the ability to capitalize on the expanded purchase, pricing, and customization options made possible by our digital world. Likewise, American consumers are becoming more confident of their power and more skeptical of businesses, more willing to use technology to find bargains, more demanding and exacting in their standards, and paradoxically more eager than ever to find solutions in the products, brands, and retailers that earn their trust. Today's consumers won't be "sold"; they want to be seen, known, and respected—and only those marketers and retailers that invest in relationships through empathy, deep understanding, and insight will prevail.

Gen Yers' confidence, knowledge of and interest in the marketplace, and love of technology have long made them a force to be reckoned with. Today those standards are even higher as Gen Yers, along with the rest of the nation, more carefully consider their purchases and loyalties and search for collaboration and partnerships with brands and retailers.

Marketers that know what works with Gen Y are poised to thrive in the new economy. Gen Yers are the young adults and soon-to-be young adults, feathering their nests, outfitting their interests, and establishing relationships with the brands and retailers that will serve them for years to come. Additionally, all age groups hoping to maximize their dollars in the new economy will cultivate their own versions of Gen Y's confidence and technologically enhanced shopping expertise—out of necessity. What works with Gen Y will increasingly work with all generations—which is why we say they're revolutionizing retail.

There's a sliver of a silver lining for those retailers and marketers catering to Gen Y—though these consumers have tightened their (low-slung) belts along with the rest of the population, they (and the parents and grandparents spending for them) have also kept shopping at a slightly higher rate and most certainly with a greater *joie de vivre*. From Starbucks lattés to plastic surgery, Gen Yers have reduced their spending less than other generations.

Nevertheless, when consumer spending dips, marketers and retailers fight for fewer dollars. But it won't be just the brands with the biggest marketing budgets or splashy ads that will win, especially with young consumers. Courting Gen Y can be cost effective—given the appeal, for example, of text-messaged pitches and counterintuitive approaches—you just need to know how to do it.

That's where we come in. As an acclaimed consumer psychologist, professor, and consultant (Kit), and an award-winning

USA Today retail and automotive reporter (Jayne), we're here to explain all the whys behind the buys of this seemingly fickle generation. Gen Yers demand an authentic relationship based on a deep knowledge of who they are and what makes them tick (and buy). We'll help marketers get there—and give some insights to anyone else who wants to get to know this unique generation better.

Between their own spending and the influence they have on their families and both in-person and virtual friends, Gen Yers' importance to retailers and marketers is undeniable. As they move into their prime adult spending years, the consumer clout of this group will only increase. They are, in short, the future of every company. So we'd best get to know them now.

Here's a peek at a couple of the people we interviewed who underscore our points:

• Isabel, eighteen, of Glen Burnie, Maryland, instant messages her mother frequently with pictures of clothes she wants and the website addresses where her mom can buy them. Isabel says shopping has a "calming effect" on her and she often just "window shops" online when she doesn't have a car to go to the mall. Like many in her generation, closet turnover is part of the equation: "I just always get tired of what I have," she says. Sure, she likes higher-end offerings from BCBG or Ralph Lauren, but she's happy to mix them with discount apparel. "I really do think that clothes can tell a lot about a person, and I love having really nice pieces paired with something I got for $7.99 at Target," she says. "I've always thought if it looks good it doesn't matter where you got it." Like many of the parents of Gen Y, this University of Maryland student's mother is a trusted shopping partner and an active participant in her daughter's acquisitions. Isabel and her generation are less ambivalent about shopping and brands than previous generations were, and they confidently acquire and mix the pieces most likely to satisfy their personal aesthetic and create a persona with impact. After all, people—just like brands—have less time to make an impression these days.

• Lawrence, twenty-five, of Washington, D.C., says his former girlfriend used to say he was a "metrosexual" because he liked to shop almost as much as she did. Lawrence and Gen Y men everywhere are certainly shopping more—and having a better time doing it—but they still have something in common with the more senior members of their gender: they spend little or no time browsing, and they rarely make impulse buys, except in the grocery aisles. Unlike previous generations, however, Lawrence is a typical Gen Yer in that he has as many female friends as guy friends. A chiseled, six-foot-three former clerk for J. Crew, he makes up to 40 percent of his purchases on the Internet, with half of that on eBay. At work, Lawrence says, "Just because someone's above you doesn't mean they're smarter," and in retail he's true to his brands—Sony, Samsung, and Banana Republic—but only if they live up to his high expectations. He's in Internet marketing by day, so he demands a lot of his Internet retailers at night: he wants product and vendor reviews, price comparisons, and speedy connections. And better prices than he's finding at J. Crew these days.

Lawrence and his generation have revolutionized shopping for all of us. Their "prove it to me" attitudes about employers are the same with retailers and brands. For example, those attitudes have contributed to an online shopping experience whose scope of offerings and services mushrooms each year, restaurants that live or die by the comments of consumers—not reviewers—and the ability for anyone to be a retailer through websites such as craigslist and eBay.

We *Have* to Go Shopping

Few women have a permanent excuse to leave work early or skip out on family chores so they can check out the latest at Bloomingdale's or take a trip to T.J. Maxx. But we two authors do have one, because it's our *job* to go shopping—or at least part of it. Admittedly the smallest part, but it's still a pretty sweet way to earn a living. It definitely makes us the envy of our friends—who forget the fact that we actually spend a lot more time interviewing shoppers and retailers, reading research, and analyzing data than we do visiting malls.

Still, there's no denying that we have spent an enormous amount of time in stores, on retail websites, and at hundreds of malls across the country. In the process, we've acquired national reputations as consumer experts—and some pretty nice shoes too.

Research and reporting for our day jobs—such as Kit's consulting work for businesses including General Electric, Del Monte, and Nokia, and Jayne's coverage of issues ranging from the demise and comeback of department stores to declining auto sales to shopaholism—have given us an impressive platform on which to build this book.

We've written *Gen BuY* in a light and lively style, but don't let the fun fool you: our foundation is rock-solid research. We're releasing our proprietary research for the first time in these pages.

Our data and our sources—many of whom are named in the Acknowledgments—include

- Hundreds of one-on-one interviews with young people aged eight to twenty-nine
- Eleven focus groups representing the range of Gen Y ages in ten U.S. cities—Atlanta; Murfreesboro, Tennessee; Westerly, Rhode Island; San Francisco; Columbus, Ohio; Portland, Oregon; Coral Springs, Florida; Wheeling, West Virginia; Chicago; and Columbia, Maryland
- More than two hundred mall and shopping venue visits in over three dozen cities
- A national online survey of more than two thousand shoppers, including a thousand Gen Yers and respondents from every U.S. state
- Scores of interviews with experts

- Insights from the team of young sleuths we've sent out to connect with other Gen Yers
- Review and analysis of hundreds of popular and academic articles, surveys, and studies

But why *shopping*? Well, for starters, shopping is our national collective pastime. In surveys of favorite leisure activities, shopping comes in first or second for nearly every demographic group in the United States. Consumer spending is a central force in the economic health of our nation. Never has this been clearer than it was in the latter part of 2008 when spending stalled and contributed to a recession of dramatic proportions. Though consumers are still shopping, they're even more particular about what they buy, and retailers are reminded of the importance of meeting consumer needs.

What we buy and have is one of the primary ways that we communicate who we are to others in today's speedy and more visual society (which also makes shopping a juicy source of celebrity—and community—gossip). It's a way to explore roles, connect with others, and socialize. Everything from the way we bling, to where we shop, to what we *don't* buy is a way to define ourselves. Similarly, what a generation buys and how it shops offers us deep insights into that group of people and, by comparison or contrast, a way for all of us to see ourselves more clearly.

Shopping is pervasive. Internationally, 73 percent of people say they shop recreationally, and, believe it or not, that figure is slightly lower in the United States—68 percent.[1] And though we may think we've just recently become a nation of shoppers, the truth is that shopping is, and always has been, an important part of every culture from the time that cultures first began. Be it selecting a particular brand of soda from a vending machine, picking up a pair of flip-flops while hanging out at the mall, planning and purchasing a new car or even electing a candidate to office—we all make brand and product selections every day.

From eighteen-year-old Robert's delight with a brand of sneakers he feels are *totally* him to twenty-seven-year-old Anna's angst at her inability to resist buying new clothes, shopping and buying are hugely emotional and deeply psychological. Through shopping and buying, we can see clearly into the minds, hearts, and lives of individuals, cultures, and generations. After all, possessions have the ability to hold such great meaning that even mummies are found buried with favorite and symbolic objects.

The tweens, teens, and twenty-somethings that are the focus of this book are upstaging baby boomers, who are often their parents, at the mall. For example, the average teen visits the mall four times a month and stays over ninety minutes per visit (nearly one full trip and twenty minutes longer than the average shopper). In January 2009, when most retailers were posting double-digit sales declines, several retailers that cater to teens outperformed even Wal-Mart.

U.S. households with at least one member of Gen Y represent the third largest buying group in this country. These households account for 37 percent of total dollars spent, 31 percent of total trips, and 15 percent more dollars spent than the average household.[2] Gen Yers are enthusiastic shoppers—and there are more of them than any other generation. At nearly eighty-four million, they are the largest segment of the U.S. population (boomers account for seventy-eight million). Today over 26 percent of American *adults* are Gen Yers.[3] The most conservative estimates of Gen Y spending exceed $200 billion a year, and this generation's spending will top $10 trillion in its lifetime.[4]

Not only are they big spenders themselves, but they hold great sway over what their mothers and fathers buy. And as the most powerful trendsetters in our increasingly youth- and technology-oriented society, their influence is pervasive. In other words, the economic impact of Gen Yers extends well beyond their own financial means—they're influencing every generation, whether others realize it or not.

While few baby boomers could ever have imagined their parents choosing a car or clothes that their kids steered them to (case in point: the leisure suits kids weren't able to stop their parents from buying!), Gen Y is influencing at least half of auto purchases and 90 percent of the apparel buys in their homes, according to 2007 research conducted for the digital marketing agency Resource Interactive.[5] At last, a partial explanation for all the skinny, low-cut jeans on not-so-skinny midlife moms.

So why is shopping so central for our well-educated, highly connected society, and especially its youth? Just as it is for their parents—but even more so—shopping serves as a mental vacation, a social activity, and a conversation starter for Gen Y. And the opportunities for this sort of escape abound as shopping centers and malls are ever more integrated into their lives. Against that backdrop, all those "things" young people acquire on their shopping jaunts become the currency of their conversation and a way to tell others who they are.

Despite (or perhaps because of) all of those reasons, it bears noting here that our book is intended to be neither a celebration nor a condemnation of consumerism, but rather a deep dive into the motivations and influences of this powerful generation of consumers. Along with helping retailers and other marketers understand—and sell to—Gen Y, we think this book will also help everyone understand why they buy and how to be better shoppers.

Insights in the Bag

Gen BuY helps explain how finding yourself, snagging a bargain, and falling in love all fit together at the mall (real or virtual). We describe how society has shaped this generation, and consequently their shopping behavior—and then, the tremendous impact Millennials in turn have had on society and the way that all Americans shop. From mobile shopping to hybrid cars, custom Keds to fast fashion, not to mention the institution of advertising now struggling to reinvent itself—it's a whole new world, and Gen Yers helped make it.

We also detail things like how technology, the Gen Y connector, has influenced the psychology of young adults (and made online shopping better for the rest of us). And how indulgent parents have set great expectations for Gen Yers and also left many dissatisfied with their choices—a dissatisfaction sometimes eased by a trip to the mall.

Retailers have responded to their buying power, shorter attention spans, optimism, individuality, and impulsive natures with great new options for all of us. Consider, for starters, the eagerness of the world's foremost designers to sell their apparel for as little as $19.99 at Target. From consumer-generated video ads to text promotions to phenomena like www.zebo.com, where young people can chronicle how many of everything they own, we investigate how branding and marketing messages are received by this group.

In *Gen BuY*, Kit and Jayne use their own proprietary research—and the best of that provided by other leading experts in the field—to help explain the psychological forces driving today's most sought-after consumers and their far-reaching impact on shoppers of all ages. All professional experts are quoted using their full names and titles, but our Gen Yers are quoted using pseudonyms because many preferred it that way, and we didn't want to compromise anyone's privacy.

Each chapter builds on the information and anecdotes in the previous one, but our book is written in a way that allows the reader to jump around if his or her interest lies more in retail strategies, sexually suggestive advertising, or, say, what's up with that shop-happy tween at home.

Here's a chapter-by-chapter look at what *Gen BuY* will cover:

- Chapter 1: The whos and whys of Gen Y explained, with an emphasis on how societal shifts contributed to a generation that's powerfully connected to shopping

- Chapter 2: The unique shopping and buying behaviors of this generation, especially the what, where, and how of their shopping
- Chapter 3: The whys behind the buys—the psychological secrets behind the purchases we *all* make, with a drill-down on Gen Y's whys
- Chapter 4: The lives, minds, and hearts of today's tweens, teens, and twenty-somethings—the key to understanding their needs and wants and shopping styles and how to communicate with them
- Chapter 5: How and why guys and gals shop differently, how shifting gender roles are affecting who buys what when and turning age-old courtship rules upside down, and the inside scoop on all that sex!
- Chapter 6: Gen Y's tremendous influence in retail, be it through their parents, the tastes and shopping styles of society, or the ways that their demands have transformed in-store and online retail—for everyone
- Chapter 7: What savvy marketers and retailers are doing that has captured the powerful purchasing power of Gen Y
- Chapter 8: Insights from some of the cleverest people we met while researching this book

So get ready—we're going *shopping*!

Gen BuY

1

GEN Y IS FROM MERCURY

Courtney, twenty-eight, a new attorney living in Washington, D.C., had a "destination wedding" in 2007 and was delighted that her parents were able to stay for the honeymoon. Her five bridesmaids (all friends from college) and their husbands also stuck around. Courtney had been a bridesmaid in each of their weddings, which had taken place in locations scattered around the globe over the past three years, and her parents and brother had attended each of those weddings as well. Courtney and her mom, who lives across the country in San Francisco, planned every aspect of the wedding together— from the custom M&M's to Dad's outfit. They emailed ideas, web addresses, and photos to each other almost daily, and both said with big grins and giggles that it was "so much fun!" Friends and family could follow along with the wedding plans on the couple's website and view photos and videos immediately following the ceremony. Gift selection was a snap thanks to a coordinated online registry, and wrapping and shipping was done in a click.

Courtney's egalitarian friendship with her parents and her enduring pack of friends from college are part of what makes this generation different. So is the technical ease with which they communicate and shop, their comfort navigating the globe and different cultures, and even their delight in (and willingness to spend big bucks for) customized M&M's.

This generation, the product of a transformed world, is to previous generations as man is to woman and Mars is to Venus. Which is to say: basically the same, but entirely different. Generation Y is unquestionably unique, and some say potentially one of the most powerful and influential generations ever.

Gen Y is diverse, adaptive, and confident. Fewer than two-thirds of them are white, over 25 percent are raised in single parent households, and three-quarters have working moms. Their generation's size—almost eighty-four million members—helps give them unprecedented influence; their confidence and their ability to connect with others guarantee it.

Raised in an era packed with cultural and economic shifts, technological wizardry, and the "self-esteem movement"—to name just a few of the major changes—it's no wonder Gen Yers are motivated by different messages, want different products, and relate to each other, marketers, and retailers differently from previous generations.

Before we spill the beans: want to test your knowledge of the world of Generation Y? Take our quiz.

Kit and Jayne's True and False YQ Quiz

1. Email is the preferred form of digital communication for teenagers.
   False. A 2008 study by the Pew Research Center's Internet & American Life Project showed that email is teens' least favorite form of digital communication, with only 16 percent of teens using email daily, compared with 36 percent texting daily and 29 percent sending instant messages every day.[1]

2. Working teens are likely to have greater discretionary spending power than their parents.
   True. According to Harrison Group's *Teens in the Marketplace Report*, working teens pocket an average of $597 each month—and without those pesky nondiscretionary

expenses like mortgage payments, on average they end up with more spending money than their parents.[2]

3. Teen girls are more likely than teen boys to have online friends that they've never met in person.
False. According to the "Marketing to Teens and Tweens" study by EPM Communications, boys ages fifteen to seventeen were more likely than any other age or gender group to have friends they've never met in the flesh, at 47 percent. In the tween category, 29 percent of boys ages twelve to fourteen and 22 percent of girls twelve to fourteen had friends they know only in the virtual world.[3]

4. More people watched Sarah Palin's appearance on *Saturday Night Live* online than on TV.
True. While fifteen million people watched on TV, even more watched on NBC.com, YouTube, Yahoo, MySpace, and Hulu.[4]

5. The U.S. Department of Labor estimates that today's learners will have nine to ten jobs by the age of thirty-eight.
False. They're expected to have ten to fourteen jobs by the age of thirty-eight.[5]

6. "Omg jk!! LOL u kno ily. nyway whatchu doen 2nite? I g2g 2 din wit da rents but bbl. u hangen out?" (a text sent to Irina, seventeen) translates to: "Oh my God I'm just kidding! Laughing out loud. You know I love you. Anyway, what are you doing tonight? I have to go to dinner with my parents but I'll be back later. Are you hanging out?"
True.

7. Eighteen- to twenty-five-year-olds are more likely than any other adult group to think that technology makes people lazy.
True. Eighty-four percent of eighteen- to twenty-five-year-olds said technology makes people lazier, compared with 67

percent of adults over twenty-six. They were also slightly more likely to believe that technology was responsible for isolation and time wasting. And almost three-fourths of the age group claims their generation posts excessive personal information on the Internet.[6]

8. Gen Yers may love their computers, but when it comes to entertainment nothing beats the television.
   False. According to Deloitte, three-quarters of fourteen- to twenty-five-year-olds view their computer as more of an entertainment device than their television. The 2009 report also found that 59 percent of Gen Yers use their mobile phone as an entertainment device (versus 33 percent of all consumers).[7]

9. A majority of young adults see their generation as unique.
   True. A 2007 Pew Research Center for the People and the Press survey showed 68 percent of eighteen- to twenty-five-year-olds found their generation to be unique and distinct from all others.[8] According to a 2008 Harris Interactive survey of nearly four thousand Americans aged twenty-one to eighty-three, Gen Y is seen as the most "self-indulgent" generation, Gen X as the most "innovative," boomers as most "productive," and our eldest generation as most "admired."[9]

10. When asked how they spend their day, average teens will tell you that nearly half of their activities are driven by technology.
    True. Four out of their five top activities involve technology. As of November 2008, the average teen expects to spend over $300 on consumer electronics in the next six months, according to the Consumer Electronics Association.[10]

11. The number of text messages sent and received each day exceeds the population of the earth.

True.[11] 'Nuff said.

12. Twitter is the chirp of a small bird and has nothing to do with technology.

    False. Twitter is a free microblogging service through which users can send and read others' major and not-so-major updates on their lives. The site, which once seemed to specialize in mindless minutiae ("I'm eating a really good sandwich!"), has now expanded so that brands, retailers, celebrities, and politicians regularly use Twitter to get their messages out. Flight cancellations, new product arrivals, job availabilities, and peanut salmonella updates can all be found on Twitter. Launched in 2006, Twitter grew by over 1,382 percent between February 2008 and February 2009. In February 2009 there were 9.8 million unique visitors.[12]

13. A new blog is created nearly every second of every day.

    False. Make that over two new blogs created every second of every day, and 1.6 million posts are made on existing blogs each day.[13]

14. If you started today, it would take you just under a year to view all the material on YouTube.

    False. It would take you over four hundred years.[14]

How'd you do? If you got nine or more right, we're impressed. And because you're the kind of person who craves information, we've got some whys behind those facts coming up, so read on. Eight or fewer? In the spirit of Gen Y, you get a trophy too, but you might also want to keep reading—you need to know Y, and you've got some catching up to do.

The Two Greatest Influences

Though some may point to social or political events such as the Columbine shootings, the Bill Clinton–Monica Lewinsky scandal, the fall of the Soviet Union, and even the death of

Princess Diana as the forces that have shaped Gen Y, there are two profoundly influential factors that outweigh the rest: *their adoring parents* and *the digital world*.

Adoring Parents

Gen Y children are considered to be the most wanted children of all time, and they've grown up in an era of exploding interest in and knowledge about child development and psychology. Unlike previous generations of parents—who certainly wanted and loved their children, but also saw them as responsibilities—or even earlier generations, who felt the same way but saw them as potential laborers—today's parents prize their children as more equal and central members of the household. Additionally, no society in history has had a greater focus on, interest in, and understanding of the child.

And even though nearly half of Gen Y children have divorced parents, and one-third come from single-parent households, those parents still spent more focused time with their Gen Y kids than any previous generation. The greater attention and parental involvement of fathers as central figures in parenting has also had a great effect on the sense of Gen Yers that they are important and central. Additionally, technology brings families even closer, thanks to the frequent contact between kids and parents that cell phones afford.

Gen Y parents have been criticized for coddling, for impairing their child's independence by hovering like helicopters, for being enmeshed in or overly dependent on their kid's approval. These characteristics are generally more true of this generation than of previous ones, and in the course of our research we certainly did see examples of just the sort of behavior that's inspired these descriptions (including moms who know who's asking whom to the prom before their kids do), and also *plenty* of parents dependent on their kids' success for their own egos. But what we also saw were "helicopters" who might also have been described as simply interested, involved parents; "coddlers" who could have been called warm, nurturing parents; and "overly dependent parents" who might have been seen as folks who value their kid's minds and opinions.

"My parents are super homey," says nineteen-year-old Brendan, a member of our Portland focus group. "My mom is the chillest of all our parents; she trusts me." Of course, one Portland participant spoke for many when he described some moms as "grown-up high school girls" or "too concerned about their image. They need you to get on honor roll so they can tell their friends 'my kid got on the honor roll.'"

We found it most helpful to view Gen Y parents on a normally distributed curve, with those clearly overinvolved, coddling helicopters at one end; some relatively disengaged parents at the other end; and most of the group in the middle—registering more kid-centric than the last generation of parents, but not 'coptering coddlers either.

Being a wanted kid in a child-centered household adds to your clout, of course. Gen Y households are the most egalitarian of all time, and Gen Y parents tend to be nonauthoritarian and to value their friendships with their kids. This is one of the primary reasons behind Gen Y's confidence and power—and also helps to explain how Gen Yers were able to earn their impressive shopping stripes so young and have such a tremendous impact on the purchasing decisions of older generations.

Their Digital World

The second most important factor that's shaped the uniqueness of this generation is their enmeshment with technology and their ability to harness the power of the Internet. This sophistication has increased their influence in their households, added a pedal-to-the-metal element to their cognitive and social styles, reinforced and equipped a team mentality, and empowered them.

Household Clout. In addition to their kid-centric clout, Gen Yers typically provide in-house tech support for their parents, which has reinforced their stature as equals—or even superiors, at least in the IT department. It's also made them *the* great force to be reckoned with by electronics marketers. When they have prized knowledge and expertise, it becomes pretty hard to discount the thoughts and abilities of a kid. Previous generations had to pretend or humor their kids ("Let's frame your Picasso!"), but in the case of this generation, their intuitive ease with technology and their ability to adapt to technological shifts is a genuine asset to any family. Having never experienced a world without computers, the Internet, cell phones, and digital cameras, Gen Yers are free of anxiety and full of playfulness when they interact with the Internet and technology of all sorts. This makes learning easier for them than it is for all but the most tech-savvy parents.

Seeing as we all know better than to tick off the techies, the glow of this expertise has contributed to the confidence of this generation. It also means that kids have more of a vote and more power in family decision making. That includes far more than technology and extends to things like vacation destinations, cars, and Dad's outfits too. To give you a sense of the pervasiveness of these junior in-house techies, according to a survey of over six thousand of our youngest Gen Yers—the eight- to fourteen-year-olds—most say that they have "online chores" that include sharing pictures with relatives (38 percent) and getting driving directions (35 percent), and a few even help with income tax returns (14 percent).[15]

Speed, Power, and Self-Reliance. Put simply, they want what they want when they want it. As the first generation raised from day one under the influence of the Internet, the world, as they know it, means speed; multitasking; instant answers; always available friends, parents, teachers, and experts; a connection to others that defies geography and hierarchy; less necessity for face-to-face (or voice-to-voice) human interaction; and free access to information for everyone.

Kit noticed, during a recent guest lecture at UC Berkeley, that at least half of her students were typing. A quick cruise around the room revealed about half of those typists were looking up her articles, an international student was checking a word definition, and the rest were on Facebook. In other words: multitasking, available to their friends no matter where they were, and instantly accessing free information.

"They are a very different generation," says Jenny Floren, founder and CEO of Experience, which helps recruits students from nearly four thousand colleges and universities for its business clients. Because they've been online often since they were toddlers, they process information very differently. "That's where their friends are, where they shop, and where they study," says Floren. "In many regards, being in person is the same as being online."

The digital world that Gen Y inhabits is credited with shortening their attention spans, increasing their need for immediate gratification, and helping them to become super speedy at processing visual data—Gen Yers live in a faster world than anything previous generations have known.

Gen Yers are also proactive and empowered when it comes to information. They seek out only the information that's relevant (or that they perceive to be relevant) to them. Previous generations, unaided by the power of search engines, acquired information in a more passive way. For example, most boomers wouldn't have had a way to learn more about a physical symptom or health malady—those answers were in the hands of physicians and households lucky enough to have a set of encyclopedias. There was no such thing as an instant answer. Not to mention that the answers available had been edited and vetted prior to publication. So when we say "empowered" we truly do mean power. From the information (though not the wisdom) of a physician to the latest Van's hoodie available to a skater living 350 miles from a mall, Gen Yers have known only one world—one in which they can get what they want when they want it.

Consequently, there has been an important social shift toward a mentality of self-reliance and the flattened hierarchy that accompanies democratized information. Contributing to this is a disappointment in social institutions ranging from our schools and religious institutions to our political leaders and even athletes and celebrities—all widely (and sometimes hysterically) reported through an increasingly competitive media. Businesses, in particular, have taken a big hit in confidence. Once the most likely villain in the movies was a Communist, monster, or alien—today it's a white businessman.

My Posse. Gen Yers, already trained in school to work as teams, have embraced technology as a way to facilitate group connections. They can and do unite with likeminded (physical) strangers from around the world to champion causes, play computer games such as World of Warcraft, stay in touch with school and business friends and colleagues indefinitely through social networking sites such as LinkedIn and Facebook, and text their moms' group about sales at Baby Gap. Whatever the interest, connections—already the social DNA of Gen Y—are enabled through technology. Gen Yers between thirteen and twenty-four tell an average of eighteen people about a website or TV show that they enjoy, whereas older adults tell an average of only ten people.[16]

Although older folks sometimes struggle to learn and adapt to technological advances, they've also had the opportunity to weigh consequences and compare outcomes. Some of the anxiety we've seen in older generations regarding Gen Y is due, in part, to their fear that Gen Y won't know what they're missing or losing by relying on technology. Will all that speed and multitasking result in superficiality? Will Gen Yers have the patience to think deeply about things? Will online relating replace or diminish intimacy? Will shorthand communication, like text messaging and Twittering, and the highly portable nature of technology result in social rudeness (like loud cell phone chats in elevators) and poor formal writing and communication skills?

We all know the answer to the social rudeness question—and it's certainly not just the younger members of our community who are at fault. As to the other questions, some of the answer resides in the asker: it's a time-honored tradition of every senior generation to ask, "What's with these kids?" And though our Gen Yers shared some serious struggles and concerns—many of which are related to technology and even more to the high expectations they have for themselves and the world—we found overall that the kids are alright. They'll have their own set of problems to solve, just as every generation before them, but they'll also have powerful gifts and new tools to help—namely confidence, teamwork, technology, and their desire to make a positive contribution to the world.

The Big Four Gen Y Characteristics

Although the kid-centricity of our society and our digital world have been the two most profound factors influencing this generation, other influences include: a reign of relative economic prosperity that lasted until the economic meltdown of 2008, globalization, the September 11, 2001, attacks, and the sheer volume of information (often unedited, unexplained, and uncensored) available anytime and anywhere.

So what's the result? What makes this generation different from the rest?

Four characteristics stand out: their confidence; their connectedness to each other, their parents, and the world; their management of an overwhelming array of choices; and their warp-speed living and all that it entails.

Confidence

Sure, we've heard others call Gen Yers narcissistic, entitled, arrogant, and inflated. We think that for the most part, or at least for the majority in the middle, they're simply, well, confident—and often charmingly optimistic as a result.

There are many reasons for this boosted level of confidence, and there's genuine support for our reasoning that this group is not simply puffed up with ego, but truly empowered. Let us count the ways.

In addition to being wanted and doted on by parents, they've been told they were special by everyone from Mr. Rogers to their grade school tutors. Kate Perry, twenty-eight, of San Ramon, California, remembers how her mother convinced her to wear a helmet when bicycling: "She told me that the government required it because my brain was so special it should be protected."

The self-esteem movement in our schools made everyone a winner. Garrison Keillor's statistically impossible Lake Wobegon exists across America today—every child is above average (at least in their parents' eyes). Grade inflation has kept pace with ego inflation: the average high school graduate today has a grade point average of nearly 3.0, and many high schools have twenty-five to forty valedictorians a year. Forty-seven percent of college freshmen enrolled in 2005 had an A-equivalent grade point average, compared with 20 percent in 1970.[17] Though psychologists and sociologists often point to the problems associated with fluffed-up feedback—most notably that when these kids start working in a competitive global economy their feedback isn't likely to get much fluffing—the self-esteem movement has also lessened competition among Gen Yers, who are truly team players, and has genuinely boosted their self-confidence.

Their ability to "find out for themselves" and share ideas on the Internet has empowered them. Gen Yers, no question, believe in themselves and their power to find solutions. And they believe in the power of their opinions. More than any other generation they blog about their experiences, interests, and opinions and rate everything from pedicures to professors online. Through these venues, they use their power to effect social change, make or break retailers, and popularize (and occasionally destroy) other people.

The Twitter campaign of a few young moms brought down a Motrin ad in less than a weekend. The ad's attempt to connect with moms over the physical pain associated with carrying a baby around hit a sour note with a blogger, who sent a tweet to her 1,018 followers. By the next day a blogger had collected tweets from offended moms and created a nine-minute YouTube video that was viewed twenty-one thousand times that weekend. By that Sunday night, McNeil Consumer Healthcare had taken down their Motrin.com site—and the offending ad.[18]

Gen Yers can get backup in a snap, and they use it to embolden themselves and to effect change. Through their natural ease at forming teams and with their ability to connect online, they're empowered and consequently more confident about themselves and the value of their opinions. If you want to get your way, "we all feel" has more of a punch than a single opinion.

Along with their doting parents and the power of the Internet, they benefit from the fact that today's society clearly values what belongs to their generation alone: youth. There has simply never been a time when simply being young has held such value. Once upon a time we had wise old men (okay, gender roles have expanded too); today, older isn't wiser—it's, umm, just old. Jessie, on the eve of her nineteenth birthday, summed it up this way: "I'm not very excited about this birthday. Eighteen was big, next year I'll be twenty, and then I'll be in my twenties!! Then twenty-one and I'll be legal. Then, after that, it's all downhill."

Beth Teitell, author of the book *Drinking Problems at the Fountain of Youth*[19], describes what she says has become a societal obsession with all things youthful. According to Teitell, "when society changed to a service economy it became more about the visual." Add to that the influence of the Internet, and now more than ever, "people get to know you based on how you appear. "There are no stores called Forever 41 or Forever 51," says Teitell. "We value youth over anything else."

Wrapping up the reasons, Gen Y enjoys the confidence that comes with a more egalitarian workplace. Many wrongly assume that Gen Y's insistence on different work values and their resilience in the face of the more traditional demands of the workplace (like putting in eleven-hour days, or doing what their bosses say without question) have *created* this shift. In fact, every generation of workers for over a hundred years has enjoyed a more empowered workforce—though Gen Y is undoubtedly speeding it along a bit faster than previous generations were able to. Just as parents have benefited from a wealth of new knowledge on child-rearing, the workplace has also invested a great deal of energy over the past twenty years in understanding how to motivate and inspire their workforce. Gen Y is bolstered and empowered by employers that *want* to understand them.

Between parenting, workplace changes, a youth-oriented society, the power of the posse, and all the Internet has to offer, it's no wonder that the 2008–2009 Horatio Alger Association's *The State of Our Nation's Youth* found that 62 percent of Gen Y college students say they are "very confident" about achieving their own goals in life. Add in the 31 percent that said "fairly confident," and you've got an overwhelmingly confident generation.[20]

Connection

This is a generation that knows how to cultivate a group. They're inclusive and team-oriented, and they harness technology to get and stay connected to each other. From parent-coordinated play dates to group dating in college, Gen Yers form families around their interests and in the workplace.

Though there are an abundance of stories about generational struggles in the workplace, in our research we found that, at least on an individual level, Gen Yers and boomers in particular seem to appreciate each other. Millennials are traditional in many of the same ways boomers are—and like boomers, they tend to be hard working, generally optimistic, and genial. People who study generational difference in the workplace—like Kate

Perry, who works in human resources at Chevron and is active in their XYZ Group—point out one other unifying similarity: both generations are change agents at heart. According to Perry, a Gen Yer herself, "Boomers identify with Yers because they had to deal with the same things we did. Boomers were after change—they brought us maternity leave, flex time, a lot of changes. We feel the same way, we want change."

The primary difference seems to be the less competitive nature of Gen Yers. Boomers—fueled by a scarcity of jobs and often raised by parents who were children close enough to the Depression to fear poverty—were taught to be competitive with each other, which makes team-building less instinctive. Perry recalls how her boomer manager had to explain to her what she means when she says she's going to get coffee: "My boss had to tell me, 'When I say I'm going to Starbucks that means, what can I bring you?' but to me, when I say I'm going to Starbucks that means that I'm looking for a group of people to go with me."

Off the job, Gen Yers are also collaborative and team-oriented. Even in their dating. To the confusion of many of their boomer parents, when Gen Yers are asked if they're dating anyone, most honestly reply "no" (as opposed to previous generations who evasively replied "no" to get out of telling their parents about their new boyfriends or girlfriends). Rather than the old "ask out, pick up, dinner and a movie" routine of yesteryear, Gen Yers are famous for hanging out in groups in which the possibility (or actuality) of romance exists. And they're also perhaps a bit infamous for "hooking up"—which we'll explore more fully in Chapter Five.

There's no place more famous for connecting than the Internet, and we're not just talking about the explosive popularity of dating sites like Match.com and eHarmony (one in eight couples married in the United States in 2008 met online).[21] From diet buddies on SparkPeople to the unique cat language that's sprung into our vocabularies from Gen Y enthusiasts on icanhascheezburger.com, Gen Y forms communities, teams, and groups online. Consider the difference between Gen X and Gen Y moms—both groups use the Internet for research and to connect with other young moms, but Gen Y moms are nearly twice as likely to own and read blogs than Gen X moms. Anderson Analytics' *2009 U.S. College Student Report* indicates that students are four times more likely to blog than other online adults, and women students are three times more likely to maintain a blog than men are.[22]

The cornerstone of Gen Y's ability to work well in teams and connect with each other is their tolerance—even celebration— of differences and their comfort with diversity. They are an increasingly diverse group themselves; nonwhites and Latinos account for more than 40 percent of the under-twenty-five population, and 20 percent of Gen Y parents are immigrants. In February 2009, only two of the top ten most highly regarded public personalities in the Davie-Brown Index, which uses surveys to quantify the marketing appeal of celebrities, were white. Gen Y is part of a globalized world—more connected with, interested in, and affected by their counterparts around the globe. Certainly, Gen Y women aren't finding the gender struggles their mothers encountered, though surveys of Gen Y girls and women suggest that gender discrimination is far from resolved. Nevertheless, women now earn 57 percent of all bachelor's degrees, 58 percent of all master's degrees, and nearly 50 percent of law and medical degrees.[23]

Choice

Gen Y is the most educated, affluent, diverse population the United States has ever seen. They belong to a global world and have been told they can do anything by parents and a society that loves them. Their options for dates, mates, jobs, and handbags have exploded with the Internet and portable, digital technology. As Jen, twenty-six, of Atlanta told us, "I found my job, my boyfriend and my apartment on the Internet, oh and I get my clothes there too."

Tom, a fifty-nine-year-old father from McLean, Virginia, notes just how much things have changed. His twenty-year-old daughter Marcy wanted to do something "exciting" recently, so she signed up for a six-week stint teaching English as a volunteer in northern Thailand. The photo she emailed home was of herself preparing to bungee jump off a bridge over the Mekong River, "proving that a new generation of daughters has developed even better methods of terrifying their parents," says Tom.

Though abundant choice has been inspiring to many Gen Yers, we've also seen that it's a double-edged sword. We've heard from a number of older Gen Yers that being told that they can have it all and do anything makes it hard for them to feel like anything other than perfection (in a mate, in a job, in themselves) is good enough. They're not sure what's "settling" and what's normal accommodation, understanding, or compromise. Emily, twenty-six, of Atlanta puts it this way: "No relationship is perfect and nothing is fun 100 percent of the time, but the expectation is that you're supposed to be passionate about your job, have this 100-percent great relationship, find the thing you love. It's not a favor to be told that I can have it all." And here is Marie, also twenty-six and from Atlanta: "There is so much emphasis on 'you can be whatever you want to be,' so much pressure. Find the thing you love and do it. I feel so overwhelmed. How do I find the thing I love when I have so many options?"

Speed

Gen Y is a high-speed generation, and as such, compared with older generations, they're easily bored and highly attuned to the power of visual symbols. But hasn't every generation thought the simple life of their elders seemed a little boring? Needlepoint in the parlor? Hanging out by the radio in the kitchen? Huddled around a black-and-white television with only three channels? Still, even compared with previous generations, Gen Y seems to have gone to warp speed.

Gen Y brains have been trained on "more and faster" and consequently process visual information quickly and get bored more easily. Older folks tsk-tsk over Gen Y's shorter attention spans because they fear that Gen Yers won't take the time necessary to think deeply, and that they'll place too much emphasis on the superficial. This, of course, has ramifications that touch everything American—from democracy to family—so it's no wonder there's an outcry. We've found that Gen Yers certainly do respond to the visual, the fast, and the immediate—*and* that their passions fuel intense and focused deep dives.

Our world, with or without Gen Y's speedy brains, simply is faster and more superficial. Consider this, and it's easy to see how Apple can launch at least one new version of the iPod every year with resounding success.

What comes with speed? Here are a few of the words and phrases we're seen used to describe Gen Y in dozens of publications and surveys: *impatient, convenience-oriented, blunt, image-driven, stimulation junkies,* and *needing immediate gratification.*

According to WeMedia/Zogby Interactive, 55 percent of adult Gen Yers say they get most of their news online. *The State of the News Media 2008* states that news is shifting from being a product, such as a newspaper or a broadcast, to becoming a service.[24] In other words, consumers are more in control of the content they wish to receive—on demand—and less passive (or patient) about being exposed to news in a broader sense. The report also says the agenda of the American news media continues to narrow, not broaden. The media covers fewer issues and focuses more intently on those that are personally relevant to consumers, such as gas prices and toy recalls—and the media has shown a "marked shorter attention span."

In upcoming chapters we'll explain how these characteristics and forces have shaped the way Gen Y shops, which, in turn, has changed the way we all shop. From their fashion authority to their shorter attention spans, the power of Gen Y will be felt by brands ranging from Starbucks to Bank of America.

2

THEY SHOP LIKE THEY'RE FROM A DIFFERENT PLANET FROM THEIR PARENTS, TOO

Megan, a seventeen-year-old Denver high school senior, helped turn the four generations of women in her family into fashionistas. She almost didn't buy UGG boots for herself in late 2007 because they were so popular and "I don't like to look like everyone else." Still, protection from the cold trumped her aversion to commonality, and she also helped convince her seventy-year-old grandmother to get a pair. Megan's clothes sense has even influenced her ninety-three-year-old great-grandmother, who's now wearing clothes from Chico's. Megan gets retail promotions text messaged to her phone and uses a search tool called NearbyNow on her BlackBerry to ensure that what she wants will be available at the mall before she goes. And she taught her fifty-year-old mother how to send and receive text-messaged pictures so they can keep each other in the retail loop (Megan also makes sure that her mom wears neither frumpy "mom" jeans nor skintight teen jeans). Like most Gen Yers, Megan has an influence on retail that extends far beyond her peers and an ease with technology that's fueled the rapid growth of mobile marketing.

Not happy to simply call the shots at home, the nearly eighty-four million members of Gen Y are about to become the largest and the most complicated and influential group of shoppers on the planet. Already they account for about 25 percent of the U.S.

population, and by 2015 they will make up 34 percent of the population. As teens, Gen Y shoppers spend five times more than their parents did at the same age.[1]

Unlike their parents, who grew up in largely middle-class settings with similar values, this generation no longer considers itself middle class at heart. That carries profound implications for Gen Yers' work ethic, career ambitions, and attitudes toward money. And it's one of many factors that influenced how they shop and what they buy.

Times Have Changed

- In 1970, the average finished area of a house was 1,400 square feet. This grew to 2,330 in 2004.[2]
- In 1976, the median age of women marrying for the first time was twenty; today it's over twenty-five.[3]
- The 1990s represented the longest period of economic expansion in the nation's history.[4]
- The average annual tuition and fees at a private four-year college, adjusted for inflation, rose from $9,903 in 1978 to $25,143 in 2008.[5]

Gen Y's unique relationships with brands, their powerful influence on marketers, their peers and their friends, their love of technology, and their speedy, visual world are reshaping retailing. Their confidence in self-expression, lickety-split decision making, and desire to have it all *now* have had a notable impact on the way they shop—and on their credit card balances.

Their influence on retail will only increase. When this generation enters its prime spending years of ages twenty-five to thirty-four, homes, cars, baby products, appliances, and insurance will be added to the long list of retail industries already heavily influenced by this generation's clout and voice.

The Giant Force of Their Digital World

Topping the list of Gen Y's retail influence is their expectation—make that *insistence*—on state-of-the-art technology. It's contributed to one of the fastest and most profound transformations in the history of retail.

Manufacturers and retailers that want to attract Gen Y need to ramp up technology—constantly. In stores, on their websites, and by making it mobile and interactive. If your website stinks, for example, so does your store.

"If it's too slow and I can find the information somewhere else, I'm probably not going to wait for the page to load," says Eleanor, nineteen, of Wheeling, West Virginia. She's voicing the opinion of her generation, who have led the charge for all of us. A 2009 Aberdeen Group report found that an additional delay of one second can lower page views by 11 percent and customer satisfaction by 16 percent.[6] Retailers have responded by pouring funds into the technology of their online stores. In 2008 49.9 percent of retailers redesigned their websites.[7] The result? Obviously faster-loading pages, better navigation, and faster checkout—and also features like catwalk videos on NeimanMarcus.com, and sites like Keds.com, where you can upload your own images and text and paint a canvas (shoe) any way you like. You can also sell your design on their site and collect royalties.

To appeal to young people, the most important characteristics websites must have are free overnight or second-day shipping (notice, that's not free *ground* shipping, which wouldn't satisfy their need for immediate gratification), fast page loads, and zooms of all views. Those are Resource Interactive's conclusions after studying fourteen- to twenty-four-year-olds who were heavy users of technology for the past three years. Other Resource Interactive recommendations from President Kelly Mooney:

- Develop user-initiated promo mobile numbers, so that shoppers can access special offers and discounts via their phones.

- Encourage opinion gathering on mobile phones. Millennials' heavy reliance on their social network and parents for validation can quickly convert to a viral campaign.
- Enable mobile wish lists. Let them shop online and send lists to their mobile phone to assist in their retail visits (and to family and friends who need gift ideas).
- Accept and promote PayPal as a payment option.

Recognizing young people's deep connection to the Web, advertisers who used to rely on print and broadcast avenues of reaching their consumers are gradually moving toward online alternatives, including the use of social media. Facebook, ranked the favorite website of college students, grew from a hundred million users in August 2008 to over two hundred million users in April 2009.[8] Such statistics have helped convince marketers that newspaper and TV ads are hardly enough to reach Gen Y shoppers.

When young shoppers are on Facebook, they typically check out their own page, which updates them on postings and pictures of their "friends"—many of whom are actually friends of friends of friends whom they have never actually talked to or met. It's the online equivalent of the distinction people in the nation's capital sometimes make, differentiating "Washington friends"—professional acquaintances good for name dropping—from their "*friend* friends." When the bar for Facebook friendship is that low and the love of many brands is so high, it logically follows that Facebook "friends" can and do often include brands, many of which have thousands—even millions—of friends.

Social networking sites are "such a game changer," says Dave Hendricks, executive vice president of operations at Datran Media, which specializes in email and Facebook marketing. The "tastemakers" in the youth market "spend all of their time in social media.

"Unlike email, the influencers in friendship groups share what they are doing and watching through social media tools," says Hendricks.

Consider Omar, a twenty-nine-year-old former buyer for Burberry, who uses a Facebook application called "what when WEAR" to communicate his style far beyond his circle of close friends. The site allows users to post pictures of outfits for specific events and poll other users for comments.

Now a resident of New York City, Om says he isn't being vain—he just wants to share his pricey and not-so-fancy brand choices. "You can put a question out there about anything," he says. "So many people are signed onto it, there's different opinions coming from all over the place."

"Working in retail you meet a lot of people from the Gen Y era," says Om. "Their number one portal of communicating is through social networking—it's almost like you gotta get on or get left."

Although such sites are especially popular with Om and his twenty-something friends, they make even more sense for tweens, who typically have less confidence in their fashion choices. Enter Allykatzz.com, a site where, says founder Denise Restauri, tween girls can see the world through the eyes of other girls. Given Gen Y's influence over family decisions extending to vacations, travel was a logical place for the site to start, with young girls like her now-teenage daughter posting items about their favorite places to go—it eventually morphed into all things tween, especially clothing. In February 2009, the site had 75,000 members and 2.5 million page views, and girls had posted more than 4 million blogs and 100,000 profiles, says Restauri.

Tween girls "want to follow but they also want to be unique," Restauri says. "Their friends are very influential but are most influential when it comes to learning about clothing brands."

This practice typically balloons during back-to-school time, when girls are seeking advice on their all-important first-day-of-school outfits, Restauri adds. In December 2008, she says the tween site's visitors ranked Aeropostale, Hollister, Abercrombie, American Eagle, and Target as their top five favorite brands.

"They really promote brands and items more than they ever think they do," she continues. "They don't specifically tell each other to go to the store's site, but they post pictures from it."

Zappos' CEO Tony Hsieh has over a quarter million Twitter followers. In addition to the occasional tweet suggesting that followers get involved with Zappos' promotions, Hsieh offers optimistic, amusing, and engaging tweets such as, "About to speak at conf. Spilled Coke on left leg of jeans, so poured some water on right leg so looks like the denim fade," and "I want to go to sleep at my hotel but the sheer number of pillows is intimidating."

Fifty-six percent of Twitter users use the site for business purposes. The intimacy and immediacy of Twitter is unparalleled. Gen Yers that we interviewed universally loved the close connection they felt with not only friends and celebrities but also their favorite businesses. Several suggested it was a great way to get first dibs on new products and hoped-for special notice of sales and special events. [9]

Despite the opportunities, 75 percent of marketers have budgeted less than $100,000 for social media over the coming year, according to a Forrester Research study reported in Adweek.com.[10] Aside from the human power required to engage in social media, traditional marketers and businesses are often wary because it's difficult to measure the effectiveness of social media.

Just as retailers and brands are racing to embrace these new forms of communication with kids, so too are parents.

Sharon, a Reston, Virginia, mother of two, travels with her eighteen-year-old musician son, Andy, whenever he goes to practices and gigs. But when he's using his cell phone to shop, Andy is in charge of the searching. He uses Slifter, which allows him to browse the inventories in malls to save his family shopping time. Like many teens and twenty-somethings, Andy will also often send photos of products he's considering via cell phone to friends.

Forward-thinking retailers such as Metropark use text alerts of sales and special promotions, such as free CDs with purchases.

"This age group is spending a lot of time typing in text messages," says Renee Bell, the forty-something CEO of Metropark. "I don't know how they have the patience." But this group is so adept, the average teen can text forty words a minute.

Brand Love

When asked, most Gen Yers will tell you that they aren't susceptible to marketing tactics, that they're "savvy" about branding (which gets our award for the most overused word to describe this generation's relationship to branding), and that advertising doesn't work on them. Many of the marketers we spoke with described Gen Y in similar terms. At the same time, Gen Yers are more enthusiastic (though fickle) about brands than any other generation. A 2007 Keller Fay Group study estimated that teenagers have 145 conversations about brands a week—which is about twice as many as adults have.[11] Need more proof? In April 2003 the top twenty songs mentioned brand names forty-seven times![12]

How to explain this contradiction? In part because Gen Yers feel they're immune to branding, they don't seem to be as threatened by marketing, branding, or advertising as previous generations were. The lower volume of hostility is related to a greater level of confidence that they're informed enough and powerful enough to see right through marketing manipulation. Therefore, clear value propositions—such as Target's devotion to design and style for a low price, and the pristine image of Coach as tasteful, modern, and luxurious—have inspired the devotion of many young consumers. And Gen Y *needs* brands to help them sift through the incredible volume of options they face, and they use brands to sort and store their perceptions. Brands offer quick and easy credibility in a TMI (too much information) world.

Gen Y is knowledgeable about old school "push the product on you" marketing and advertising, and they abhor manipulation.

More than anything else, this generation does not want to be lied to, or to be told what they should want or who they should be. Though they want to be understood, they don't want outsiders acting like they know them. "You don't know me" is a way to protect the sanctity of the group.

Gen Y rejects brands that appear to court them, preferring instead to pull in the brands that resonate with them. They want to do the picking—which is made all the more complicated (for marketers) by the fact that, with a few notable exceptions like Apple, they'd like to think they're not part of a pack of followers. Gen Y's ultimate brand relationship is collaborative—they want to be asked for their opinion and have the ability to influence the product.

In a speedy, visual society, brands provide a way to join with others and feel part of something. Where clubs, neighborhoods, and hobbies might have unified previous generations, brands are a way for many members of this generation to connect. Due in part to the deeper psychology that marketers have been able to cultivate in brands, consumers have gotten closer to the products they feel represent them and connect them with likeminded others. Through the use of images and symbols, of sponsorships and affiliations with celebrities and causes, and by harvesting the multitude of tactics that new technology affords, marketers and branders have upped the ante and are using tactics that slip past the vigilance of consumers.

So although Gen Y does seem to catch on quickly to the more overt and traditional forms of marketing communications, they're not immune to branders who support their local sports, play hard to get, or appeal to an emotional lifestyle that resonates with them—quite the contrary. The key that unlocks the more resilient Millennial heart is to subtly pursue her until she catches you.

The passion Gen Yers displayed for Barack Obama during his presidential election campaign is a lesson in Millennial marketing. Peter Feld describes in *Advertising Week* how Obama's "brand management" showed "pitch-perfect understanding" of how to appeal to Gen Y. Obama's tactics included an Apple iPhone app, "Countdown to Change," that tracked the seconds until Election Day; an iconic logo on a par with the world's most successful brands; his mastery of social media; and his campaign's use of "brand ambassadors" and celebrities like Scarlett Johansson.[13] In other words, a sophisticated use of technology, imagery, and emotion and the connectedness of this generation.

Another factor played an important role: Obama used a bottom-up approach to connect with supporters. He relied on his supporters to tell others who he was and what he stood for, rather than a top-down approach of supplying all the talking points. Obama once described himself as a Rorschach—people project onto him what they wanted to see. He depended on his supporters to communicate about him through social networks rather than to direct the flow of communication through traditional media. This allowed supporters to project and communicate to others the values *they* held most dear, and it empowered them—which is inspirational to Gen Y. As both a reward and a symbolic proclamation of his alliance with Gen Y values, he let supporters know that those who signed up to receive text messages from his campaign would be the first to learn about his choice of Senator Joseph Biden to be his running mate. Those attending Obama's acceptance speech at the Democratic convention were urged to send text messages to family and friends to get the word out about his campaign. During his campaign, Obama was the most popular Twitterer in the world (as of April 2009 he'd been overtaken in popularity by Britney Spears and a few others, but he still had over a half-million followers). The Obama campaign was awarded *Advertising Age*'s Marketer of the Year. Other Gen Y favorites, all savvy Web 2.0 connectors, rounded out the list: Apple came in second, Zappos third, and Nike fourth.

People who worked with Richard Costello in the twenty-two years that he was manager of global branding for General Electric called him "the brand guru." He was an essential part of the team that brought General Electric from a sleepy bureaucracy to a world-class brand, and he has a reputation far and wide as one of the most respected marketers of our time. Richard is also "Dad" to two Gen Yers, Anna and Luke.

Gen Yers aren't more brand savvy, they're more media savvy, Costello says. "The massive change has been the Internet. The accessibility of information by consumers puts more control in their hands, and it's made the whole relationship between customers and vendors much more transparent—from pricing to choice options to information. Consumers are much more informed than ever before. You can't bullshit people—you have to be straightforward."

Costello says most Gen Yers have been taught by someone in high school who "has no real marketing knowledge and often has a negative and suspicious bias against marketing" (by the way, we certainly found this to be true of most of the Gen Yers we spoke with).

According to Costello, "A brand is fundamentally a promise to consumers about what it will do for you that will make your life better. It has to be a promise that is relevant and enticing and sets up obligations for the marketer to fulfill that drive the business model. Yes, it's biased because it's made by the marketer, but it ultimately has to deliver."

The brands that deliver today are not just well-performing products—there are bazillions of products that work well. The brands that deliver also have the power to unite, inspire, and speak for their owners.

Consider the appeal of, umm, undergarments. It wasn't too many years ago that underwear, certainly for men and usually for women, was mostly an afterthought except when it came to girls trying to hide their bra straps; obscure their panty lines; or plan for their honeymoons or, well, a really big date. Now that underwear is almost as important as outerwear (and often doubles as it anyway), a multitude of Millennial marketers are trying to further ensnare young consumers with what goes under the fashions they already sell. With the late 2007 debut of Abercrombie & Fitch's racily promoted Gilly Hicks line and Juicy Couture's entry into loungewear and undergarments, young women can go even further—financially and fancifully—in the pursuit of the perfect panty and bra drawer.

Heidi, twenty-two and a journalism major at a Boston college, started her collection of sixty-plus bras and countless pairs of underwear in high school with the hopes of impressing her steady boyfriend.

"But I also felt it was my way of expressing myself and my sexual identity," says the bubbly blond from Old Lyme, Connecticut. "I felt very sexy when my bra and underwear matched."

Her near infatuation with her own décolletage created an addiction to the store she considered the epitome of femininity.

"I love my boobs," says Heidi. "I naturally started finding myself drawn to Victoria's Secret. When you hear Victoria's Secret, it's synonymous with sexy bras and lingerie. That's just where you go to find a sexy bra."

Eleanor from Wheeling, introduced earlier, may not have Heidi's vast collection—or an equal cheerfulness about her chest—but like many other teens and twenty-something women these days, she shares her passion.

"I spend more on underwear than I do on my regular clothes. I just really like underwear," says Eleanor, who buys it only at Victoria's Secret. "I blow so much during the semi-annual sales. I'm such a sucker for their advertising."

The lingerie advertising and marketing that's luring these young women is often only a baby step away from pornography. Mothers have picketed at Victoria's Secret stores where the window displays have looked like peep shows, with sexually suggestive poses and lots of black-and-red lace garters. But though some of that's been toned down—thanks in part to the entry of the more collegiate-looking "Pink" line—Victoria's Secret's advertising is hardly demure.

"I definitely think the provocative ads associated with [Victoria's Secret] make me more interested in buying their lingerie," says Beverley, sixteen, of Pasadena, California. "I mean, I like their clothes because they're a good product, but it certainly doesn't hurt that everyone looks so good in their commercials. Women want to look like that, and men want their women to look like that, so they pretty much rope in every audience."

Abercrombie decided to test its brand loyalty with its Gilly Hicks lingerie line, which takes a page from its parent company in its online marketing. The photo on the homepage of Gilly Hicks' website in April 2009 featured seven naked men lined up against a fence with their behinds facing the camera. One young woman in the middle was facing the camera wearing a bra and bikini underwear and with her hands on two of the backsides.

Abercrombie's advertising, says brand and store design expert Steve McGowan, is intended to make young people feel like somehow they'll be transformed into one of the guys with the six-pack abs if they spend the extra $25 for a T-shirt there. Besides, getting the Abercrombie catalog is "like getting hold of *Playboy*," says McGowan, who believes Gilly Hicks has gone "way overboard."

"The kids find the ads and in-store graphics appealing, as it is part fantasy and part lifestyle alignment," says McGowan, whose Gen Y children include a twenty-something daughter with spiked hair and a tween girl who loves Hannah Montana. "There is a sexual attraction to the models, but more so the action or activities taking place in the ads or graphics. From nearly naked co-ed touch football to beach parties, the target audience finds this stimulating. It attracts them into the store."

Like it or not, there's no question that the products and their pitches entice young people, whose enthusiasm for underwear draws them even closer to brands they already love. In the process, Gen Y helped redefine and expand a category once called *lingerie* that now includes pajamas that double as pants and tops that were once called *camisoles*. With the word "Pink" or "Juicy" emblazoned across the clothing, there's an unspoken knowledge of just who the Juicy or Gilly or Abercrombie girls really are.

Many kids also hope the brands they *don't* buy say something about them, even though they're actually responding to the sort of stealth branding just mentioned that's become about as common as the provocative pitches. Stores including Gap's Old Navy, Banana Republic, and Gap brands, and American Eagle typically steer young customers toward generic, understated fashions with advertising messages that sometimes suggest the wearers are defining their values by eschewing other brands—and embracing this one.

When Jayne asked an auditorium full of high school students in Murfreesboro, Tennessee, how they felt about Abercrombie & Fitch, the students were loud and proud in their opposition. Many agreed when one student declared as ridiculous both the prices and the free advertising customers gave the store by wearing their prominent logos.

No matter what their store of choice, Gen Yers like to make their own decisions once they get there. Gen Yers are so knowledgeable about what's out there and what suits their style, they can't really trust their boomer parents or, God forbid, *grandparents* to get it right. That's contributed to their insistence on gift cards and helped propel these slim slivers of plastic into the #1 most wanted holiday gift in America. Beyond that, gift cards satisfy Gen Yers because they love to shop and a gift card is more than cash; it's permission to go shopping. In fact, it's the gift of shopping! The National Retail Federation's 2008 gift card survey found more than 60 percent of those aged eighteen to twenty-four ranked gift cards as their most wanted gift.[14]

Transparency and Authenticity

Gen Y craves authenticity. They want to have relationships with brands and companies, but it better be honest. A whiff of manipulation can lead to a brand's destruction in a viral tsunami of mockery. As pointed out by Costello, the Internet is making everything more transparent anyway—it's pretty hard to hide the truth. Authenticity has also become the antidote to a generation raised to be skeptical about businesses.

Advertising is an industry in transition, trying to respond to comments like these: "The whole purpose of advertising is to make you feel unhappy with your situation so that you think you have to buy," says Jillian, twenty-six, of Atlanta. Allie, twenty-nine, of San Francisco, says, "I feel guilty when I buy things sometimes because it means I've been stupid enough to fall for the manipulation."

Struggling to adapt to a breed of consumer that's more confident, communicative, and connected than any before, those in the persuasion business have had to add to their repertoire of tools. Marketers are investing in understanding the psychology of their consumers; playing with stealth event sponsorships, product placements, promotions, and social networking; and releasing some of their authority to speak for the product—instead, as Obama did, letting consumers take some control.

Without any training as a formal makeup artist, Lauren Luke became the go-to gal for makeup techniques by posting homey, chatty YouTube videos of herself applying everything from prom night and wedding makeup to Kylie Minogue looks for aspiring superstars. Many of her videos have reached over a million viewers. Within eighteen months, the twenty-seven-year-old single mom had acquired a contract with Anomaly and Zorbit Resources—a manufacturing and branding company for the cosmetics industry that's worked with companies such as Nars and L'Oreal—her own cosmetics line, a newspaper column, and a book deal. The authenticity, sincerity, and likeability of Luke are key factors in her success. That she was championed by consumers, rather than pushed onto them, is another.

Vans' authentic skateboard heritage coupled with their ironic, barely-above-the-surface graphics on their hoodies, T-shirts, and shoes has resulted in a passionate, Gen Y–generated following.

Seattle-based Trevor, seventeen, cracked the tiniest of smiles when an adult noticed the tiniest of skulls nearly hidden on his Vans T-shirt. A guy as understated as his style, Trevor had a one-word response: "Subtle."

The forty-four-year-old brand was bought in 2005 by VF Corp. (which also owns Nautica and The North Face), giving it the capital to really capitalize on the seemingly unstoppable interest in so-called "board sports" stores, even by kids who have never been on a skate, snow, or surfboard. Buoyed by a 2001 documentary, *Dogtown*, that was turned into a movie, *Lords of Dogtown*, in 2005, Vans has made board-sports-oriented apparel a bigger part of its offerings and, at the same time, returned to the more classic vulcanized-sole shoes that the movie helped popularize. Though its competitors now include Zumiez, PacSun, Hot Topic, and often even Hollister, some carry Vans shoes and no one would question the Vans claim to be the granddaddy of them all—a claim that is cemented with Vans-owned skateboard parks and its sponsorship of the biggest surf competition.

Indeed, one of the more popular means of getting close to Gen Yers is through their interests and their favorite causes. Gen Yers, in part by virtue of their age but also because of our more superficial society, are yearning for purpose and want to belong to something bigger than themselves. They are often genuinely attuned to and passionate about causes, but there are other reasons why this technique has worked so well. Causes also add purpose and meaning to shopping—and sometimes just enough added benefit to rationalize a purchase. Being *seen by others* as being passionate about a cause is *en vogue*—and it unites people together.

Businesses that support causes also appear to be more compassionate and socially responsible than those that don't, which is reassuring and a stamp of quality to Gen Yers. Many Gen Yers make it their business to support the brands and retailers that they perceive to be good to their employees, good for the environment, or doing something good for the world.

Karen, twenty-six, of Morgantown, West Virginia, stands out from many of her contemporaries with the fairly conservative fashions that she buys so as to not alienate the senior citizens in the Lutheran church congregation where she is a pastor. ("I can't stand up there with a keyhole back in my top in front of all those eighty-year-old women," she says.) But when it comes to socially conscious shopping, Karen could write the book for many twenty-somethings.

When she's not at Macy's or Lane Bryant, Karen tries to do most of her shopping through fair trade–oriented websites and stores. The newlywed and her husband also looked for appliances that were made in America, leaning toward Kitchen Aid, which manufactures more in this country than many of its competitors, she says. When New Balance sneakers pulled its manufacturing out of the United States, she lost her last American-made casual footwear option.

"Our goal is to buy from the fairest company, so we avoid most of the Asian companies," says Karen. "There are *some* things you can buy with a clear social conscience."

It's the Glue

Shopping is the tie that binds for many members of Gen Y, and it's a trend we predict will stick around for a while. Whether by shopping in packs at the mall, connecting with each other through what they purchase, or shopping online while IMing friends who are looking at the same site from across town, Gen Yers demonstrate their love of teams, groups, and real or created families by shopping together.

Irina, seventeen, is a boarding school student in Indiana who speaks Latin fluently, plays on the varsity fencing team, and has done missionary work with farmers in Greece. Still, shopping is the theme of most of her conversations with her friends, siblings, and cousins. "Everyone I know loves to shop. It's what everyone wants to do and talk about. It's just what you do," she says. Their consumerism, no matter how it may differ in dollars or type, brings them together.

While much of the thrill of shopping is simply social, teens in particular are also looking for that all-important approval from their friends before they buy. Sixty-eight percent of teens and twenty-somethings shop with other people at least half of the time; only 44 percent of older consumers can say the same, according to our research.

Although her bohemian style and layers of jewelry make her look like a fashion trailblazer, seventeen-year-old Tara really is more of a trend follower. She wants to be darn sure that what she buys meets the approval of her peers, so she shops in groups.

"We want to know that our friends 'accept' what we're going to buy," says Tara, who lives in Fort Myers, Florida. "Nothing sucks more than thinking that you found something really cute just to hear your friend tell you hours later how hideous it is or how it doesn't 'flatter' you. I could shop alone, and often do, but prefer to shop with a friend whose opinion I trust."

When retailers discovered how often kids were not only shopping together but trying on clothes together, they realized they better make their fitting rooms a lot bigger—and even more unisex. Andrew McQuilkin, vice president of design at the retail consulting firm FRCH, says stores are going far beyond the seat in the dressing room—now known as the girlfriend *or* boyfriend chair—and replacing spaces that were once three by four-and-a-half feet with eleven-by-twelve-foot areas that give you room for a party. Which is precisely the point.

It used to be "like dressing in a shoe stall," says McQuilkin. Now, retailers are "glorifying and celebrating the fitting room."

They're also occasionally making them unisex, a more gender-neutral trend in retail selling. American Eagle and Gap have unisex dressing rooms, but McQuilkin notes that Aeropostale has the most extreme example. Four dressing rooms are clustered in the middle of the store, and the doors are not full height. The lack of privacy—and the prospect of literally being the center of attention in the store—pushes the boundaries of most people's typical expectations for dressing rooms and wouldn't work for most places in retail.

"There's a very social aspect of this whole fitting-room experience," agrees retail expert Ken Nisch—his firm designed the Metropark stores, which have "futuristic light" in the fitting rooms and LCD monitors that feature music videos. The chain targets young people from about eighteen to thirty-five.

The focus on fitting rooms makes perfect sense, says the National Retail Federation's Dan Butler, because young people try on clothes more often than older people, who tend to become more confident in their ability to judge size as the years go on. For certain categories, such as couture or bridal, it's always been almost like a fashion show for the whole store—"making emergence from the fitting room important," says Butler, who heads merchandising and store operations for NRF. But now, thanks to the influence of Gen Y, "the process of buying the product today becomes the entertainment" in nearly all categories.

When there's room for others in and around the fitting room, retailers are encouraging more interaction among shoppers, who most young people would rather hear from rather than a sales clerk working on commission.

The interactive dressing room mirror that Christopher Enright helped design is part of what he calls "social retailing." The mirrors, used in the Nanette LePore department at Bloomingdale's in the SoHo section of Manhattan, stream high-definition video of shoppers trying out clothes to their friends' computers or mobile devices. Friends or family can comment on the outfits and even choose other designs in the collection for the shopper to try.

Along with better fitting rooms, retailers are responding to the tendency to shop in groups, offering wider aisles and lounge areas with plasma TVs. Metropark has a whole area outside the fitting rooms where they sell magazines and bottled water and other beverages. The goal is to keep young people around as long as possible—to both increase the chance they'll make a purchase and boost the stores' image as hip hangouts.

And who does that better than the über-popular Apple stores? Ronald, sixteen, says he counts Apple as one of his favorite stores, along with Foot Locker and Champ's. But the Houston, Texas, high school student says it's not because he necessarily buys anything—it's "just to hang out."

Youth-oriented retailers including Journey's and Guess also stream their own branded versions of MTV-style programming in their stores to encourage more kids to take a seat and watch.

Seeing Stars

Celebrities—long a source of admiration, envy, and great gossip in the U.S.—are inspiring new peaks of fervor and hoards of fascinated followers. Glossy gossip magazines like *Star* and *US Weekly* spurred things forward, but it was the Internet's ability to provide instantaneous updates and infinite content that really moved things to a new level. In 2008, despite a historic U.S. presidential election, an economic meltdown, and Michael Phelps' eight Olympic gold medals, the most popular search term on Yahoo! was "Britney Spears."[15]

In our increasingly disconnected communities, celebrities, as a source of common interest, unite us. And it's not just movie stars, athletes, or recording artists; a celebrity can be anyone with a following. Reality television, blogging, YouTube, and Facebook fame have made it seem more attainable than ever. Having been raised to be special, many of today's youth identify strongly with celebrities. Previous generations of young, particularly teenage, consumers might have simply emulated their favorite stars; today's youth feel a much more intimate connection with celebrity culture.

And they can look to Mario Lavandeira for inspiration. This shy, overweight thirty-year-old guy achieved his goal of becoming "the gay, Latino Oprah," otherwise known as Perez

Hilton, in three years. His website, PerezHilton.com—a snarky, sharp celebrity gossip blog—grew from fewer than one million page views a month in 2005 to over 250 million impressions and 12 million unique readers a month in 2008, and now rakes in millions from advertising sales. Young fans line up to meet him when he appears at venues such as goth-grunge retailer Hot Topic, and record industry executives clamor to sign artists who have his blessing. Always on top of things, Hilton was one of the first to launch a mobile website on which readers can share posts through SMS texting and search archives from their mobile phones.[16]

Far more members of Gen Y than of previous generations can and do dream of being famous. Hilton was little-known and starstruck in 2004, but as Hilton told *Wired* four years later, "Now, the people come up to *me*." Lavandeira's success is a testament to both our newfound ability to leverage the Internet to become famous and the great value our culture puts on fame. Fully 31 percent of American teens believe they'll become famous, according to a 2006 *Psychology Today* survey.[17]

Fame validates. At one time greatness often resulted in fame; today fame itself is often the goal—those who acquire it are assumed to be great. It's no wonder then that those who have achieved celebrity influence the shopping styles and tastes of many Gen Y consumers—who often want the latest "it" outfit almost immediately after they've seen it on a favorite celebrity.

TV shows such as CW's *Gossip Girl* are some of the key drivers of the phenomenon. Celebrity-inspired fashion has "definitely been amped up," says *Gossip Girl* costume designer Eric Daman.[18] A former assistant designer on *Sex and the City*, Daman was amazed by how much faster word flew about *Gossip Girl*'s fashions in these social-network-driven days than it did in the heyday of his former show.

CW's website links to stores where retail versions of the stars' clothes can be purchased. Even though it can't track actual sales, show executives know that when actress Leighton Meester dons a new headband or colored tights, she starts a virtual race to the checkout.

"Younger people of this generation are much more interested in fashion than they were when I was in high school," says twenty-nine-year-old Meredith Barnett, founder of Store Adore.com, a guide to retail boutiques. "Most of the reason they are so interested is they are so much more exposed to it. They are highly influenced by what they see on TV and what they see celebrities wear."

So StoreAdore, which already attracts many young shoppers because boutiques tend to respond quickly to trends, helps the girls get the *Gossip Girl* look. Shortly after the headband trend accelerated, thanks to *Gossip Girl*, StoreAdore provided its picks for the best headbands sold on the Web.

Not only are young women trying to achieve the Serena or Blair look (Serena is Blake Lively's character; Leighton Meester plays Blair), but stores including Barney's are specifically showing them how to do it with in-store displays.

"The girls' names are becoming like labels," Daman says. "It's almost kind of crazy to see how great the reaction is to it."

Similarly, when Miley Cyrus shows up at Jaye Hersh's Los Angeles boutique, Intuition, young people in the store watch what she buys closely and typically ask for the same thing—like the red and black plaid messenger bag that Cyrus posed with for the store's website. Hersh—whose sister, celebrity wedding planner Mindy Weiss, did the weddings of Ashlee Simpson and Eva Longoria—has been able to launch her small, off-the-beaten-path (of Hollywood) shop into the retail stratosphere with red carpet clients including the stars of *Desperate Housewives*, Demi Moore, and Halle Berry. Hersh's star-studded clientele helps guarantee that Intuition's fashions are regularly featured in magazines including *Lucky* and *In Style*.

While young girls may and do flock to headbands, messenger bags, and other clothing and accessories worn by headline names,

Hersch says her baby boomer shoppers steer toward celebrity style too because it makes their "lives appear a little more shiny."

Interestingly, most consumers of all ages report in surveys that they're not influenced by celebrities (except perhaps for the hoards that lovingly follow Oprah's advice). After all, it's uncool to copy, and it flies in the face of our love of individuality. But as is often the case with surveys, what people say and what they do aren't always in sync, especially when asked to endorse something out of alignment with the respondent's self-perception. Nevertheless, the products that celebrities pick are the products that consumers want. First, there's the glow of association that a product receives if it's also chosen by a celebrity. Additionally, many consumers believe that an influential person has access to everything, therefore the things she picks must be the best in that category—it's an assurance of quality and style. Last, in a subtle emotional way it unites the consumer with the celebrity through their shared purchases.

Celebrity style has, in turn, given a big boost to so-called throw-away fashions—trendy apparel with low price tags and often second-rate quality.

Fast Fashion

Laurie, a nineteen-year-old student at a Maryland state college, says she and her sorority sisters frequent Forever 21 in part because when "Green Lemonade" and other mixed-drink soirees are a regular part of the social calendar, they know they'll spill on—and likely ruin—their party dresses. The notion that the dresses might not hold up much longer even if they don't drop drinks on them is of little concern. Besides, the sorority girls may well be on to a new style in a month.

"It's all about once and done," says retail strategist Madison Riley of the global consulting firm Kurt Salmon Associates.

While the economic recession has put a damper on the throw-away consumption of older generations, many Gen Yers have yet to break the habit. They may be buying less, but the emotional thrill of sampling styles and the realities of their "hot today, boring tomorrow" world have carried retailers of affordable fast fashion safely through the tough early months of 2009.

Retailers such as Wet Seal and Charlotte Russe are trying to hit a certain low price point and have to be "spot on from a trend standpoint," says Riley. "To hit it, they're not going to have a quality level that's enduring, but they know what they're doing and they know who they're serving. They're playing into the times."

Short attention spans and the quest for stimulation, variety, and attention makes "closet turnover" important—and consequently makes fast fashion a necessity for retailers hoping to get the nod from young women in particular. A bonus to retailers is that frequent merchandise turnover in stores results in more regular visits—and as we know, the more we shop, the more we buy.

Fashions aren't the only things coming and going in the blink of an eye. Retail outlets are popping up for seasonal—even weekend—visits too. Hence the name "pop-up" stores. Once reserved for Halloween costume or calendar shops, pop-up stores tap into the same emotions as fast fashion—the thrill of the hunt, a sense of exclusivity, and the excitement of something fresh. In malls, empty storefronts, and museums, pop-up shops inspire chatter. The knowledge that it's here today but not tomorrow inspires impulse purchases.

Similarly, "concept stores" that rotate themes and merchandise throughout the year keep their Gen Y shoppers engaged. Gap has a concept venue located next to its flagship store in New York City. In April 2009, Gap turned it into a dance studio and provided free ballet classes on weekends. Naturally, there was a product linked to the promotion—the launch of GapKids' summer collection with a ballet-inspired theme.

Buying High—and Low

They may want some fashion that's cheap and fast, but Millennials are also big spenders when they think it's worth it. Gen Yers have helped demolish demographic typecasting in their quest for quality in sufficient quantity to satisfy their ever-evolving tastes and interests. At least when it comes to the middle and upper classes, Saks Fifth Avenue is for everyone, and so is Target. Gen Yers calculate a value equation that includes elements like style, length of usage, impact, and functionality as they navigate through a much broader array of options than previous generations would have considered at that age.

Rhonda and Janie, eighteen-year-olds from Potomac, Maryland, shop the best departments at Nordstrom (whether or not there's a sale going on), wear Tiffany's jewelry, and love Target fashions. Janie, the daughter of an optometrist, wears Chanel sunglasses, carries a Marc Jacobs tote bag, and proudly buys clothes from Target.

The willingness of Gen Yers to mix ten-dollar tank tops with Jimmy Choo sandals brought forth a shift in retail that's ultimately delighted the masses: high-end designers creating affordable options for discount stores. It started with Isaac Mizrahi at Target and has since mushroomed to include a Max Azria line at Walmart; ALLEN B and I (♡) Ronson at J. C. Penney; Project Runway winner Christian Siriano at Payless Shoes; and a constant parade of top designers, such as Alexander McQueen, at Target.

Target's Sally Mueller calls it "masstige." Housewares designer Michael Graves calls it a "design democracy," and Target VP of nonapparel design and development Jill Sando says, "That's what Target is trying to create."

Despite the economic meltdown of 2008, that November, when a limited-edition collection of Commes des Garçons clothing hit H&M, lines of shoppers stretched down the block in San Francisco, New York, Chicago, and Los Angeles. The available stock of a $350 dress and a $60 scarf sold out almost immediately.

Here are some highlights about how Gen Y shops differently from the over-thirty crowd, from our survey of two thousand U.S. consumers:

- One-third of Gen Yers said, "I love to shop," and rated shopping an enthusiastic "9" on a nine-point scale. A full 65 percent of Gen Yers put shopping in one of the top three "love" boxes—well above simply enjoying it. Older Americans often also love to shop; however, less so than Gen Y. Only 43 percent of older respondents rated shopping in one of the top three "love" boxes.

- Young, old, male, female—in every group, "clothes" averaged well above everything else as the most favorite thing to shop for. Not surprisingly, Gen Y girls and women were the most enthusiastic about shopping for clothes—fully 94 percent said it was a favorite thing to shop for. Even 71 percent of Gen Y guys picked clothes too. Among non–Gen Yers, clothes got the nod from 73 percent. Gen Yers are generally more enthusiastic about shopping for everything, except for books and gifts for other people and high-ticket items like furniture and cars. Not surprising, given that 44 percent of the Gen Yers surveyed were under twenty.

- Sixty percent of Gen Yers use advice from their friends when deciding what to buy, and 41 percent say they are influenced by their parents. Though generally speaking, the over-thirty crowd says they make their own decisions, 41 percent admit to being influenced by their spouses or sweethearts.

- A strong majority of all categories of shoppers feel that service is a problem. Gen Yers are particularly irritated and annoyed by discourteous and unfriendly salespeople. And although that's also an issue for older shoppers, the thing that bothers this group the most is poorly trained or unhelpful salespeople. Two-thirds of our over-thirty respondents endorsed this complaint. Other areas of irritation for Gen Yers are high prices, long lines, disorganized displays, and out-of-stock merchandise (each being cited by nearly 50 percent of respondents). These things were also problematic for older shoppers, but not to the same extent.

- Gen Yers are slightly less likely than older folks to agree that women and girls like shopping more than men and boys—though most people of all ages feel this is true.

- Forty-eight percent of Gen Yers feel guilty about shopping— even when they don't spend more money than they have— compared with 35 percent of people over thirty.

3

THE WHYS BEHIND THE BUYS

Robert, an eighteen-year-old from Fort Lauderdale, Florida, owns fifty pairs of sneakers and a shirt to match most of them; he has a job at a shoe store to support his passion for fashion. After each exciting purchase he does a "happy dance" inside the store or when he gets home. Robert hopes that the fact he was voted "best dressed" at school will impress his children someday. He says his father can't figure him out—but we can. Robert, like many other eighteen-year-olds, lets his sneakers do the talking. He's found a way to get proof positive that he's recognized and appreciated—no wonder the happy dance!

Like most Americans, Gen Y consumers don't "need" (in the truest sense of the word) much. So why do they buy what they do? What motivates them to love one brand over another, to buy a handbag when they have a dozen already, to shop until they drop? Why will one teen or twenty-something buy Keds and another Nikes—and why will they even stand in line for fifteen hours to get the latest pair of Nikes? What's behind impulse buying, saving strategies, brand devotion, collections, hanging out in malls, and other shopping and buying behaviors?

These behaviors may appear nonsensical, but there are deep emotional and social reasons why Gen Y buys. And we can all become a little wiser about our own buying and shopping—no matter what the generation—through comparison. After all, wouldn't all of us love to know the real reasons why we buy what we buy? To have a little consumer X-ray vision? Understanding the whys behind the buys is a glimpse into the hearts and minds of your customers—not to mention your neighbors, friends, celebrities, and most important of all, *you.*

Marketers who understand the psychology of their consumers can better address their needs and communicate more effectively—in fact, in today's tighter economy, it's essential.

Consumers who understand why they buy get more control over their spending and consequently less guilt and more enjoyment out of what they do buy. And everyone gets a deeper look at our society and generational differences.

"Shopping" Is the New "Weather"

At a time when talking about the weather is a political discussion and party chatter is loaded with political correctness land mines, talking about clothes, music, cars, and the latest techno gadgets (not to mention who bought the new Kooba handbag and who should have worn Spanx with those linen pants) brings us together and keeps us engaged. As much as (or even more than) politics, books, or religion, we share a knowledge of brands and products that provides fodder for an exchange of ideas. In other words, where and how we shop, and what we buy and think about buying, is the new common denominator of social discourse. And with hundreds of channels to choose from, not to mention YouTube, Netflix, and TiVo options, we're more likely to share an interest in Nordstrom's anniversary sale than we are to share any other form of entertainment. We understand each other by sharing ideas, and today, more than ever, the most common, universally shared knowledge and entertainment revolves around shopping—and saving strategies.

"My friends and I talk all the time about where we got the best deals and if somebody bought something new," says Annie, twenty-one, a college student in Denver. "It's just fun;

it's interesting. And if you meet somebody new it's a good way to start a conversation, and if you like something they're wearing then there is a better chance you'll get along."

Considering that there has never been a generation with more "stuff requirements" than Gen Y, the opportunity for this common language is richer.

- Required by an eighteen-year-old in 1978: the right Levis, tops you'd wear for at least a year or two, one purse if you're a girl, and one pair of great shoes if you're a guy. Plus, depending on your groove, a couple of disco outfits or a couple of chambray shirts, some cheap jewelry (for both sexes, of course), a blow dryer, about one-quarter of the skin care and grooming products you'd use today, one bottle of cologne or perfume. A car, if you were lucky, and a cassette or record player and lots of albums.

- Required by an eighteen-year-old in 2008: A wardrobe of jeans, an array of tops refreshed monthly rather than annually, several casual and "party" dresses and an assortment of purses, shoes, jewelry, caps, sporting equipment, or accessories depending on your interests and gender. Hand, nail, feet, face, body, and hair products galore (NPD Group reported in 2006 that eighteen- to twenty-four-year-old girls were actually the heaviest users of fragrance of all-aged women, and nearly 70 percent of teen boys reported wearing cologne), a car if you're lucky, an iPod loaded with iTunes, a computer and software, a cell phone and headset, an X-Box or Wii, and games, lots of games.

Clearly, there's a lot more to talk about today—not only in terms of product requirements, but also in the brands to consider.

Things Create Community

Taking it one step further, shopping helps to create a sense of belonging and connection—in other words, community. As we increasingly relocate, spend more time online than in person, and have less time for neighbors and clubs, many sociologists note that Americans long for a greater sense of community. For better or worse, in a shopping mall you're part of something, and through our tastes and shopping interests we connect with others. As noted in Chapter Two, there is a greater cultural emphasis on the superficial, appearances, and quick visual communication.

Jim, fifty-six, was sitting at a San Francisco stoplight in his BMW 750i when a bass-booming beat-up BMW from a decade or two ago pulled up alongside. The young Latino in the passenger seat looked over at Jim and his watch, then lowered his window and asked, "Is that a Panerai Radiomir?" Jim nodded, and the twenty-something young man smiled and said, "Cool. I'm getting one of those. I've been looking at them for a year now." Everyone exchanged a wave, and they drove off—united, if only for a few minutes, over BMWs and Panerai watches—regardless of age, race, or income.

There is an enormously powerful need for people to belong to groups—back in caveman days it was essential to stay alive. Today, when we're ever more likely to bond over our interests than we are over our gender, age, or race, we look for things to show belonging. Like that need to belong, a strong interest in buying and having things isn't something new—people have wanted special things since there have been people.

Like it or not, the things we choose to buy (and not buy) really do say a lot about who we are. More important, they reinforce to others and to ourselves that we're part of something bigger. This goes well beyond the idea of status purchasing—it's about human connection. As Miuccia Prada said in a *Wall Street Journal* article about her company, "What you wear is how you present yourself to the world, especially today, when human contacts are so quick. Fashion is instant language."[1]

Critics of consumption often mistakenly assume that the motivation to purchase is to one-up your friends and neighbors; they view purchasing as simply a way to tell others that you're in some way wealthier, more successful, or more privileged. It's much more than that—in fact, today purchasing is more likely to be about belonging and a way of connecting and joining than simply a means to impress. It's still often used to get attention, but status is related more to personal influence than money. Gen Yers use consumption to showcase and share their creativity and interests, attract (and sometimes repel) other people by their selections, and let (even demand that) others know who they are through what they buy and own.

When it comes to creating a community, back-to-school time is like a shared national birthday. It's a time when parents everywhere reflect on their kids' getting older and the passage of time. Purchasing is a way to both celebrate it and, well, stop getting all welled up about it. Back-to-school (and college) shopping is reinforced by the fact that "everyone is doing it" and, in addition to the required notebooks and thumb drives, "everyone" also wears new clothes to school. Back-to-school shopping is hardly new, but the amount of money being spent each year has grown tremendously. It's now the second most important selling season of the year for retailers, after Christmas.

It's a gigantic example of our powerful instinct to belong and connect though clothes, cell phones, backpacks, and sneakers. "The two most important days of the year are the first day of school and the last day before Christmas break," explains Shanna, sixteen, of Chicago. "What you wear the first day of school kind of sets up who you are and, you know, first impressions and all. Then, the last day before break you want to wear something good because that's how people will remember you."

Gen Y's love of individuality may *appear* to throw a wrench into this idea that groups are formed—or at least aided—by possessions. In fact, for many Gen Yers anti-brand brands, or thrift store finds *are* the connection. Just as one group of Juicy Couture–loving sophomores may scoff at the kids who wear Goodwill goodies, the latter group may hold in equal contempt the carefully selected Juicy garb of the former group. Connecting by not buying a brand is as powerful as connecting through a brand—the medium is still retail.

From our youngest Gen Y focus groups to the oldest, and with both guys and girls, the message was the same: what you wear says who you are. In our group of nine- and ten-year-olds we heard Katarina's angst on visiting New York and seeing different styles: "I felt like I'm so weird because I'm dressed like a California person and not a New York person." And at ten years old, Carmen's already thinking about what her outfits say: "When you go to a funeral, if you don't wear something fancy it looks like you don't care, that you don't respect the person."

James, nineteen, of Portland, is a YouTube-worthy skater. When questioned about what he and his friends wear, they showed us their shoelace belts, which are badges of authenticity and worn for a reason by real skaters: to minimize injuries. They noted that others copied their look right down to the belts, but the nuances gave them away. "We see the worn-out-looking clothes in Abercrombie and think, geez, that's the way ours look when we get done with them; we could probably sell the clothes we've skated in."

For Gen Y, the use of possessions and clothing as a way to communicate and bond is ramped up exponentially by the visual media through which they stay connected. "We post on Facebook what we wore out the last night and have to have different outfits and looks each time," says Amber, twenty, who lives in Charleston, South Carolina.

This sense of community is facilitated not just by clothing, but by well-developed brands and retailers of all sorts—for Gen Y young men and boys, nothing seems to top video games. Danny, seventeen, of Rockville, Maryland, says he and his friends would sometimes get together on a Saturday afternoon and play the World of Warcraft computer game until three in the morning. "It's not as intense as the word addictive is," says Danny. "Some kids do turn to video games as a way to escape. For me, it's more of a socializing thing."

Similarly, many Gen Yers are so connected to their favorite retailers and brands they often feel like they are investing in a relationship, not unlike one they'd have at school or their jobs.

"The young girls are obsessed with it," Gela Nash-Taylor says of the Juicy Couture brand she and Pamela Skaist-Levy launched in 1996 with a line of pricey track suits. Sitting in the VIP room of their Rodeo Drive flagship store, surrounded by flowers and giant decanters of candy, Nash-Taylor and Skaist-Levy explained why they think their brand has clicked with kids—both young and older. It's the attraction of collecting things, the obvious close friendship between the founders—who call themselves "girls"—and the cheeky marketing. And, of course, the clothes.

"Celebrating friendship and girl power—that's very Juicy," says Nash-Taylor. "We're not alone in our obsession with stuff; we do live in a disposable world, and it's human nature to want to collect things."

Shopping Is a Mental Vacation

Karen, forty-four, began the hunt for a new chandelier for her dining room nearly a year ago. Since then, she's purchased three—a retro chic one for her dining room, which was subsequently moved to the kitchen; a new, larger, and more stately replacement for her dining room; and recently a festive little sparkler for her Gen Y daughter's room. When jokingly asked if she'd become a chandelieraholic, Karen said that it started as a task and a hunt for one chandelier, but then it came to be a relaxing and enjoyable mental break to scroll through chandeliers online.

Karen's not alone. More than half (56 percent) of our survey respondents said shopping provided a "mental vacation," and a great many of the folks that we interviewed described shopping using terms such as "soothing," "relaxing," "deliciously mindless," and "a stress reliever." That makes sense—online or in a store, for most, shopping can be a pleasant, mindless activity. There's lots of positive stimulation; you can have as much or as little social interaction as you like; and perhaps most important, it's something to do to give yourself time to think and to process information.

After all, our society isn't big on "sitting and thinking." Imagine this: your boss sees you sitting at your desk seemingly doing nothing; she asks why you're not working, and you tell her that you're "thinking"—you'd probably hear some version of "Get busy" in response. So we all have "doing" activities that are actually a way to sneak in thinking time—and shopping is a popular one. It keeps the conscious mind busy so that the subconscious mind can solve problems and mull things over. Psychologists who research creativity have found that creative ideas and insights come from "unconscious incubation" that occurs most often when people are engaged in "mindless" activities. It's no wonder, then, that Gen Yers were even more likely to call shopping a "mental vacation" than older respondents. In their heavily scheduled worlds, milling around a mall may be one of the few times in a week that they get for mindlessness.

Kimmi, twenty-seven, one of Kit's graduate students at Golden Gate University, admits to shopping almost every day. With her school located just a few blocks from Saks, Macy's, Neiman Marcus, Nordstrom, H&M, and Zara—to name a few— it is hard to resist. But with only a part-time job and student loans, how (and why?) does Kimmi do it?

"I know when things will go on sale, and I sort of stake them out. Sometimes I end up buying something full price, but then I usually return it and wait for it to go on sale. I know what the best looks are, and if I can find something close at Zara I might pay full price there."

Talking with Kimmi, it's clear she's an expert shopper. Though Kimmi's always enjoyed shopping, she says that she shops more now as "sort of a hobby, to relax, and a way to help my friends." Graduate school has been a stressful transition for her, but when it comes to shopping, she's confident, in control, and masterful. Kimmi, like many people, uses shopping to bolster her confidence, as a mental break, and to reward herself.

The Potent Psychology of Sales

Here's why sales work. They:

- Take away that rational process of considering if something is "worth it." If it was $100 and it's now $30, we tend to think, "It must be worth it" and buy impulsively. Incidentally, that part where we wonder whether it's worth it is where our logical brain kicks in, which slows us down. Without it, we're more emotional and less rational about our purchases.

- Pare down choices—which most shoppers find overwhelming. This makes it seem easier to shop and consequently easier to buy.

- Create a sense of urgency and a fear of missing out. We think, "If I don't buy it now it won't be there later." For competitive-sport shoppers this is particularly irresistible.

- Allow us to rationalize purchases, thereby giving ourselves an excuse to buy.

- Make us feel like we're saving, rather than spending, money. We tend to focus on what we saved rather than what we spent. "Wow! I just saved $300 on this coat! We can go out to dinner now!"

- Prime the pump. It's a well-known consumer fact: the first dollar comes out of the wallet slowly, but once someone starts spending, it gets easier.

Shopping Is a Way to Prepare and Feel More in Control

When people get engaged to be married or find out they're pregnant, they often can't wait to go shopping. When people want to go on diets, go green, even save money—ironically enough, they will most often start by buying something. Buying makes what we're feeling seem more real, and it makes us feel committed to new causes.

Shopping is also a way of mentally rehearsing new things. As we go through the process of considering purchases, picking things out, and looking at things, we visualize and more powerfully anticipate the new events; this helps us feel more prepared and in control. To illustrate this point, imagine preparing for a dinner party—as you think about what you'll serve, you think about your guests while visualizing and mentally "tasting" your considerations to determine what things will go together well and whether or not your guests will agree. Similarly, as we consider purchases of all sorts, we often imagine how others will react or what they'd be like in a different environment. In short, we take a mental trip into the future as we shop, and in addition to helping us figure out what to buy, those mental excursions help us to anticipate and prepare for the future. And that in turn gives us a greater sense of control.

It's no wonder then that over two-thirds of our survey respondents said they particularly liked to go shopping when things are changing in their life—like a new job, school, or home, or a special event. It's not just the things we buy that make shopping so alluring during transitions and changes; it's also the shopping itself!

Finally, an explanation for why Americans stockpile wool in August. Fall clothing is traditionally purchased months before it's worn—and in most parts of the country during the hottest month of the year. Retailers like Zara and H&M can turn a fashion idea into reality-on-the-rack in less than a month, so it's no longer about lead time. And our annual pilgrimage to the malls for fall fashions isn't just for the back-to-school crowd anymore either. Though we all have a bit of the squirrel in us (instinctively preparing for the winter and all), and those early competitive sales are hard to resist, we're also responding to shopping's unique ability to catapult us into the future, generate excitement, and help us feel prepared.

In addition to the allure of shopping as a means of mental rehearsal, shopping during life transitions also calms anxiety. As pleasurable as most transitions can be, there is always stress and anxiety in the unknown. Because shopping is a "doing" thing, it fosters a sense of control. Here's an example using Gen Y's particular twist:

College spending has dramatically increased in recent years. Between 2003 and 2008, back-to-college spending—on everything from apparel to computers but not including textbooks— nearly doubled, from $16.7 billion in 2003 to $31.3 billion in 2008, according to BIGresearch.[2] In addition to kids just having, wanting, and expecting more these days, spending has also increased because of the important emotional role that shopping plays in helping today's more involved parents adjust to this big life transition. Psychologically, parents are using off-to-college shopping as a way to visualize their child's future environment, feel more in control of the transition, and be with their child through a shared activity so that everyone has the chance to process this new level of independence. Simply put, it's an emotional rehearsal: as parents buy and consider items, they're imagining their kids using them, and it helps them to feel more secure.

With the closer relationship that kids have with their parents these days—and the greater dependency that parents have on their friendships with their kids—it's no wonder off-to-college shopping has become a much bigger event for parents, kids, *and retailers* in the past few years. Smart marketers like Target and Kohl's have raked in sales with matching dorm ensembles and mini-kitchen essentials.

Here are a few comments from our special survey of college-bound kids—note the brand love, parental involvement, and gender differences, some of which we'll explain in more detail in the next chapters.

"I enjoyed buying my sheets because they are hot pink and I loved them the moment I saw them. When we were shopping my mom said that college would probably be the only time in my life

when it would be acceptable to own pink sheets, so she told me to go for it even though they were more expensive than the other options. My dad and I went back and forth before we settled on the perfect computer. It made me feel like I was much closer to being a college student."

—*Robyn, University of Michigan*

"Being that it was my first year in college, I was willing to pay a lot of money to be comfortable and prepared. Clothes and electronics were the most enjoyable to buy. My favorite memory was going to Marc Jacobs to get a scarf and ending up getting a really expensive pair of shoes instead."

—*Iko, UCLA*

"Buying new clothes was fun in a very manly way."

—*Thomas, University of Michigan*

Thomas also said that he did most of his shopping "whenever girls were in the mood" to accompany him.

"Last year I was heading off to my freshman year of college so I felt really pressured to buy a lot of nice clothes so I could make a good impression on the people I would meet. I wanted a variety of 'going out shirts' since I knew I would be attending parties more than I had in high school. These tops include tanks, halter tops and in general, tops that are fancier and kind of showy! I wear jeans a lot and don't think spending $200 or more is excessive for something I'll wear every day."

—*Rachel, University of Missouri-Columbia*

"I loved shopping for clothing and for my room! My mom and I argued a lot though over what would look good in my dorm room. I bought Uggs, North Face, Juicy sweats and zip-ups, and Citizen Jeans."

—*Paige, Penn State University*

"For my birthday I got a Chanel purse, a classic item that would last me for the rest of my life, that I picked out with my mother. It was for my eighteenth birthday and is by far the most expensive thing I have been given. For school, I look up things online first, then I go to the stores and I get to see everything, then I decide what I like the most."

—*Ana, Southern Methodist University*

"My favorite memory about shopping for college was when I was shopping with my mom for things for my room. I got a blender and she told me she only wanted to hear about the smoothies I made, but enjoy the margaritas."

—*Blair, Loyola Chicago*

"Clothes are always the most fun to buy! My mom and I spent a whole lot of time together shopping for all my college stuff."

—*Kari, University of Michigan*

Shopping Well: A New Olympic Sport?

"I always, and I mean always, get the best deal of all my friends. If I can't get it on sale—like really on sale—I don't want it. Even if I had the money, well actually I could afford to buy stuff for full price if I wanted to, but it's no fun. I love the hunt."

So says Gayle, fifty-two, of Walnut Creek, California. We call Gayle, and the millions of Americans like her, competitive sport shoppers. Some wait in line for hours to be first inside for "Midnight Madness" sales, some have finely tuned radar for sales and specials, and still others cultivate insider relationships with sales people from their favorite stores. In the end what they all have in common is skill, stamina, and a special talent for finding special products and getting great deals. Just like knitting or skiing, great shopping is an accomplished art and, for many, a hobby that defines them. For other, less-Olympian shoppers, it's an area of competence that—like cooking—just feels great to have. To be masterful and competent at anything, especially something so valued by society as getting the right stuff at the best price, is psychologically rewarding.

For Gen Yers shopping well means more than getting the best bargains—it's also about finding something special and unique, or creating a custom pair of Nikes online that everybody admires, or downloading the perfect play mix for a party.

Technology has created a world waiting to be customized. Creative Gen Yers can use websites to design the fabric of their bed sheets, create custom energy bars with just the right mix of not only flavors but also nutrients, have real outfits made based on the ones they designed for their online avatars, and craft clothing of all sorts according to their tastes. They can also sell their work to others on many of those sites. It's just a question of time before you'll be able to get a commission for selling everything from memberships at your gym to the outfit you're wearing in a Facebook photo through widgets from the manufacturer's web store on your page.

Shopping Centers and Malls Are Increasingly Integrated Into Our Lives

Malls have become community centers and a safe (well, at least physically safe) place for kids to get together. Mall developers have done a great job of incorporating entertainment into shopping centers—from movies and sports to coffee shops and fine dining, there's something for everyone these days. At the same time, many communities have lost places where young people can hang out. So while kids are socializing in malls, they come to feel right at home—and along with that comes a familiarity and comfort level that results in a very unguarded, open, and positive perception of malls and shopping. How could you not have warm feelings about the place where you got your first pair of jeans, your first iPod, and, for many, your first glimpse of Santa Claus? Consequently, although they are safe in some ways, there's some risky psychological training going on too. After all, malls are built for the purpose of selling things; the entertainment is there to attract people—ultimately, to sell products.

As we all know, proximity fosters intimacy. Consequently, when kids feel close to and familiar with brands, owning them seems only natural. Some of the "entitlement" that shocks parents is really an expression of familiarity. Old-fashioned luxury stores, where kids get dirty looks from suspicious salespeople who know they can't afford the goods, are losing ground to places like Prada. Prada's artistic, techno-advanced design (including "responsive" dressing room mirrors in some of their stores that give shoppers the chance to simultaneously see images of themselves in all the outfits they've tried on) lures folks in—if only to check out the store for now. Shoppers are encouraged to linger, make themselves at home, and maybe now or maybe someday come back and buy. Likewise, Apple's playground of computers showcases new products, and also creates familiarity that's proven to blossom into ownership.

All this is compounded and reinforced by the Internet, where kids learn and play and socialize—when they're not at the mall. "How can I not feel like I should be interested in all that stuff when I see it every day splashed all over Facebook?" complains Fiona, twenty-six, of Atlanta.

Not only does this close relationship with malls, stores, and shopping websites integrate buying and having more fully into Gen Yers' lives, but it's also resulted in the sense of ownership that many Gen Yers feel they have of the places they shop and the products they're considering. As such, they feel it's their right to expect retailers to cater to them—and pity the shop or web merchant that disappoints. Gen Yers use their ability to connect with others through word of mouth, online reviews, or a Twitter bomb as revenge.

We Buy for Hopefulness

With a few exceptions, people buy *in anticipation*. Every new item offers hope of something better, even if it's just quenched thirst (or antioxidant-infused, revitalizing, and tasty quenched thirst). It may be something new and transformative, or it may be a replacement for something that's worn out or not working. But one way or another, there has to be a psychological expectation that the money spent will improve life in some way.

The most hopeful new purchases even cross the line to inspirational. New products with promise can bolster confidence. Much as we want to think we're immune to an artificial retail boost, the fact is that the right outfit *can* make someone feel more confident on a date or in an interview. A study by U.K. professor Craig Roberts, reported in *Advertising Age*,[3] found that men who used Lynx deodorant (the British version of Axe) were seen as more attractive in videos than those who used a deodorant without fragrance—at least until they started talking. Obviously, their boosted confidence was apparent to the women who viewed the videos.

For most Americans, the purchases we make are not intended to satisfy simply basic needs. We don't buy clothing, for example, primarily to say warm or dry. If we did, last year's coat—or a blanket, for that matter—would be fine. And we're not buying food just to sustain our lives. We want *particular* foods that satisfy our tastes, celebrate our guests, impress our families, or provide the basis for creative expression. Incidentally, those in culinary circles point to Gen Y as the driving force behind more complex, ethnic, socially conscious food preferences.

So what are people really buying when they think they're buying cars or clothes or sports drinks? The most accurate answer lies in our fundamental emotional needs: security, confidence, self-esteem, respect, adventure, expression, love, sex, belonging, aesthetic pleasure, power, and freedom.

The key is to go beyond the obvious, empathize with your customers, and understand their deepest needs. Is it really sex, or the attention that comes from being sexy? Admiration, or the security of knowing you're OK? Greed, or the anxiety of emptiness? Perfectionism, or a fear of being wrong?

Gen Y is even more hopeful than previous generations. They've seen the power of technology, and they believe in "new" as better. A product that "hasn't changed its formula for twenty-five years" sounds tried and true to many baby boomers; to a Gen Yer, "tired" would be more like it, so the product would be beyond consideration. So it's thanks to this younger generation that we have constantly and rapidly evolving skin care products, fashions, and most especially technology.

"They are the primary drivers moving all technologies forward," says Steve Koenig, director of industry analysis for the Consumer Electronics Association. "They innovate by adopting altogether new technologies without any qualms."

From Bridezilla to . . . Promzilla!

For decades, the wedding has been society at its most glamorous and, often, ostentatious. It's created a being known as Bridezilla, who can become so overcome with *The Event* that all else gets lost in the picture—even, for some, the marriage.

These days Bridezilla is at the mercy of—well, so much. But it's her ability to convince herself that she's doing the right thing by loading up her (and often her parents') credit cards with debt for her wedding that sets the stage for it all. Granted, she lives in a world that gives her a lot of ammo. We've all heard these words gushed when it comes to weddings (especially by those hoping to cash in themselves): "It's a once-in-a-lifetime event!" "It's *your* day." "It should be perfect." "Make your dream wedding." "You're making memories." Bridezilla separates herself from the pack by *believing* it, and believing it's worth going into debt to achieve.

Which brings us to a new phenomenon. Bridezilla's baby sister . . . Promzilla! As kids marry later, proms are a stopgap big formal event that serves the emotional purpose of showcasing a teenager as an adult for the first time. Prom is the multicultural *quinceañera* or modern debutante ball. And as such, it's an event that now often includes the egos and involvement of parents—who, themselves, have contributed to the elevated stature of prom.

Though a healthy chunk of prom expenses are paid for by teens themselves, parents still have the authority to approve purchases and are compensating for gaps in budgets.

Leslie, eighteen, of Charlotte, North Carolina, found her dream prom dress online and then convinced her mom to drive two and a half hours to buy it. The straight dress with bold pastel prints and a crisscross of sequins down the back cost more than $500. "When my mom saw the dress I wanted, she was like, 'What are you thinking? You're only going to wear it once,'" Leslie said. "But she knew it was the one I wanted. When something like that [prom] comes up, you just want to go all out."

Most parents behave responsibly, but there are always a few who overspend on their kids, either to make a statement to the community or to buy their kids' affections. Those families set unrealistic and even unhealthy standards for other parents, who sometimes feel pressured into spending more than they'd like in order to avoid feeling as if they've deprived or disappointed their child. The community nature of prom makes this an event ripe with peer pressure for both the kids and their parents.

It's no wonder, then, that prom spending is on the rise. Dramatically. Prom spending nearly doubled between 2003 and 2007—it's now estimated to be a $6 billion industry.[4] And it's not only the girls that are driving it; though they're certainly leading the charge, boys are more interested in spending for prom than ever before.

Just like Bridezillas, Promzillas can get swept up in the idea that they're "creating memories" by buying the right props. Emphasis is placed on the role of preparatory purchases—from pedicures and jewelry to limos and pre-parties—rather than emotions and the relationship, as a way to ensure a successful event. In some households kids spend more time at the pre-photo session than they do at the prom.

As we know from earlier in this chapter, shopping for events is emotional preparation, and for many it heightens the excitement of the event. Promzillas, however, become so enraptured with the shopping preparation that they lose sight of the event—and anybody else who might be involved.

The principal of a Long Island Catholic high school cancelled his school's 2006 prom because of all the extravagance and "bacchanalian aspects." "It is not primarily the sex/booze/drugs that surround this event, as problematic as they might be; it is rather the flaunting of affluence, assuming exaggerated expenses, a pursuit of vanity for vanity's sake—in a word, financial decadence," Brother Kenneth M. Hoagland wrote in a two-thousand-word letter to parents quoted in an October 2005 Associated Press article.[5]

Just like today's brides, today's prom-goers are subjected to loads of pressure from retailers. Prom is now a full-fledged spending season, and retailers of anything from flashlights to acne cream look for opportunities to promote their products as prom night necessities. Most of the kids we spoke with got ideas about what should be part of their prom experience either from shopping or from magazines—both of which are saturated with prom-specific advertisements and promotions.

Prom dress designer DeBora Rachelle has noticed a steady increase in the attention—and money—devoted to prom. "It's like a mini-wedding, and it's the first time for them to have a huge event in their lives," said Rachelle, who's been designing since 1990. "Now it's twenty to thirty kids renting a Hummer limo. People are even renting boats." Rachelle's main prom line retails for between $250 and $600, but she can custom-design dresses on request—and has—for between $5,000 and $11,000 for pop stars and just regular girls from New York or California.

The Dark Side

It's easy to see why shopping is so popular and pervasive. And it's also easy to see how shopping can turn into spending problems. How people can go way beyond shopping as the "retail therapy" we know, love, and laugh about, to becoming overly dependent on shopping as a serious psychological crutch.

Although most Gen Yers are not in debt, as a generation they're more in debt than any previous generation, and many worry that their love of merchandise, discerning tastes, high expectations, and impulsive natures are a setup for irresponsible spending. Of all generations, Gen Yers were the least likely to cut back their spending after the onset of the 2008 recession,[6] though it's true that they are also less likely to have mortgages, kids, and other major financial encumbrances that might impede spending than those in older generations.

They're certainly more pampered more than previous generations—in 2009 they averaged over twice what their parents got in allowances in high school (in inflation-adjusted dollars).[7] Nearly half of all U.S. apparel expenditures in 2008 were made for or by Americans under twenty-five years old, according to the NPD Group.[8] Over half of kids aged six to eleven and 75 percent of teens have a television set in their room, according to a 2007 Experian Simmons study.[9] In 1960, the average wedding cost $3,500; in 1980 it was $6,000. In 2009 the average cost of a wedding topped $30,000.[10]

Gen Yers are also far more likely than previous generations to go to college and more likely to be in debt when they graduate. Sixty percent of degree recipients in 2007 borrowed to fund their education, and the average debt upon graduation was $22,700. In addition to college loans, 66 percent of college undergraduates have at least one credit card, and in 2007 college seniors with balances owed an average of $2,632.[11]

Gen Y has been hit with a triple whammy—lots of spending influence, without the necessary education about the consequences of spending to go with it; high expectations (and great taste) from having been indulged; and abundant confidence in their ability to make as much money as they'll need.

Shelly Banjo, a reporter for the *Wall Street Journal*, interviews hundreds of twenty-somethings a year and researches and writes about young people and finances (and she's a Gen Y high achiever herself). "Our generation has little exposure to the financial basics that we need to live our lives," Banjo says. She's found that many Gen Yers "haven't learned the basics like how simple decisions can have repercussions throughout life and lack sophistication on finances, debt, and long-term planning." Banjo adds, "People go to universities and graduate with expectations of maintaining that standard of living. Most entry-level jobs pay $25,000 to $50,000 a year, which isn't enough to maintain that lifestyle." And according to Banjo, they don't want to miss out on anything, so they go into debt or neglect saving for the future. According to a 2007 Charles Schwab study, most Gen Y teenagers believe they are prepared to deal with finances, but when asked about things as simple as paying bills, they clearly are not.[12]

Most financial experts believe it all starts with their parents. Everyone acknowledges that today's parents are under much more pressure than previous generations to accommodate their kids' desires and demands. And as you'll see in the next chapter, products—especially clothes for girls and electronics, games, and sports equipment for boys—are part of a normal age-related need to figure out who they are and try on different roles and personas. But in today's society of closer parent-child relationships, more powerful kids, and more emphasis on "stuff," those normal needs have inflated.

Parents are essential in teaching kids the more rational, less social and emotional components of purchasing decisions. According to Dotson and Hyatt, in a 2005 *Journal of Consumer Marketing* study,[13] kids' greater influence on parents, coupled with their increased media consumption and spending power, jeopardize the influence of their parents.

All this is made more difficult by the few parents in every community who raise the bar by overindulging their kids. Some do it because they're stressed out and short on time—and, let's face it, it's easier to give in. Others do it to compete with *their* peers and showcase family wealth through their kids' wardrobes, cars, and indulgences. And of course, some parents simply lack financial sophistication and discipline, which is ever more urgently needed, given the pressures to spend that Gen Yers face. For whatever reason, kids are powerfully influential in getting their parents to fork over money to meet their demands. For example, according to 2007 research conducted by the Harrison Group, 75 percent of parents will give in to their kid's requests for new video games, half of them within two weeks.[14]

Though the economic crisis has contributed to a slowdown, relatively speaking, kids today are still far more influential than in previous generations.

In the end, kids who are overindulged develop expectations and standards that lead to disappointment when they're forced to live within their own means as adults. They're also ultimately less confident than those who are taught to use their own ingenuity and resourcefulness to get the things they want, to delay gratification, and to avoid relying on retail fixes to make them happy.

We met lots of Gen Yers with ingenuity who had found ways to satisfy their expressive and creative needs by doing things like altering clothes, trolling thrift stores, selling on eBay—or simply saving for something special. Their pride—not only in their video games, clothing, or skateboards but also in their resourcefulness—was obvious.

For others, however, there's a dark side to always getting what you want. In addition to missing out on the personal pride of earning and enjoying the fruits of their labor, those who are overindulged often develop a sense of entitlement. "Entitlement" has become a nasty term, and one all too often used to describe Gen Y. A July 2007 *Wall Street Journal* article, "Blame It on

Mr. Rogers: Why Young Adults Feel So Entitled,"[15] was the most frequently read and emailed article of the week—clearly it's a hot-button topic for many.

In our research we did not find this to be a hallmark of this generation, but we did see higher expectations in general and confidence that might appear to be arrogance. Nevertheless, the continuum that ranges from "hope" to "expectation" to "entitlement" is shifting toward entitlement, particularly for the youngest members of Gen Y, but frankly for all of our society. Teenagers at least have an excuse—self-absorption during those years is normal.

Gen Yers who fall squarely on the entitled end of the spectrum are in the minority, but they're getting a lot of attention. After all, it's just not pretty. We'd like to point out that the irritation faced by those who are asked to accommodate them is much less significant than the emotional wreckage faced by the entitled. When unrealistic expectations are unmet (which is often the case), the result is anger, disappointment, and frustration. Ultimately, those emotions become the soundtrack of their lives. Pleasure, appreciation, and the ability to think about other people's needs are replaced by negative emotions, and this makes relationships—the cornerstone of happiness—difficult.

The seventeen- and eighteen-year-olds Ken Reed teaches financial planning to at Blackman High School in the Nashville suburb of Murfreesboro, Tennessee, regularly tease him about his Levis, off-brand Crocs, and Nike sneakers, which they think aren't nearly trendy enough. Although the area has a mix of welfare families and college-educated professionals—thanks in part to a nearby university and Nissan's new headquarters—what kids wear often has little to do with their family's income. The 15 percent who get free or reduced-price lunch are as likely to be wearing $180 sneakers or similarly pricey designer jeans as kids from more well-to-do families.

"They confuse wants and needs," says the thirty-eight-year-old Reed, who worked as an accountant before he became a teacher. "They feel almost peer pressure to live above their lifestyles."

And though parents are lately slowing their spending, the urge to indulge is still alive and well. Manhattan-based Tina Tang boutique manager Chloe Caldwell recalls an instance when an eleven-year-old girl came in with her mother and spotted a $98 dollar necklace she liked. Initially the mother resisted the girl's pleas for the jewelry, but shortly she gave in and sprang for one—and another as a gift for the daughter's friend.

Once a standard is set, it's hard to go backward. Just as Shelly Banjo pointed out, we also found that many of the twenty-somethings we interviewed often felt frustrated or deprived by their beginning salaries. Beverly Winslow, Ph.D., a psychotherapist who specializes in young adults and families, works in one of the wealthier suburbs of San Francisco. She's seen this attitude cause problems with young Gen Y couples. "Young people today become independent later. They become used to shopping and buying a lot and then go through a crash when reality sets in and they don't have much money to spend. Especially when all of a sudden they have kids, it can put huge pressure on a couple." Dr. Winslow adds, "There's a lot of interest in expensive things, and kids often have an attitude that if they want it they should have it—now."

Marketers appealing to what they believed to be Gen Y's inflated sense of self-importance were actually tapping into something more important—the need to rationalize purchasing. "You deserve it" and "only the best for you" resonates not only because it appeals to a sense of superiority, but even more so as a way to assuage guilt when wanting to purchase quality. After all, Gen Y knows quality.

"Gen Y is a privileged generation—we had everything—we learned our consumption habits in our childhood and teens," says twenty-six-year-old graduate student Melody from New York City. "Now we struggle to maintain a quality of life that, for many of us, may even be unrealistic. Because many of us are committed to having disposable income, even when we are all just entering the workforce and are all a ways off from our money making peak, many of us are in debt. Shopping is an activity—like a vacation, or a bike ride, or a trip to Six Flags. I often find myself using language like 'I deserve it' or 'I work hard' to justify spending money. Shopping is a reward much more than it is a necessity."

Lisa, a twenty-eight-year-old systems specialist who grew up in Connecticut, says that she feels really conflicted about her spending values. "On the one hand, I don't know if I'll ever be able to save enough money to buy a home, and I really resent that it was easier for my parents' generation. On the other hand, I eat out in restaurants at least twice a week. My parents eat in restaurants for special occasions. What I spend on a weeknight dinner with my husband would be a special occasion for my parents. They sacrificed, and I've just never done that."

Ally, twenty-nine, of San Francisco, concurs with a story of her own: "When my parents celebrated their twenty-fifth wedding anniversary my dad gave Mom a Rolex, and it was *such* a big thing. My roommate's boyfriend gave her a Rolex when they'd dated like six months! I mean, where do you go from there?"

Gen Y parents have treated their kids to the best they could afford—often sacrificing their own extravagances (and even retirements) to do so. As Emmy—mother of the self-described "diva" Lexi, twenty-three—explains, "My mom wasn't as close to me as I am to Lexi—I think it was easier for her to say 'You can have these nice things I have when you're my age and work for them.' I could never do that with Lexi. If I was getting Diane von Furstenberg, it seemed like she should be able to have it too. I'd feel guilty buying her cheap stuff when I'm buying quality things for myself." Unlike the experience of previous generations, more equality in the household has resulted in higher expectations that kids will also have an equal share of their parent's discretionary funds. So if Dad's just purchased new shoes, his teenage son feels justified holding that against him in an argument about getting a new cell phone.

We'd like to point out here that most of the adult Gen Yers we spoke with appreciated top-quality goods, but they were not necessarily overspending. Many had, however, learned those lessons in frugality through a painful process of overcoming debilitating credit card debt. Which brings us to the second factor contributing to financial woes of this generation: previously easy credit and impulsive purchasing.

According to research conducted by Fidelity Investments,[16] "young consumers are more likely to use credit than to save for short-term purchases, which results in an ongoing struggle with debt management." The study also found that 40 percent of Gen Yers with workplace retirement plans cash them out when they change jobs.

Credit cards create a detachment from money that often makes spending precious funds seem less relevant than the gratification of buying something tangible. That, coupled with the speedy, often impulsive nature of this generation, can cause problems.

The nosedive in the economy has reined in spending, but not necessarily the desire of parents to indulge their kids, or the desire of kids to have the best. Gen Yers and their parents have shifted from conspicuous consumption to more considered consumption. They're clearly more value oriented than they were in the past; however, Gen Y tweens and teens and their parents have proven to be the most resistant to belt tightening.

We found a difference in attitude and expectations between the over-twenty-two and under-twenty-two Gen Yers. Older Gen Yers were less prone to extravagance even as teens and were already in the process of cutting back before the recession began. Younger Gen Yers were more optimistic than ever that their ability to earn would always match their abundant desires. We found this group, who grew up with more of everything—connectivity, prosperity (until 2008), and freedom—to be less inclined toward budgeting than their older counterparts. It's not that they don't care; they're just finding it hard to believe that they won't be successful enough to finance their wants.

Take 2008 holiday spending, for example: while the rest of the country dramatically trimmed spending, in surveys Gen Y, and teens in particular, reported the least intention of any group to cut back.[17] And certainly video games, purchased more by Gen Y than by other age groups, haven't been hurt by the economic slowdown—even at full price. The same is true for the vampire-themed merchandise sold at Hot Topic in celebration of the movie *Twilight*. So enthusiastic were Gen Y shoppers that Hot Topic was one of the few retailers to post increased sales during one of the most dismal holiday retail periods in history.

Asked by BIGresearch in January 2009 to describe their feelings about the chances for a strong economy in the first six months of 2009, 33 percent of eighteen- to twenty-four-year-olds and 32 percent of twenty-five- to twenty-nine-year-olds were very optimistic or optimistic, compared with just 23 percent of those over thirty.[18] In the same survey, adults aged eighteen through twenty-nine were far less likely to say that they planned to reduce their spending on clothing and electronics, despite the negative economy, than those over thirty. The youngest members of the group, those aged eighteen through twenty-four, were even less inclined.

The exuberance, optimism, and extreme confidence of many Gen Yers can be charming and inspiring—and also cause for concern in tough economic times. Depending on their personality, the challenges that inspire fortitude in some provoke a fingers-in-the-ears "la, la, la, I can't hear you" in others.

A post by twenty-three-year-old Ypulse managing editor Meredith Sires, "The Power of Positive Thinking: How Gen Y Will Get Through the Recession,"[19] is loaded with optimism about their job prospects (because boomers will retire and there aren't many Gen Xers), their ability to keep a cool head (because they haven't known anxiety in the past), their ability to plan (a proven talent, as they see it; after all, they made it through high school and into college and landed a job), and finally, "If all else fails? We'll move back in with our parents. No, it wouldn't be ideal, but it's still a viable option if we need it. Unlike Gen X, this move backwards isn't synonymous with failure. It's more like a reset button."

The Most Common Psychological Reasons Why We— All of Us, Not Just Gen Y—Overspend

- To compensate for feelings of deprivation—feeling unappreciated or unloved, overburdened, or overworked.
- To avoid dealing with anger in personal relationships.
- Because we're not taking control and personal responsibility and instead blame others or situations for our financial decisions.
- We shop when exhausted or under stress, which sabotages reasoning and dissolves will.
- We have a distorted sense of entitlement and a feeling that we deserve things and the rest will sort itself out.
- We buy to fill a sense of emptiness. An overemphasis on what we have and how we look can create a sense of emptiness—which is momentarily filled by approval and attention for new purchases and appearances. This "mini-fix" isn't deeply satisfying but offers just enough relief to become a distracting addiction, ultimately exacerbating the emptiness—which leads to more buying.

You Need to Know Y's Whys

The whys behind the buys are complex and emotional for this generation. Given the abundance of options available to them, understanding their surface needs isn't enough. Marketers need to go deeper. Shopping plays a gigantic role in helping Gen Yers connect with each other, learn about and understand themselves, and feel more in control of the future. Products are more important than ever in their ability to satisfy social and emotional needs. Marketers and retailers have a great opportunity, more so with this generation than any other, to be a central part of these customers' lives and to be adored. And just like any other meaningful relationship, it's earned through listening, understanding, and satisfying emotional needs.

4

THE LIVES, MINDS, AND HEARTS OF TODAY'S TWEENS, TEENS, AND TWENTY-SOMETHINGS

Rachael, twenty-three, and Ally, seventeen, are both shopping with their mothers at Caché in San Francisco. Rachael and her mother evaluate dresses together. They're giggling and sharing frank, figure-specific evaluations and a closeness that previous generations would have found only with their best girlfriends. Meanwhile, seventeen-year-old Ally dutifully takes the dresses her mother suggests into the dressing room—but she doesn't try them on. She and three of her friends picked out the dress she wants her mother to buy for her a week ago. She's simply humoring Mom—a process she knows is effective. Chances are that when Ally is twenty-three, just like Rachael, her mom will once again be her shopping buddy and confidant. But for now Ally needs to figure out who she is—that's been the developmental task of all teenagers for all time—and as it does for many teens, that process often includes rejecting Mom's advice on clothes. Those teen years, dotted with rejection and independence, are especially tough on today's moms who have previously enjoyed friendships with their kids. That's why Ally, who only two years ago relied on her mom's advice, instinctively humors her by trying on gowns she has no intention of buying—she's protecting her mom's feelings and their friendship, while making sure she gets the dress she wants. Ally and Rachael share scores of generational characteristics—but because of their age differences, right now they'll shop and buy in different ways.

Winning Y's Heart Means Investing in a Relationship

Applying cookie-cutter techniques and tactics to reach Gen Y is as effective as thinking your cologne or perfume will make you irresistible to the opposite sex. Though it may help, only in 1960s advertisements did it actually work.

No, with this generation you're going to have to jump in all the way and really get to know them, empathize with them, and invest in a relationship. There's no faking it with this group. And there's no how-to manual of what Gen Y wants, except this: they want to be genuinely seen, known, and appreciated; offered meaningful solutions; and be respected as part of the process.

There are four things a marketer can do to win with Gen Y every time:

- Train yourself to "think like a shrink"—in other words, to get psychological, go deep, and understand what's beneath the surface.
- Get Gen Yers on your team and listen to them. Not for $n = 1$ research studies, but to remind you of how fast things change and to pepper your world with new ideas and insights.
- Keep up with technology and the digital world.
- Take the time to know what their lives are like and how things have changed.

To that end—read on.

Generation Chasm

Have you ever found yourself saying something like, "Back when I was _____ [a teenager, in college, starting my first job ...]"? Though it's human nature to try to understand young people through our own "back in the day" experiences, that automatic comparison will get in the way of understanding any generation in their own terms, especially this one. Not to mention that you'll get the same eye rolls from today's kids that you once gave your elders. Or you might be thinking, "Kids are kids, isn't that what really matters?" That sort of attitude will get you into as much trouble as it did the marketers of the 1970s (R.I.P.) who thought "women are women" and ignored the cultural shift of feminism.

Today's young adults are experiencing 90 percent of the same thrills and challenges you experienced. But make no mistake: their world is different from the one you knew, and they are different. Every generation has a gap, but this gap is a chasm. As the world moves faster, the gap widens more quickly. So though teens are still teens, and starting out is still starting out, Gen Y has an entirely unique set of opportunities, resources, expectations, and problems.

Whether the buy is an impulsively purchased iTune or a carefully considered car, people don't spend money unless they think it will improve their life in some way. And when we say "think," it's more like "sense"—most consumers aren't really aware of the real reasons why they buy what they do. Although someone may buy food because she's hungry, the kind of food, brand of food, and when and where it's purchased all come down to more complicated, deeper motivations. Though we're aware of when we're hungry, most of what we desire isn't even conscious to us—we experience a shorthand version that sounds something like "I need something to wear to that party" or "I saw the coolest iPhone application." Underneath that is a complex web that includes the tremendously powerful developmental tasks that kids must conquer to move from one stage of life to the next.

It's often through an understanding of the problems Gen Y faces that we see opportunities for retailers, brands, and products. Gen Yers will look for solutions to their unique challenges through the marketplace and identify with marketers and retailers that "get them," empathize with them, and can help them.

Every dollar spent (except maybe for taxes) is accompanied by an expectation or hope of a problem resolved. Knowing both the surface needs and the deepest secret ones that lead to purchases, and the subtle nuances of desire that explain why one product is chosen over a seemingly identical one—that's what it takes to compete when Gen Y is your target.

For example, currently *Cosmopolitan* magazine is the best-selling young women's magazine in the world. About eighteen million people in a hundred different countries read *Cosmopolitan* every month. The cover of every issue is pretty much the same: sex, sexy clothes, sex, a celebrity to admire, sex, and makeup techniques to look . . . sexier. Though you'd be correct in thinking that *Cosmopolitan* owes its success to an understanding of the psychology of teens and young women, you'd be wrong if you thought that it was really about the sex.

For sure, young women do want sex, but that's not why they're drawn to cover headlines like "The Sex He Craves" and "62 Sex Moves: Guys Share Tons of Totally Original and Mind-Blowing Tips." As you might have gathered, these articles focus on what *men* want and how to make an impression on a man, rather than on sex itself or women's sexuality. That's because what's important to these readers is not the sex itself; what's important is trying on and exploring roles. And, depending on the age of the reader, it's also about learning how to attract attention, which they've discovered sometimes has something to do with . . . sex *appeal*.

Developmentally, one of the strongest subconscious motivations of sixteen- to twenty-four-year-old women is to prepare to form a couple and to learn how to love. Most of the young women who read *Cosmopolitan* are not seriously honing their sex skills in order to conquer a man, but they are interested in learning about how to be desired—which widens the pool of applicants.

Being sought after and desired satisfies the other major developmental task of this age group—the need to find a unique identity. People in this developmental stage of life often see themselves most clearly through the eyes of others. From how people respond to them to what they say about them to who courts them, the reactions of others offer insights about who they are. Consequently, these young women are also hoping to attract a certain amount of attention. As many a young man can tell you, a woman in this age group may try hard to get a man's attention and interest, but that doesn't necessarily mean she actually wants him. Although most young women do want relationships, they're also interested in knowing that they're desirable and in finding out more about themselves through the feedback they get from a man's attention.

Picture the women who read *Cosmopolitan* on a continuum. According to a research project Kit conducted for *Cosmopolitan*'s launch in Finland, only about 10 percent of the magazine's readers are anything like the fiery, fun sex kittens described within. The rest, in varying degrees, are sampling, fantasizing, and learning about new roles, sexual power, relationships, and themselves. For most readers, *Cosmopolitan* is more like a textbook of ideas than a how-to manual.

Marketers who understand the subtle difference between wanting sex and wanting to be desired will be successful with these readers; those who don't will feel the cold shoulder of a misunderstood woman. Also successful will be the products and pitches that appeal to this young woman's interest in exploring new roles and identities. *Cosmopolitan*'s global appeal is a testament to the magazine's ability to address these two developmental tasks.

Life's Lessons and the Mall

The bridge between childhood and adulthood—otherwise known as the teen and tween years—is a high-impact, vexing time for everyone. Often for parents, certainly for kids in the throes of it all, and especially for the marketers and retailers brave enough to try to reach these groups. Understanding their fickle fascinations requires dedication. Then the twenties offer a whole new set of challenges. Despite their advantages, in many ways this generation has more to deal with than previous generations, and, just as they have their entire lives, they'll often look for solutions in the marketplace.

Social, emotional, and psychological development takes place in steps and stages. Each age-related transition creates needs, insecurities, and opportunities that are addressed by the flip-flops, iPhones, and eventually baby strollers that tweens, teens, and twenties crave and buy.

The age-related, subtle shifts from needing to belong, to needing to be seen, to needing to express themselves and to care for others are all reflected in the details of Gen Y's shopping styles. So while teens and twenty-somethings, like Rachel and Ally, sometimes end up in the same stores, the ways they shop, the whys behind the buys and the snubs, and their decision-making processes will be vastly different.

For forward-thinking marketers, human resource managers, and businesspeople wondering how this particular generation will impact their business now and in the future, this chapter will sort out what's enduringly age-related and what's uniquely Gen Y. For folks hoping for a deeper understanding of the social and emotional needs of today's tweens, teens, and twenty-somethings as they mature, this is your chapter.

It's a Revolution!

From a developmental perspective, tweens, teens, and twenty-somethings are going through nothing short of an internal revolution: a physiological, cognitive, and psychological upheaval. It can also feel like a revolution to the rest of society. Like the boomers who brought us civil rights, feminism, the seeds of globalization, and a technological revolution, Gen Yers are determined to change the world.

Does it seem like Gen Y has more influence than previous generations of youngsters? Are you concerned that Gen Y seems to be getting into more trouble than previous generations? Do you think that, except for our World War II heroes, Gen Y has done greater things at a younger age than previous generations? You may be right—or it may just appear to be the case.

Confidence and technology have empowered this generation. They've also made the extremes visible to everyone. Which is why in any given month you're likely to have found blogs or articles summarizing Gen Y in contradictory ways. Are they eschewing materialism, or hopelessly in debt from credit card binges? Starting successful businesses at sixteen, or lazing around in their parents' homes well into their late twenties? Tartish or wearing purity rings? Because they have more latitude, and because we can (and want to) see it all through enabling technology, all these examples are true for some, but not a blanket summary of this generation. There are genuine shifts in the values, thought styles, and ways that this generation connects with each other and the world. The specifics, however, vary greatly. Which is one thing that Gen Yers all have in common—more freedom and opportunity in the way they choose to live their lives compared with previous generations.

By the way, when you read an alarming article, it helps to keep in mind that every generation thinks, "Today's kids are in trouble." Eventually those kids become adults and think, "Today's kids are in trouble."

A Generation Gaplet and The Facebook Factor

Gen Y is often described as the first generation that grew up on the Internet, but the Internet and digital technology have evolved a lot since the oldest Gen Yers were in high school. There's a mini generation gap between under-twenty and over-twenty Gen Yers, due to the swift progression of technology in the past two decades. When our older Gen Yers were tweens and teens, they did not have sophisticated video games, Guitar Hero, or Wii; an iPod and iTunes; or a MySpace account, YouTube, Skype, or their own blog. Most important, they didn't have a high-speed Internet connection and their own computer in their room. They were also less likely to have had their own cell phone, and certainly they weren't texting or Twittering. Though the first cell phone call was made in 1983, few twenty-somethings had one as a teenager. Today four out of five teenagers have a cell phone—a 40-percent increase just since 2004.[1]

The first commercial text message was send in December 1992; as of this writing, over six billion text messages are sent and received *each day*.[2] To further demonstrate the mini generation gap: by far the most avid texters are teenagers, thirteen to seventeen; they average an amazing 2,272 text messages a month.[3] The over-twenty Gen Yers would find this unimaginable.

As Kimberly Palmer, a senior editor at *U.S. News and World Report* and a Gen Yer herself, points out, "There's a misconception that all of our generation had the same experience with technology. There's a generational difference between older and younger Gen Yers, and the main one is the result of our vastly different experiences of the Internet in our teens." Palmer feels that high school kids are exposed to much more through the Internet, and consequently parents are more protective. She also points out that older Gen Yers are less materialistic and had idols like Kurt Cobain, whereas many of today's teens might think that what's cool is "pedicures and getting their hair done."

Nearly all of the over-twenty-four Gen Yers that we spoke with pointed out this "gaplet." "My younger sister is way more into stuff than I was. She not only wants more, but she's so much more particular about what she wants," says Regina, twenty-five, of San Francisco. "I see young kids with $300 jeans and Coach bags."

Says Jessica, twenty-nine, also of San Francisco, "It's alarming. What concerns me is, if you start at that level, what expectations will they have when they get to my age?" Dawn, twenty-nine, also of San Francisco, wonders if it's a reflection of society: "Look at the size of engagement rings: once it was a symbol of love, now it just has to be the size of a muffin."

And then there's the technology gap: "It's like this hyperactivity. They are always on the Internet with IMs and texting," said Marie, twenty-six, of Atlanta. Parents of teens point it out too. "We went to the beach and there were all these teenagers there together, but they were texting, not talking, to each other, and definitely not enjoying the beach," says Jim, of Seattle. Forty-seven percent of teens say that their social life would end without texting, according to an MTV study, which also found that 45 percent of teens IM their friends to "talk" about a television show they're both watching.[4] Two-thirds of fifteen- to seventeen-year-olds prefer texting to email; for eighteen- to twenty-four-year-olds it's an even split; and among twenty-five- to thirty-four-year-olds, 75 percent prefer email to texting, according to ExactTarget's 2008 Channel Preference Survey.[5] Teens spend approximately four hours each school day devoted to technology-related activities, and nearly half of teens' activities are driven by technology, according to research conducted by the Consumer Electronics Association.[6]

The question of how our relationships are shaped by technology isn't a new one, nor one unique to Gen Y or teens. High levels of Internet use have long been linked to depression and loneliness. Human beings need intimacy and physical contact. A phone call is more intimate than an email exchange, and an email is more intimate than a text message. With limited hours in a day, those spent on a computer or focused on a cell phone are potentially replacing time spent with other people. Anyone who's tried online dating will tell you that a person can feel smitten with someone after email exchanges, enamored after a few phone calls—and the whole thing can end after meeting in person. Obviously something irreplaceable happens when humans connect face to face. The unguarded, spontaneous communication that takes place in real time—accompanied by facial expressions and body language—is a form of intimacy you can't get any other way. Although teens have loads of interaction in school and at home, when they're on their own they can feel lonely—and lack the tools necessary to truly connect with others. This can lead to even greater use of technology as a temporary stopgap.

Given the near ubiquity of online social networking among Gen Yers, it's no wonder members of this generation care about their image. Sometimes this takes the form of carefully crafting an image of someone who doesn't care about their image—either way, the emphasis on the persona is still there. Social networking, by its very nature, requires that users focus intently on how they appear to others. It's not that young people haven't always done this; after all, it's a normal part of being young to learn about who you are by how others react to you. It's just that social networking has taken this to new heights, and for many it's *replacing* rather than enhancing time spent with others. Worse, the more focused people are on their persona, the less likely they are to truly feel connected with and supported by others. After all, a persona isn't intimate—it's controlled. It accompanies the knowledge deep down inside that people are responding to—and liking—only what you've allowed them to see. Not all of you.

About fifty thousand readers a day turn to the blog "Radical Parenting" for insights on teens and parenting. Vanessa Van Petten, twenty-three, has written a parenting book and has worked with thousands of clients on teen issues. Van Petten coined the phrase "cotton candy friends" to describe the Facebook friendships that she and many of her clients rely on after college. Though Van Petten is a fan of Facebook and admits to visiting the site first thing in the morning and a dozen times a day herself, she's also found some problems. According to Van Petten, there's a propensity for relying on friendships that are filled with meaningless tidbits of information, a superficiality, and a numbness that comes from mindlessly skimming without real connection. Worse, it inspires a quantity-over-quality mentality that can create a void—one that can be filled only by genuine real-life friendships.

Obviously these problems aren't unique to Gen Y, but the potential is greater—even more so for today's tweens and teens.

Only half of Americans today say that they have a friend, besides their spouse, to confide in and rely on for support. That's a big drop from 1985, when nearly three-quarters of Americans felt they had such a friend. One-quarter of Americans say they don't have *anybody* to confide in—that number is double what it was in 1985. One of the authors of the study, which was conducted by the National Science Foundation, made a point of saying that hundreds of Facebook friends and dozens of daily email exchanges don't cut it when it comes to feeling the safety and support of close friends and confidants.[7]

Another gaplet? The fashion faux pas, squabbles, and assorted embarrassing moments that all teens have can now live forever and be shared with anyone through technology. Between camera phones, email, text, IM, MySpace, YouTube, and Facebook, today's teens are exposed. At a time when egos are fragile and identities are shaky, the pressure is tremendous. Because 48 percent of kindergartners and first graders are already interacting with people online, according to a Rochester Institute of Technology study,[8] the risks are starting even earlier—long before kids have the impulse control and immunity to racy news that they need in order to stop themselves before clicking the send button. Imagine how much more difficult it is to figure out who you are when mishaps and mistakes can be so public, permanent, and consequently devastating. Besides, how can you learn from mistakes if you never make any?

Once Gen Yers get to college, they have things like JuicyCampus to contend with. JuicyCampus.com had over five hundred colleges participating and hundreds of thousands of anonymous posts that include the names of people who are presumed to be "easy" (the actual terms were more blunt), have STDs, or have had plastic surgery; and polls such as "Have you ever used Adderall?" (51 percent had used the drug, which is intended to treat ADHD but is also used by college students as a "cognitive steroid," Joshua Foer wrote in *Slate*). Though JuicyCampus folded in February 2009 for lack of revenue (after all, not many advertis-ers *would* be attracted). New versions, like Peoplesdirt.com, will continue to pop up. With all of this, and gossip about everything from personal hygiene to personal body parts, it kind of makes the pressures that older Gen Yers and the generations before them faced when they were in school (like whispered gossip and notes passed in classes) seem quaint—and relatively benign—in comparison.

One last point: independence and growth mean lessening your connections to old groups to make room for new alliances. Although most people look at new friends and affiliations in a "the more, the merrier" sort of way, the truth is that you have to create space for change. Additionally, it's harder to reshape and grow in your identity if you're always part of past groups. Without physical contact, people will always see you the way you were when they knew you. Their memory of you will guide their expectations, which in turn creates a subtle urging to stay the same.

Social networking is influencing a bounty of social and psychological shifts. Users have access to a constant influx of ideas, the ability to stay in contact with people forever, and the influence that comes from having followers to name a few. The impressive, game-changing power and possibilities made possible by online networking have also created challenges and new needs for Gen Yers, particularly the younger members who have grown up knowing this as life. They include an emphasis on appearances that can rob an individual of genuine intimacy, a fear of over-exposure that can hamper spontaneity and creativity, and a pull to the past that delays connecting with new groups and exploring new interests.

An Opportunity Through Empathy

It's no wonder, then, that Gen Yers—particularly the younger ones—look for community and belonging through brand rela-tionships and the products they share. The need for connection and a sense of belonging will only increase as today's younger Gen Yers age. It presents an opportunity for marketers who can join people—through websites, emotionally meaningful products, contests, causes, and mobile technology that bring people together, and through authentic and engaging experiences. The challenge, and the greatest reward, is in humanizing a company or product, not just by giving the brand "personality" or a spokesperson but by taking every opportunity to connect in a genuine, empathetic way with customers.

Marketers are often rewarded for their analytical skills, and it's those very skills that sometimes interfere with empathy. Judging makes simply understanding more difficult. Marketers who rely on data without also knowing and interacting with this generation are likely to miss out on a compassionate and genuine understanding of the complex lives of Gen Yers—and consequently, ways to make their products and pitches more relevant.

Looking for Safe Harbor in a Sea of Hormones

This is your brain on teen hormones: *She is evil. OMG I love her. Sex? Wonder where my key is? I am a star. I could be a star. If I were a star I'd be much nicer to people than most stars. I wish everyone would just go away.* $(\cos x + i \sin x)n = \cos (nx) + i \sin (nx)$. *Sex. Why hasn't Jen called? I have a hideous nose.*

In other words: confusion, anxiety, and moodiness—as in frequently changing moods and also scaling the highest of highs and descending into the pits of despair. Oh, and we can't forget the ol' sex-on-the-brain syndrome. It's easy and fun (as long as it's not happening to you again) to see the physical changes—sprouts and spreads of all sorts. The physiological changes we can't see, those brought on by hormones, are even more dramatic.

Those highs and lows, deep feelings and confusing changes—not to mention an awakened libido—put teens in a vulnerable position. And despite an often bullet-proof and sometimes combative posture, we all know that the teen years (the early ones in particular) are a time of insecurity. Today's teens learn about what to expect through all the usual sources, like parents and friends, but also, and more emphatically than previous generations, through an examination of the marketplace, in stores and online, and through the omnipresent media in their lives.

Tweens also learn by watching (make that studying) teens. Which explains why today's tweens, with more freedom of expression—and money—are looking a lot like teens. Previous generations wanted to do it too, but they weren't given the latitude.

The tweens and teens we interviewed pored over magazines and websites and combed shopping centers and malls for tips and inspiration. As we noted in Chapter Two, shopping is preparation for future events. To tweens and teens, who are often focused on the future, shopping can feel almost vital. Add to that their higher levels of exposure to malls, which are the place they're most likely to hang out (not to mention the Internet, also chock-full of shopping inspiration), and the practice they've had influencing their parents' purchases, and it all makes sense.

There is also and most certainly an emphasis on appearances and "looks" that corresponds to tweens' and teens' rapidly changing physical appearances. Unlike those internal moods and feelings, outward appearances feel more manageable. According to OTX's Teen Topix study, 61 percent of teens worry about their looks, and 50 percent said that looks and physical appearance are very important when it comes to respect.[9] Consequently, tweens and teens, especially girls, get a sense that they're more in control and *doing something* by learning about, shopping for, and trying on new appearances.

Teen boys also care about their looks much more than they let on, but they're more likely to get that sense of control, preparation, and bonding by shopping for equipment—most notably video games and electronics—than for clothes. Though Gen Y teen boys are shopping more, and they're more interested in shopping than in previous generations, shopping at the mall doesn't come close to playing video games for that sense of control and power over their universe, not to mention a heavy dose of fantasy. As it is for girls and shopping, the mall is also a place where they hang out with friends and sort things through. When it comes to shopping, for guys it's hanging out at Apple or Best Buy—or near girls. "When I was in junior high we used to go to the mall to be around girls. Girls buy a lot more stuff. Guys actually use everything we buy," said nineteen-year-old Raymond of Cleveland.

In much the same way that school is a preparation for their intellectual future, shopping is preparation for their social and emotional future.

"I love to read magazines. We all do. I really like it when they have advice, like how to bring out your face shape more and what to do to get a look for less," says Jeannie, sixteen, of Chicago. Knowing what to expect calms anxiety, as Tara, also sixteen and from Chicago, points out: "It just feels good, like calmer, to see what's at the mall."

Though the hormonal influence pipes down as teens become twenty-somethings, the urge to prepare for the future through shopping remains. Seventeen- to twenty-five-year-olds were significantly more interested in learning about fashion from magazines, television, runway fashion shows, and especially celebrities, than older adults were, according to a November 2008 American Pulse survey conducted by BIGresearch.[10]

Obviously this is a boon for marketers—this generation is yearning for and actively seeking ideas and inspiration in the marketplace and media. They believe in products as solutions and can find heroism in the right brands.

Reason and Rebellion

Also going on in the teen brain is a whole new way of thinking. Teens are developing higher-level reasoning skills and the ability to be more logical, abstract thinkers. Teens often appear so sophisticated in their dress and manner that we forget that early teen brains aren't fully matured.

Great reasoning skills don't come overnight; when we're first learning how to use them, the tendency is to seize onto a concept and then block out contradictory information. That's why teens tend to be more idealistic, perfectionist, and judgmental than adults. Newfound ideals are often wholeheartedly and dogmatically expressed—partly for the sake of the ideal, and partly to defend the sanctity of those newfound analytical skills. Add to this the fact that most teens are protected from and unencumbered by many of the constraints of the real world, and you've got a recipe for idealized heroes, idols—and enemies. It's no wonder that teens are often passionate champions of causes and movements and relate so strongly to products that carry emotional messages or that are endorsed by their heroes.

And it can start as early as their tween years. Jamie, eleven, of Cheshire, Connecticut, stopped eating meat, fish, or poultry when she was eight. The Bonne Bell Company is one of a growing number of companies that doesn't test on animals; they believe this makes their brands even more appealing to tweens and teens. Hilary Bell, who oversees creative development, says the company often gets emails from girls thanking them for their kindness to animals and suggesting what they like and may want to see in products in the future.

The first hurdle of adulthood is to come to know who you are and what you stand for. The part of the teen brain that's carving out an identity is looking for two things: to have something in society to feel passionately part of, and for it to be different from their parents' interests. In the teen years this is likely to take the form of a battle cry familiar to all parents: "I'm not you." What appears to be a rejection of the characteristics, hobbies, or lifestyle of one's parents is really the first step toward independence and a social identity.

Andy, twenty-one, of Avon, Connecticut, still sports the ear gauges and piercings that define the time during his teen years when he was feeling rebellious. His big goal was to be like the members of punk rock band Blink-182, he said. "Now I'm kind of past wanting to be like someone so bad that I'd do something to myself for it," says Andy. "Modifying your body is the ultimate thing to do. You're really committing to a lifestyle when you get a tattoo or piercing. Anyone can just go out and buy a T-shirt or pair of jeans."

However extreme Andy may appear, rejecting the family's values is nothing new. Mark Twain expressed this universal experience well: "When I was a boy of fourteen, my father was so ignorant I could hardly stand to have the old man around. But when I got to be twenty-one, I was astonished at how much he had learned in seven years."

Kids start out temporarily rebelling against their parents' world because they know it extremely well and it's easier to stand *against* something than it is to start from scratch. Creating a case for something new requires complex and creative thinking and lots of data. In contrast, rejecting something that exists is relatively simple. It's also emotionally satisfying to be against something. Those who are "against" feel a sense of competence, even superiority, and get the opportunity to express passion. All of these things—feeling superior, expressing who you are (initially by expressing who you're not), and feeling passion— are compelling and satisfying beyond words to young adults and teenagers.

Be they James Dean, Elvis, Bob Dylan, or Eminem, every generation has idolized rebellious heroes. Gen Y also has brands and product ideals that, just like a celebrity or artist, represent something important to that person. "The Mac Guy," who represents Apple's computers, was profiled in *Advertising Age* as resonating with Gen Y because he represents Gen Y's personality. The article noted that Mindset Media's independent survey of 7,500 online consumers found Mac users to be "more assured of their superiority, less modest and more open than the general population." But it's not just Mac Guy's personality that works—he's positioned against Mr. PC, who represents the old way of doing things.[11]

Gen Yers' closer relationship to their parents means that this generation has gone about "rebelling" in a slightly different way—more respectfully, often with the help of their parents (who are less insulted than previous generations), and with more authority. Jenny, a forty-something salesperson at Bloomingdale's in San Francisco who has been working in retail for over a decade says, "In the last year I've had more than one mom and daughter come in and buy exactly the same top. I would never have even tried on tops with my mom when I was that age."

Though we found many moms and daughters who shared a few outfits, teens still want to have their own look, their own opinions, and their own stores. Parents and marketers who try too hard to enter their sacred territory without an invitation are (as they always have been), well . . . gross. The key is to be invited.

Twenty-somethings often come back to their parents' choices. Once the options have been considered and their independence is made clear, many of the tastes and sentiments they learned in childhood resurface.

Whether for rebellion or identity, there's no mistaking the connecting role of brands in Gen Y's life. Almost 65 percent of the 1,200 young women aged thirteen to twenty-four polled by *CosmoGirl* magazine in 2007 agreed with the statement "Stores are like friends."[12] That's a reflection of their potency in Gen Y's life—and the shorthand way that Gen Y gets the emotional gist of products and brands. In this oversaturated marketplace, brands that connect through personality, emotion, and relevance trump those that rely on reasoning. The more visible and iconic brands are membership organizations. Purchasing that brand buys you entrance into the club.

Need further proof? In January 2009, the trade publication *Internet Retailer* reported that more than 40 percent of the web retailers on its Top 500 list "have a presence on Facebook," and 29 percent on YouTube.[13] The article further reported that when surveyed in the fall of 2008 by the marketing research company Rosetta, about 60 percent of the one hundred top retailers said they had a Facebook page for their fans. The percentage had doubled since the spring of 2008.

It's proving to be a savvy business move: in April 2009, H&M and Apple each had well over a million fans; Gucci nearly four hundred thousand; American Eagle, Van's, Prada, and IKEA were all in the quarter-million range of admirers. A Facebook application that lets you send a virtual can of Coke to your friends had over ten thousand active monthly users and nearly a half-million fans.

Think Different

In addition to these traditional cognitive changes, Gen Yers, particularly those who are teenagers, think differently from previous generations. We don't mean just the old-fashioned way of thinking differently—as in looking at the world differently and having fresh ideas—we mean that they literally think differently. They consume and process information differently. Our brains are malleable and shaped by our experiences. What we use the most becomes stronger, and what we neglect weakens. Repeated experiences reinforce neural pathways (in other words, use it or lose it).

The majority of Gen Yers play video games; add to that the near ubiquity of the Internet and the often simultaneous use of other media, music, and cell phones, and it's safe to say that today's kids are experiencing loads of fast, high-impact stimulation. It's the stimulant equivalent of kids in the 1970s going to Disneyland, but it's daily, constant, and ingrained. So ingrained that when the Consumer Electronic Association took teens' cell phones away from them for day-long focus groups, the kids "described it, in a word, as 'horrific,'" says CEA's industry analysis director Steve Koenig. Koenig says the comments included, "I felt completely disconnected from my friends," "I was depressed," and "I never want to do this again." "Consumer electronics are almost like food to them," says Koenig. "They need this stuff to survive, to maintain their social network, even to be productive."

The reach and influence of technology is growing exponentially. In 1984 there were a thousand Internet devices, in 1992 there were a million, and in 2008 that number had mushroomed to a billion. In 2006 the average number of Google searches each month was 2.7 billion; three years later, that number had grown to over 31 billion a month.[14]

Gen Y brains have no doubt adapted, and the result is their speedy style, that famous fleeting and flitting attention, and their ability to attune to a wider variety of stimulants at the same time. According to Anastasia Goodstein, founder of YPulse.com and author of *Totally Wired*, "Lots of input, multitasking, going from one screen to the next—it's changing the way the brain processes information. Everyone who works with or teaches young people has seen this."

Nicholas Carr's widely discussed article, "Is Google Making Us Stupid?"[15] explores the effect of technology on the way that we think. "As the media theorist Marshall McLuhan pointed out in the 1960s, media are not just passive channels of information. They supply the stuff of thought, but they also shape the process of thought." Carr wonders if concentration and contemplation are sacrificed by the efficiency and immediacy of the Internet. Considering the popularity of Carr's article and the response to it, many are wondering if deep thought is a casualty of the Internet.

In *iBrain: Surviving the Technological Alteration of the Modern Mind*[16] neuroscientist Gary Small suggests that technology has altered the way that young minds develop. Small paints a picture of accelerated learning, speedy decision making, and enhanced creativity—and also one of social isolation, difficulty concentrating, and stress. Meanwhile, others—including a November 2008 MacArthur study—suggest that online activities facilitate self-directed learning and independence.[17] Don Tapscott, in his book *Grown Up Digital: How the Net Generation Is Changing*

Your World,[18] points out that growing up playing video games and using the Internet has resulted in brains that process visual information more quickly, notice more stimuli, and are better at multitasking—all of which are ever more vital in today's world. After all, as the world changes—and certainly the Internet and digital technology have changed the world—we'll need a different set of skills to be successful.

Gen Y has the gift of resources. It no longer matters whether you're a small-town teenager or a doctoral student at Yale; if you're connected to the Internet, you've got (literally) a world of information at your fingertips. Along with that comes the task of learning how to best harvest and intelligently use and process those tremendous resources. We mentioned that Gen Y has its own unique set of challenges: this is one of them. Sifting through choices is often overwhelming and anxiety-provoking for Gen Y; they're constantly confronted with choice overload and a more complicated analysis. This elevates the role of "sorters" in their lives—the people, brands, and institutions that they can rely on.

Nordstrom, one of the only department stores that both our teen and older focus group members consistently mentioned, serves this important purpose for Gen Yers, especially young women. From the funky shoes in the BP section to the designer clothes that are available to them starting when they are toddlers, Nordstrom has managed to attract and keep girls longer and more consistently than perhaps any other department store. The same is true for Apple's attraction for young men, who take a product's presence at the Apple store as the only stamp of approval they need.

Peer reviews on websites help sort through the clutter and are considered more credible than merchant descriptions. Increasingly popular are websites devoted to merchandise reviews, such as www.wists.com (think "wish list"), where members bookmark products they recommend from any site on the Internet.

Not only do Gen Yers have loads of information at their fingertips, but the time it takes to access it is dramatically reduced from previous generations. Most Gen Yers would be shocked to learn what their parents are likely to have gone through for their book reports and college research projects—actually going to a library, perhaps even using a card catalog, locating books and articles on foot, and taking the time to read them while taking notes (unless they were lucky enough to use a library with a cheap copy machine at their disposal). And that doesn't even include the time it took to type on a typewriter without the ability to cut and paste (except literally). Learning in this manner would be unthinkably boring to Gen Y, and the contrast is a vivid example of one of the many ways in which Gen Yers are just plain accustomed to moving more quickly. Their tolerance for boredom is understandably low.

Visual and symbolic communication has always been particularly potent with younger consumers; its ability to tap into emotion is unrivaled by written communication—and all that's ramped way up with Gen Y. In its infancy, communication on the Internet mimicked written communication. Within a few years, contributors learned that shorter, more visual ways to acquire information were more effective. Viewers (no longer called readers) responded to "snapshots," not lengthy text. Today's clever marketers and retailers have gone way beyond that—and as Gen Yers continue to lead the way in all things technological, there's one thing we can be sure of: in the future it'll be even faster, more realistic, more interactive, and more stimulating than it is today. After all, their way of thinking was shaped by their interaction with technology. They will in turn create (and demand) according to their faster, more visual way of thinking.

The saying that "a picture is worth a thousand words" has never been truer. And today a picture really *needs* to say it all—because that's all the time a Gen Yer may give you. Tag clouds, wordies, histograms, bubble charts, and scatterplots are visual representations of data—and they're soaring in popularity. These fast data snapshots capture the attention of Gen Yers in a way that a block of text can't, particularly on a website.

Christopher, eight, designs his own video games and sells them to his friends on the Internet for $5. Instead of the old-fashioned lemonade stand, he sells his CDs in front of his house. His uncle says when he watches Christopher and his friends play on their Xbox, their adaptations to new games are entirely intuitive. They're also highly opinionated about how the user interface works: "Part of their enjoyment comes from the critique. They think they could do it better—they're critiquing it at that level."

Socially and Psychologically

What's alluring to tweens and teens are activities that allow them to express their tastes and be creative, and to care for, connect with, and compete with others. Shopping does it all.

Psychologically, teens are working hard at figuring out who they are—just as every generation of teenagers has done before them. They have an idea of who they are within their family, and now it's time to develop and define their identity and personality on the larger world stage. Which explains several things: why most teens seem so concerned about what other people think about them, why they're self-conscious and often self-critical, and why they seem self-absorbed. It's all part of the process, and it's their job.

Tweens begin by forming a friend collective. They want to fit in with their group and revel in the ways they are alike; they tend to bond through their activities and interests. By doing this they're establishing a stepping-stone identity. It's unique from their parents, but within the safety of their group.

As tweens move into their teen years, they become more interested in establishing a unique identity, but still rely heavily on their peers for security. This is an age of exploration. Their friendships and relationships are part of the process of self-discovery, and a safe haven throughout the process. In Columbus, Ohio, fourteen-year-old Joanie says Juicy Couture's $100 velour hoodies are such a big deal that girls kept going up to her friend, who was wearing a Kohl's velour sweatsuit top at school, to see if it had the trademark "J" on the zipper pull. The two bonded over their view of this as silly.

Her sixteen-year-old sister Allison, talking about her group of now high school friends, says, "A few years ago we were on the conveyor belt of Abercrombie. When you're at that age, you need to conform."

Twenty-somethings, now more secure about who they are and what they like, are ready to turn their attention to the world and other people. They're steadily less dependent on others for the feedback that contributes to their self-identity, and friendships become more selective and less security focused. Groups take on a different flavor as the inevitable pairing-off of couples takes place. Young adults are more able to focus on other people and things in their own right, rather than as part of their own self-discovery. Obviously, twenty-somethings are now more interested in products and tools that'll help them in their relationships with their boyfriends, girlfriends, spouses, kids, or in-laws. The primary focus of their attention is no longer simply themselves; they're defining their role in society through their work, interests, and hobbies—and products help.

As society has changed and traditional rules have relaxed, Gen Yers are blazing trails and figuring out the best new ways to parent and partner with others. The comfort of just doing what your mom did doesn't always take into account things like how to parent without extended family nearby, how to coparent in a more egalitarian relationship, or how to be a single parent or a stepparent. Though there's great opportunity and freedom to redefine roles, there's also the anxiety of both figuring it out and wondering whether you're doing it right. As they always have, this generation will find support and solutions through technology and the marketplace.

Money, Money, Money

With each age break, our focus group participants "loved" shopping a bit less. Though clothing and personal goods were still exciting to buy, they were clearly more carefully considered purchases once Gen Yers reached their mid-twenties. We also heard more comments about things like "fiber content" and "cost per usage." In addition to the role of finances, the "gaplet" mentioned earlier plays a role—older Gen Yers were less shopping oriented as teens than today's under-twenties are.

"My habits have absolutely changed," says Sandra, twenty-four, of Weymouth, Massachusetts. "When I was a teenager, I was so conscious of brands. I was the girl with the big GAP shirt or an outfit with more Nike swooshes than you can count." Back then, Sandra, now an assistant account executive at a public relations firm, was working and could and did spend all her money on clothes. She had at least eight of the same pairs of Nikes in different colors. They were about $125 a pair at the time. "I would buy new shoes every month, and give my mom my hand-me-downs every month," she says. "Now, brands could matter less. It is all about price." As Sharon, twenty-nine, of San Francisco put it, "I changed. I'm more mature and conscious about what I buy."

The recession has taught everyone to be more conscious of spending. Though Gen Yers are no exception, the youngest of this group remain the most wedded to a lifestyle that includes shopping and buying.

KGOY or KGOL?

Although the adult dress and sophistication of tweens has caused many to wonder whether kids are getting older younger (KGOY), psychologists are wondering whether kids are getting older *later* (KGOL). Their close relationships with their parents have led to record numbers returning home after an initial "launch" into college or a first job, and the emphasis on group relationships makes leaving the pack for an intimate relationship more difficult.

Many of the young adults we interviewed described a "quarter life crisis"—in those exact terms. The "crisis" or anxiety associated with becoming independent is occurring later—closer to twenty-five to thirty now than eighteen to twenty-five. As Ansley, twenty-six, of Atlanta put it, "When you're younger it's laid out for you, you don't have to know much about yourself. But then it hits you that you don't really know yourself." More than 80 percent of respondents to the "Golden Age of Youth" study conducted by Viacom Brand Solutions International said that the twenties should be about exploring life and having fun, and 52 percent of twenty-five- to thirty-four-year-olds feel that they still have "a lot of growing up to do."[19]

This is particularly true of Gen Y men, who often think of themselves more as "guys" then as men well into their late twenties and identify with their pals and freedom much more than responsibilities or "settling down."

"There's a prolonged adolescence, which is a stage of safety in numbers," says renowned psychotherapist and author, Dr. Michael Bader. "Men in particular have a hard time leaving their peer groups; there's pressure to remain part of the pack."

Some wonder if it's evolution—people work longer and live longer, so why not wait awhile to feel "older"? Others say it's our youth-focused culture, which makes growing up seem much less desirable than it did to previous generations. Still others point to the greater involvement of parents.

Family therapists have long noted that homes where families are closer also tend to foster less independence in kids. It makes sense that today's much closer relationships between parents and kids would also create more dependence.

What's important is for older retailers and marketers to recognize that what they wanted or expected of themselves in terms of responsibility or independence when they were in their early twenties isn't necessarily going to resonate with today's young adults, who are marrying later, delaying parenthood, are more dependent on their parents, and much less willing to be constrained by an employer.

Sampling Roles to Find Your Style

Paco Underhill, author of *Why We Buy: The Science of Shopping*, describes the apparel and equipment as "costumes and props."[20] This is never truer than in the teen years. Costumes make "getting into character" much easier during those role-sampling years. For example, of the thirty-five thousand fans who attended Kenny Chesney's concert at AT&T Park in San Francisco in 2008, a healthy proportion were young women dressed in cowboy boots and hats, shorts or short skirts, and wide belts (along with a complementary number of young men). Never has San Francisco seen such a gathering of country music lovers—or so it appeared, at least. According to Jasmine, twenty, whose group of friends are more likely to attend a Rhianna concert, "Oh my gosh we had so much fun and we all wore cowboy hats and stuff and it was a blast." Jasmine went on to say that she thought many of the young attendees were "dressing the part" and though they enjoyed the concert "sooo much" they weren't what you'd call "major fans" of country music or likely to wear their cowboy hats again—until the next concert, or Halloween.

Style sampling works pretty much the same way as tasting ice cream flavors before buying a cone—a sample isn't a commitment; it's how you learn what you like. Similarly, it's through sampling, experimenting, and testing roles that young adults get a better idea about their style. They can try out the kind of person they want to be. Here are a few words of wisdom acknowledging the importance (and fun) of finding your style, compliments of our sixteen-year-olds in Chicago:

- "It's interesting how our style changes as we get older; it's looking to find out who you are."

- "First you don't know your style, then we all end up getting different things—like we have our own style!"
- "People have to mature into a style."
- "I like expressing myself with my style and showing my personality."

Obviously this group has given it some thought!

And then there's Jamie, a seventeen-year-old senior from Milwaukee. She's replicated Paris Hilton's puffy pout to perfection. When we spoke with her, she'd just purchased a long scarf to tie around her new blond bangs and a dress about the same size as that scarf. Jamie's mom worries: "Kids today are so much more sexual." Though Jamie's mom is smart to stay on top of things, it's not necessarily true that Jamie's replicating Paris's values. She's doing what everyone did at seventeen: exploring different, more adult roles by trying on costumes. But she's doing it in a Gen Y way. That means with more access to information about a celebrity's life, more freedom of expression, within a more casual and accepting society—and with a lot more spending money for "costumes."

To be sure, today's sexy tweens (yes, tweens, as in eight- to twelve-year-olds) and teens have caused some controversy. Almost 65 percent of those responding to a poll by BIGresearch agreed with the statement "Fashion for young people has gotten too provocative."[21] In 2007, the American Psychological Association issued a widely discussed report in response to an increased emphasis on the sexuality of teen girls. The report found that an overreliance on sexual desirability as a primary identity stunts girls' development as well-rounded individuals.[22]

Brenda Sharman, the national founder of the modest-clothing group Pure Fashion, couldn't agree more. She works to teach the hundreds of girls who are part of the group and the more than twelve thousand who attend the dozens of fashion shows around the country that "what they wear sends a message and to choose wisely." The "modesty movement," as it's often called, is putting pressure on retailers to offer less suggestive alternatives to the typically revealing casual clothing sold even to middle schoolers. Sharman says there are too many apparel designers advertisers "who are crossing the line from beauty into indecency, lust, and sensuality."

Still, there are plenty of girls and guys who are lured by what Sharman and others might see as lurid. "'Sexy' I think is universally appealing, a universal style, at least for women," says Ellen, twenty-one, of Vienna, Virginia. "I think when women look at advertising they are looking for things that they think are going to make them look sexier."

Sexy or not, as always, tweens want to look like teens and teens want to look like twenty-somethings (this trend seems to reverse at forty, which, as we all know, is the new thirty). Irina, seventeen, offers this insight: "People believe Abercrombie is targeted towards older teenagers because of how promiscuous the clothing is. They assume that these kids will relate better to the highly 'sexed' image of the store. Quite on the contrary, older teenagers find little attraction to these stores because it's only *at* their age—but not a step up. What's the appeal of shopping at a store if you already feel that 'age' in your image?" Irina feels it's the younger teens who are most likely to be attracted to what she refers to as the "naked advertising" because it'll make them feel older.

By the time teens turn into twenty-somethings, they've found their style. And though it may shift and accommodate new jobs, locations, or relationships, the role-sampling period has pretty much ended. Twenty-somethings will now shop to solidify and personalize their identity—through cars and clothes, and through the deeper knowledge and more exacting standards they've developed for their camping gear, cocktail accoutrement, or book collections.

Retail advertising, catalogues, and websites seek to appeal to the psyche at each stage, notes Ken Nisch, chairman of the retail branding and design firm JGA. Whereas a high school–oriented teen retailer might show a group of kids "jumping off of a bridge together," the marketing for college age kids is more likely to show them "backpacking in India alone."

Crafting Your Identity from the Reaction You Get from Others

Role sampling requires feedback. Teens, especially, get information about themselves from the way that other people react to them, and it's through that feedback that they see themselves most clearly. It's a slightly deeper and more obsessive version of "Do I look fat in these pants?" Despite the mantra of the day, "I don't care what other people think about me," teens value and crave this information and are keenly and acutely attuned to it, which explains how teens can think they're hideous one day and bound for stardom the next. It often just depends on the latest feedback—or their perception of the latest feedback. This is a giant difference from the carefree days of just seeing other people and not evaluating their evaluation of you.

Remember the intensity of your first love? Assuming you felt this way in high school, it was probably awe-inspiring. What teens are feeling could more accurately be described as self-love and the bliss of seeing themselves very positively in the eyes of someone they admire. Though teens certainly admire and "love" their romantic partner, it's more about self-discovery than about the other person.

Similarly, kid's morals are based on the approval of other people—their greatest fear is getting busted by Mom or disappointing a teacher or another authority figure. Teens are in the process of internalizing their morals in the form of a conscience; in other words, shifting their center of authority from what others think to what they think of themselves.

Given the overwhelming importance of what other people think and the tremendous range of options available to today's teens, it's no wonder they get such relief from shopping, trying, and buying. Phones, Wii's, and purses are the costumes, props, and equipment that enhance performances, bolster egos, fuel imaginations, and, most important, inspire feedback.

The Kid-to-Marketer Relationship Is Like the Kid-to-Parent Relationship

In the progression from kid to adult, teens tend to swing between extremes: feeling bullet-proof and feeling babyish; wanting to fit in and wanting to stand out; wanting responsibility and wanting to be taken care of; and between craving new experiences and wanting the safety of "sameness."

- They want you, need you, like you
- They hate that they want you, need you, like you
- They really hate the idea that you might know that they want you, need you, like you

Marketers walk the same fine line as parents—kids really do want you and need you during this transition, but it's ... complicated. So as any good parent knows, the best course of action for a marketer is to stick close but—as Lakisha, seventeen, of San Francisco advises (with tongue in cheek)—"Try very hard not to be inappropriate." In other words, you have to be present and seen without being intrusive; listen, listen, listen; provide guidance when asked; and, most important, offer reassurance. Kids needs to feel respected and to have a sense of their own authority in order to respect you. It's no surprise that what works are things like product placements, sponsorships, celebrity endorsements, contests, ambassadorships, and consumer-created online content—these are all ways to be unobtrusively integrated and present in a teen's life, while they provide opportunities to listen and new usage ideas and reinforcement.

It makes more sense to focus on helping young people feel smart and good about themselves than it does to try to convince them that your brand or product is smart or cool. Talking about yourself is never as effective as talking about *them*. This goes well beyond flattery. It means designing products that are intuitive and easy to master, like technology that doesn't require a manual to understand and website interaction that's seamless and responsive.

Using Stuff to Manage Group Relationships

Style, clothing, and possessions also provide a common denominator through which Gen Yers can talk to and about each other and the world around them. "Things" are simple and easy to understand, a relatively unsophisticated way to know someone else. It's subject matter—like talking about the weather—but it's personal.

And on another level, clothing and possessions represent style, which represents character and personality—and that's how many Gen Yers get to know each other. Consider how deeply interested Americans were in the fashion selections of the potential first ladies and running mates considered in the 2008 presidential election. Some say Sarah Palin's Neiman Marcus shopping spree was a seminal moment in the election. It was widely contrasted with Michelle Obama's J. Crew outfit selection the following week.

Using style to figure out who's in and who's out begins with a vengeance in the tween years, especially among girls who are more verbal and connection-conscious. Style and fashion is the fodder with which girls create a social structure and establish a hierarchy. In our tween and teen focus groups, discussions about each other's clothing were a way to exclude, include, rank, praise, and admonish each other. Nothing new—teenagers did this in the 1970s too—but with these differences:

1. They didn't have as much stuff, so there was less to talk about.

2. They didn't get it all year round, so chatter ebbed and flowed around the start of the school year and the winter holidays.

3. They didn't have as much control over what was purchased, so they could always blame their parents for mistakes.

4. There was a very conscious social effort not to define people by their style in the 1970s.

5. They didn't have the same level of information about style options (the 1970s popular fashion and style culture pretty much revolved around *Seventeen*, *Glamour*, and a couple of other magazines).

According to the ten-year-olds in our San Francisco focus group, the right clothes are important for two reasons—because "when you're wearing new clothes you feel cute, and fresh and new and more confident." And also because, "they won't talk bad about you." The group described a process whereby over the course of a day at school most of their class would hear about someone's fashion flaw. It starts with "Don't tell anyone, but I hate so-and-so's outfit" and ends with "Don't tell anyone, but everyone thinks that so-and-so's outfit is cheesy." The girls acknowledged that quite often a rivalry or jealousy was at play, more than poor clothing choices—but having the right outfit is a safeguard. By the way, here's the definition of "cheesy," according to our San Francisco girls: "LA is cheesy; too flashy, metallic, gross. Six-year-old is cheesy too."

Clothing and style were discussed and analyzed, and emphasized as a very important way of signaling that you belong and should be accepted and respected. Style is also used as a way to establish and maintain group standards, which often are really not about clothes but about behavior—and gossiping is a way to enforce those standards. Individual style is important. According to Martina, ten, if you purchase the same thing that your friend has, "Other people would be, like, 'she's a wanna-be.'" Incidentally, it wouldn't bother the friend—who would most likely be flattered.

Shopping and style appreciation are also a way of bonding and validating connections. The sixteen-year-old-girls we surveyed in Chicago showed their support for and appreciation of each other through clothes shopping: "Susie helped me and Beth helped me a lot, they took me to stores and said, 'This is cute.'" And each of the nine girls in attendance was able to describe the look each of the others was known for—or at least a special stylish accessory each was associated with, such as red boots, a stack of cause bracelets, or wearing skirts a lot.

Tweens feel the same way. "My mom's usually pretty in, but it's way more fun to just shop with my friends," says Jen, ten, of San Francisco. "I don't get to do that very much now, but I think it will be, like, 'Oh that's so *cute*, and sometimes, 'No, not that one.' I can't wait to just, like, go to the mall with my friends, and we would try on everything and tell each other what we think. We would browse and look at everything together and give our opinions."

"What's important for marketers to understand is that for most teens, shopping is a purely social experience," says Bruce Friend, president for media and entertainment insights for OTX, in an article published by *MediaPost*. Their 2007 survey found that 84 percent of teens prefer to shop with others—of those, 74 percent with their friends and 26 percent with their parents. Although 65 percent say they learn about new products on the Internet, 62 percent say they learn from friends, 54 percent from television, and 48 percent from magazines.[23]

The process of using visual cues and style as a shorthand way of knowing and understanding others is common to everyone—it's just ramped up a bit for most Gen Yers of all ages. This is a generation with an emphasis on the visual, and with an urge and the ability to evaluate quickly. With all the options, latitude, and emphasis on individuality and creativity, even the youngest

Gen Yers are aware that their possessions say something about them. But unlike previous generations, it's not just what you buy, it's what you *do* with what you buy. Having a coveted cell phone, custom-designed Keds, or Lauren Hill's latest dress is great—but the magic is in the mix. The idea is to showcase your taste, not the item.

Though we humans like to think that we're independent and self-sufficient (an anthem for Gen Y could even be, "I don't care what other people think of me"), the truth is that belonging to groups is an unshakable, fundamental aspect of being human. For most of our existence it's been essential for survival—a caveman without a group didn't survive long. For Gen Y, style is communication and connection—and ultimately a sense of belonging.

Individuality is a double-edged sword for Gen Y. All ages struggle with the desire to be unique and independent, while still maintaining unity and a sense of belonging to groups. Gen Yers' love of individuality and belief in their own leadership capabilities can be in conflict with their need to conform to group standards. Their acceptance of diverse interests and their comfort in working with teams is what makes it all work.

According to Nolan, twenty-four, of Charlottesville, Virginia, "It's all about image. Our demographic hunts ceaselessly to craft a certain 'look' for themselves. Whether that be preppy, jock, scene, gothic, bohemian, punk, rock, urban, country, east coast, west coast, or the 'I have no image' image, everyone is still working towards something." Pete, nineteen, of Boulder, Colorado, states plainly that "I want to have a presence everywhere I go, and I don't want anyone else to have a presence like mine." Even "ugly" is a look for some Gen Yers, especially once they hit the college years—an "I don't want to look like I'm trying too hard" look, or "I want to look like I think focusing on looks is superficial" look.

Ten or twenty years ago, you could fairly accurately break down the shopping habits of young people based on their racial groups, says Ted Chung, president of Cashmere Marketing, which targets urban and often multicultural young people. Now, he says, there is so much personalization and customization of products that tastes fall more into lifestyle and culture subsets, and ethnic stereotypes should be out the window. A group of white, African-American, Asian, or Hispanic kids could just as easily be wearing J. Crew, Van's sneakers, or clothes from the Salvation Army.

Indeed, Resource Interactive futurist Nita Rollins says young people can't even predictably be divided into clear groups, because a preppy or a goth is rarely defined the way a baby boomer, Ralph Lauren stylist, or Hot Topic buyer might define them.

"They do not create identity by associating with a certain category, like jock or nerd," says Rollins, a petite forty-something Ph.D. who can rattle off Gen Y jargon like a twenty-year-old. "If anything, they feel the need to take the best of their ethnic heritage, the best of music, pop culture, and peer influence. They are very, very flexible and fluid in their identity construction."

Call it "mashinality," suggests Rollins, because that's what it is: A mashup of all the element of their personalities.

That certainly defines seventeen-year-old Stephen, an automotive enthusiast from Cleveland who plays football, "sags" his shorts (wears them so low his underwear shows), and has an earring in each ear. His friends, however, call him a preppy.

Stephen "is not the East Coast, Nantucket, pastel-wearing preppy with sweaters tied around his shoulders," explains his friend Irina. "He's a California preppy, which has a similar style in that they wear Lacoste polos and plaid pants and like to golf, but they have a more laid back, 'too cool for school' attitude, which includes listening to rap, piercing their ears, and wearing stylish sunglasses."

By the time Gen Yers are in their twenties, their jobs, colleges, interests, and relationships provide insights about who they are and what they believe that go beyond the fashion, phones, and family vacations that differentiated them from their peers in their younger years. They've also developed deeper and richer ways of knowing and understanding other people. Not to mention that they are now in a position to choose their groups. Tweens and teens, on the other hand, carve out groups from within their school and the smaller options of the immediate community.

Nevertheless, Gen Y twenty-somethings are a product of a more visual society and are still more likely than other generations to use "stuff" to understand and connect with others. They're more particular and more budget-minded now though. Greer, twenty-six, of Atlanta, bought two pairs of "Melissa" shoes that she saw on a design blog during the summer 2008 Olympics. She hunted online until she found the shoe and bought it without hesitation. "I *loved* the shoe. It reminded me of the Beijing stadium. So timely!" Judy, twenty-six, also of Atlanta, says she avoids "anything too mainstream" and particularly likes to buy secondhand clothing that she recrafts herself to suit her image (and her self-described short legs).

It's not just the downturn in the economy that's fueled Gen Y's interest in secondhand outlets like Goodwill and eBay. Nearly every age group we spoke with found delight in the treasure hunt of shopping in secondhand stores. They also enjoyed the notion that they would have an entirely unique look—not to mention the prices. Four skaters from Portland, now nineteen but formerly high school buddies, recall their rainy-day shopping excursions to Goodwill as "adventures." "It's an experience, some of that stuff is goofy and everything is like a dollar or $5. We bought a crazy scientist oven once and had fun with it for a day." They would go "with at least two or three people," and because there are multiple thrift stores in the area, they were sure to run into other people. "I get 50 percent of my wardrobe from those stores; it's cheap, but it's also different from what other people have."

Celebrities Are Our Hometown Hotties

Remembering that teens are only beginning to get the complexity of things and people, you can also see why they find celebrities and role models so fascinating. We use the term "role model," by the way, in its most neutral form—as someone modeling a role, not as someone aspirational.

There's no denying a huge jump in our fascination with celebrities today. The bottomless pit of interest in their love lives, drug problems, fashions, and figures is actually serving a psychological purpose. They are today's version of the town sluts, heroes, and drunks of yesteryear, who also served a psychological purpose. We gossip about and revel in the lives of others (the more charismatic the better) as a way to discuss and explore our values and decide social norms and standards. What is right, wrong, indecent, worth valuing; the consequences of unusual behavior—we discuss (okay, gossip about) other people's lives to create understandable, relatable stories about our values and to learn about life. It's no wonder, then, that gossip is at its most intense in high school and tapers off a bit each year thereafter—because it's in our teens and twenties that we need input the most. We're thinking about the kind of person we want to be and the sorts of groups we want to belong to—and now we're thinking about what *our* standards will be, rather than just accepting the views of our elders.

The Internet has made the world (especially Hollywood) everyone's hometown. While our connection to each other in our geographic, non-virtual towns and cities has decreased, our access to the lives of celebrities has increased. And our forums for discussion have expanded way beyond the local restaurant and front porches to blogs, Twitters, and Facebook and *People* polls. So really, the folks who fill the pages of *People* feel like part of our community, and our gossip and interest in them is serving a purpose.

It's also worth mentioning that they provide some exciting style: one step away from "OMG I love that outfit" is "That would look great on me—where can I get one like it?" So in addition to the social monitoring and values exploration, today's celebrities provide inspiration (*she looks gorgeous; maybe I should get my teeth whitened too*) and validation (*if Misha Barton has cellulite, mine can't be that bad, and if Britney can't keep it together, with all her money, I'm doing okay*).

Ned, twenty-four, says he was influenced by movie characters during his teen years—Tyler Durden from *Fight Club*, Jack Sparrow from *Pirates of the Caribbean*, and Johnny Cash from *Walk the Line*. This doesn't mean he wanted to actually fight, sail on a pirate ship, or take drugs, but certain elements about the glamour behind these characters and their attitude helped him decide what to put on in the morning.

Celebrities are also fodder for fantasy—a favorite pastime of teens. Fantasy allows us to explore potential roles, consider heroic futures, and explore our own potential. Part of the allure of video games is in their ability to let us do the same thing—even more realistically than daydreaming.

The Fame Game

Considering all the scrutiny and knowing the ways we psychologically use celebrities, it's a wonder anybody would want to be famous. But they do—for many Gen Yers, fame is validating. At one time you became famous for being great—today, you're great when you become famous. As exemplified by Perez Hilton, fame in and of itself is an aspiration.

Fame is not just for validation and proof of your hotness, coolness, or brilliance. It's also influence, and influence is a more important symbol of status than money. It's also recognition, feedback, and acceptance for a generation that's been more recognized and rewarded in their childhood than any previous generation.

It started with reality shows—once a small part of television and now some of the most popular and prolific programming available. It's mushroomed, however, through the Internet. Fame seekers have a place to display their wares, but more important, everybody gets to have a vote (or twenty votes). The involvement and ability to voice your opinion is an essential draw. This is not only in the hope of being noticed or influential; it's the medium's power to give a voice to everyone.

For example, Justine Ezarik, known as iJustine, at least in Gen Y circles. In case you didn't know video blogger—and the most famous of her nearly two hundred blogs, about her three-hundred-page iPhone bill, resulted in over 1.6 million YouTube hits. She's also attracted over a hundred thousand viewers when she's made cotton candy or poked dead birds. According to her website, "I am the Internet" and "I make movies that make no sense." Did we mention that she's also highly photogenic?

IBeatYou.com is "the place to compete online with anyone in anything." There are categories for text, video, and photo contests with titles such as "If You Were a Donut," "Best Useless Fact," "Fastest Texter," "Best Water Spit," "Best Photo of You Driving," and "Shake That Hair!"

HotorNot.com (as in hot, or not) has millions of members who rate and date each other. Each contestant's profile can include photos of the products and things they think are "hot." We found lots of sports teams, cars, and beer brands on the guy profiles and lots of frilly drinks on the gal profiles.

About 80 percent of the comments, questions, and ratings on Internet sites are produced by only 9 percent of users. Over half of those heavy contributors are under age twenty-two, according to a 2008 study by Rubicon Consulting.[24]

Not Just Fame, But Influence—and Opportunity

Unique to this generation is its members' ability to become famous through their own channels. They don't need to wait for the existing hierarchy to find them, and they don't need the anointment of the older folks who are likely to be in charge of traditional channels. Bypassing the "system" and the established hierarchy has also allowed this generation entrepreneurial opportunities never before seen—the empowerment is a great fit for confidence of this generation.

Chamillionaire (born Hakeen Seriki) told attendees at a ford venture capitalists conference that he became a millionaire in two weeks selling his music online because he couldn't deal with a record company. He asked fans to repeatedly click on his MySpace and YouTube pages to move him up in the rankings. Chamillionaire went on to win a 2007 Grammy Award for his number one single, "Ridin'."

EBay has proven to be a popular source of extra money for several of our focus group attendees of all ages. Many, some as young as thirteen (with the help of their parents), sell their own games and clothes when they've gotten bored with them so that they can buy new ones. And several of the older Gen Yers that we spoke with—including college student Robby, nineteen, of Seattle—have turned it into a profitable business. According to Robby, "I make all my money selling on eBay. I was working at a skate shop, but it was so boring, so I sold my own skate stuff on eBay and then my mom's old stuff. Nike shoes are all collectors. You hang on to them for six months and then sell them. I'm trying to figure out how to earn money in my own way."

Just as our needs and interests evolve as we age, so do our feelings about shopping. After all, shopping is a way to explore and share—especially for Gen Y. You can see how the age of the respondents of our two-thousand-person survey influenced their feelings about shopping in this chart:

Through the Ages

	I especially like to go shopping when things are changing in my life.	I enjoy shopping more now than I did three or four years ago.	Though I don't spend more money than I have, I still often feel guilty about buying things.	I love shopping.
15 or under	60%	69%	23%	57%
16 to 20	85%	42%	52%	51%
21 to 25	81%	32%	51%	41%
26 to 30	70%	21%	49%	36%
Over 30	53%	18%	35%	30%

5

SEX, LOVE, AND SHOPPING

Brad says he thinks that shopping is boring. Nevertheless, he finds himself at Atlanta's Perimeter Mall, which is close to his home, at least twice a week. The twenty-four-year-old, who's living at his parents' house again while he looks for a job, doesn't consider hanging out at the mall "shopping." He meets friends, plays with computers at the Apple store, eats at the food court, and, though he knows his way around most of the stores we visited pretty well—especially the Sports Fan Attic—he still doesn't think of it as shopping. Brad buys a new video game every other week; he likes buying basketball clothes and equipment—and he knows his fashion.

So what's at the heart of what motivates Gen Y? And how do gender differences play out at the mall?

Among Gen Yers, women and girls still rule at the mall—nobody we've surveyed has said the guys can keep up with the gals. Studies show, and our research bears out, that men shop less frequently, don't stay as long when they go, and spend far less than their female counterparts on clothing, shoes, and accessories—not to mention groceries.

But teen and twenty-something guys are shopping more than their counterparts in any previous generation, and each year more than the last.[1] Because it's more fun and social than it used to be; they like being with their friends (many of whom are women and girls); they've gotten more particular in their tastes; and retailers have gotten better at catering to them.

There's also an important ongoing social shift away from distinct gender roles. Men and women are becoming increasingly similar in what they do and therefore less wedded to the traditional gender roles of our ancestors. And last, guys are on their own longer these days and can't rely on their moms or partners to shop *for* them.

Men are, in fact, outpacing women in increased apparel spending. During the economically turbulent period from March to November 2008, women's apparel sales fell 6 percent, but men's apparel sales grew 1 percent, according to MasterCard SpendingPulse data. Though women's apparel spending is still more than four times that of men's, many retailers, such as Saks and Bloomingdale's, consider men's apparel to be the area of greatest potential growth. As Marshal Cohen, chief industry analyst for NPD Group, told the *Wall Street Journal*, "Men's was always the first one to lose momentum and the last one to gain. That's not the case this time, because men have grown more fashion-conscious and continue to update their wardrobes with slimmer silhouettes."[2]

Wanting More

During a research visit to a mall in South San Francisco, we counted thirty-seven kids under seven years old playing with other kids in a protected indoor playground area in front of Target. Their parents watched from the side while chatting and snacking on Target popcorn and hot dogs. Clearly, there's something to the notion that the mall has become America's playground. Across the country, from the swanky suburban malls of Chicago to Seattle's glorious outdoor shopping district to the outlet malls of Las Vegas, we saw similar scenes: toddlers and their parents (dads too), packs of teenage boys and girls, twenty-something couples, and Gen Y girls and their moms, eating, laughing, talking . . . and sometimes shopping and buying, too.

The recession may have thinned out their numbers, but malls and shopping areas have evolved into full-on community centers, fulfilling the purpose of the old Main Streets. Movie theaters, banks, shoe repair shops, health clinics, and massage chairs are becoming commonplace. So are ever-changing opportunities to see new products, such as the latest Lexus (no test driving in the aisles, though); or to play with new Wii games; or to meet celebrities endorsing stores and products. Shopping areas have the best holiday decorations in town—not to mention Easter Bunnies and even leprechauns, if you're lucky. And then there's the food: with kids today having ever more particular tastes, food courts make sure there's something for everyone. Truly *everyone*, because we also saw food courts equipped with china and silverware (and food that doesn't come in a paper wrapper), ethnic food vendors of all sorts, and—tucked into the corners of some of the malls we visited—even upscale cocktail lounges.

Yaromir Steiner's Easton Town Center in Columbus, Ohio, the first lifestyle shopping center, was designed for precisely these reasons: to lure kids when they're young and dipping their toes into one of several wading pools, through the time when they're furnishing homes for their own kids, and even later on when they're shopping for their grandkids. To avoid late night trouble, the center doesn't allow kids under sixteen to be there after nine, but Steiner says that makes it all the more attractive when they are older, especially when they can drink.

"Everyone is our customer—from the five-year-old looking at the electric train to the fifteen-year-old who, if you treat him well, will be back someday to watch soccer games at the Irish bar," says Steiner, known as the grandfather of the open air shopping centers, which are rapidly replacing enclosed malls. "If you don't serve multiple generations, you serve a narrow window. When malls just focus on the retailers, they die."

Around the world, malls and shopping areas are increasingly integrated into our lives. The most notable impact has been on men and boys, who, unlike their dads and grandpas, feel more comfortable in stores and malls. Gen Y boys who played in malls while their moms (and, increasingly, their dads) socialized, years later found this same arena to be the place where they went to hang out with other kids and meet girls. How many baby boomers can say that they got their first kiss in a mall? We're not sure how many of the kisses we saw were "firsts," but we did see some action and attraction at malls—especially around 3:30 P.M.

Socializing in malls also means that today's young people have a subconscious, emotional relationship with the shops and brands they encountered. Even if they weren't yet a candidate for a particular product or brand, while hanging out and bumping into retailers and brands, their minds processed impressions that last a lifetime. Clotaire Rapaille, a French psychoanalyst turned brand consultant and author, makes the case that our earliest childhood memories of brands form an emotional template for our adult thoughts and feelings about those retailers and products. We're generally not even aware of those impressions, and they're formed by not only those initial interactions with the brand itself, but also our mood and the social circumstances within which we encounter the product or retailer. In other words, if we're having a good time or feeling good and stumble across a product in that mood, there's a rub-off effect on the brand. Which bodes well for any retailer within sight of that first kiss!

On a more conscious level, young Gen Yers will naturally develop impressions of retailers as they interact with them. Tiffany made a brilliant move in adding a line of (relatively) inexpensive silver trinkets to their inventory. They became drool-worthy hits for hordes of high school and college girls—and those wishing to impress them. Years later, parents and suitors of those girls know that nothing quite matches the thrill of the blue box—though the gift of choice may now have to include gold, platinum, and possibly diamonds.

Bookstores, including Barnes & Noble and Borders, have long treated their customers like family, creating early impressions that are actually emotional bonding experiences as customers are encouraged to linger in comfy chairs, read, sip coffee, and snack, without pressure to buy. You'd be hard-pressed to find either one of the chains' locations that don't have a coffee shop. Barnes & Noble has also been trying to draw customers into stores and drum up more interest in books by adding hundreds of videos and video programs about authors and books to its websites. And Borders has been working to lure technophobes with the addition of digital downloading centers in some stores.

Retailers that consider the emotional experience of the consumer—not just in how the store looks, but also in how it makes the consumer feel—and that give young consumers the opportunity to interact with a variety of products, even outside of their current purchasing mind-set, will enjoy long-term benefits.

Because Gen Y men have been exposed to more merchandise in their teen years, they have a greater storehouse of information about a broader array of products that they're therefore more likely to at least consider than their elders would have been. Which is a partial explanation of the increase in sales of men's shower gels, sunscreens, moisturizers (still not a big hit, but with huge growth potential), body spray, hair products, and a much broader array of casual clothing and shoes. Though still a fraction of the size of the women's fragrance industry, men's fragrances are growing at twice the pace.

So incredible has been the success of Unilever's Axe Body Spray that industry insiders have a name for it: the "Axe effect." Axe connected with young men through MTV, ads in video games, and interactive websites—all with a direct boy-gets-girl message.

Ironically, the soaring success of Axe Body with preteen boys may be responsible for a recent dip in sales. Axe, which is officially targeted to men aged eighteen to twenty-four, was a runaway success with middle school boys. Older men taking note may have felt they didn't want to be using a "kid product" and lost interest in Axe. And kids don't want kid products either; they use products that help them feel more manly and mature—that means men have to want them too.

Lisa, fifty-three, of Seattle, recalls gagging in her car from the thick fog of Axe Body Spray after picking up her then-fourteen-year-old son and two of his friends from a trip to the drugstore. So enthusiastic (and lacking in restraint) were young guys about Axe that many schools banned the product altogether. Lisa's inside (that is, overheard) information is that the guys think girls love the smell—and hey, if a little is good, more must really drive 'em wild.

Lisa says that her son recently abandoned Axe in favor of Procter & Gamble's Old Spice, and he's not alone. Besides the "kid product" image, Axe is in a heated battle with Old Spice, a brand that, according to *Advertising Age*, has become "very introspective." Rather than "run away from its grandfatherliness, Old Spice instead embraced a big-brother persona," which was described as "helping guys navigate the seas of manhood." The manifesto of Old Spice's brand team is, "I didn't have an older brother to steer me down the aisle to the Old Spice shelf. Needless to say, I spent my formative years watching a lot of *Star Trek: The Next Generation* on Friday nights. Now I have the chance to be that older brother I never had. I want to help the kids of today become the men of tomorrow. I want to sell them some Old Spice." It's exactly what young men want, and it's delivered in Gen Y terms—which means with ample doses of campy humor.[3]

Axe is hardly down and out, though—be it body spray, deodorant, body wash, or hair care, catering to the expanded grooming needs of Gen Y men is a sizeable and growing opportunity. A dab of Brut or splash of English Leather on the weekends won't cut it with this generation.

Girls, who are already comfortable in shopping environments, are also influenced by the deep familiarity they have with stores and products—they aspire to own categories of products such as high-end designer clothing and luxury skin care products that their parents wouldn't have considered (or even felt comfortable exploring). More than half of tween girls use skin care products, and four out of ten use cosmetics, according to a 2008 NPD Group report.[4] Luxury designer brands are purchased more by younger consumers than by their parents[5] —who may have dreamt of owning a Chanel handbag someday, but wouldn't have considered it a realistic option in their early twenties. Be it the real thing or a less expensive version of the real thing, such as Sigerson Morrison shoes or Shabby Chic furniture available at Target, Gen Yers know what's out there, and they know what they want.

Of course, familiarity isn't the only thing behind this trend—a compressed social strata, more product information on the Internet, more marketing and media targeted toward Gen Yers, and more indulgent parents also contribute.

No Substitutes, Please

It's no secret that Gen Yers are particular about what they want. Their birthday, graduation, and holiday wish lists are unlikely to simply read "new computer" or "brown suede boots." They will specify brand, make, and model. This increase in specificity has two sources. First, Gen Yers know their stuff. There are precious few remaining retail categories for which parents teach their kids these days; in fact, the reverse is more likely. Second, Gen Yers care about what they own—they crave specific things that are exactly right.

The alternative to a brand, make, model, and color gift request is Gen Yers' very favorite gift of all: the gift card. Gift cards have boomed in popularity in the past few years, and as usual, Gen Yers have led the way. As we've noted before, gift cards not only guarantee that just the right gift will ultimately be acquired, but they also provide the "gift of shopping." Shopping with permission to buy in the form of prepayment is way more fun than shopping just to see what's out there and to socialize.

Guys and gals are equals when it comes to wanting what they own to be just right. And they're becoming more similar in the types of products that they want, too. Gender-related interests are still apparent, but traditional role distinctions in product categories are falling away, particularly as they age. To demonstrate, let's take a look at the Holiday 2008 wish lists of a few Gen Yers we interviewed. By the way, speaking to our point that Gen Yers "want more," the average retail cost of a ten-year-old's holiday wish list was $794 in 2008, according to Node Research.[6]

- Eleven-year-old Nishelle of Denver wanted an iPod; gift cards at Abercrombie, Gap, and Old Navy; a puppy; concert tickets for Alicia Keyes, Beyoncé, and Gwen Stefani; a Wii; and earrings.

- Timothy, a twelve-year-old boy from Fairfax, Virginia, asked for "an iPhone, failing that an iTouch, failing that a 120GB iPod; also a hockey net and hockey skates." He says he doesn't want clothes, because "clothes are not a gift."

- Neil, fifteen, of New Orleans, asked for Fifa Soccer '09 for his PlayStation, Nike Air Zoom Control II FS Premium soccer shoes, Volcom Volitile shorts, a USA baseball cap, and a digital camera so that he can post photos on his MySpace account. His list was submitted electronically to his parents along with URLs and thumbnail photos.

- Nellie, sixteen, of Oakland, California, says that money is always first on her list. Following that, a Samsung Rant cell phone; gift cards from Express, H&M, Target, Forever 21, Visa, or Footlocker; a Mac or Bare Essentials makeup set; a big purse or jewelry from Forever 21; Uggs winter boots; and a peacoat from Old Navy, Forever 21, or H&M.

- Eighteen-year-old Kenneth of Simi Valley, California, wanted a Bauer 5500 maroon hockey helmet, a Synergy S19 hockey stick, Abercrombie "Fierce" cologne, a gift certificate for jeans, a senior class ring, a Gait Torque lacrosse head, black Nike socks, and a Grenade snowboard jacket.

- Nineteen-year-old Bree of Santa Barbara told her dad that she would like ... cash. When he wondered if there wasn't something more specific, she said, "We could go shopping together if you want! I need a new purse and boots."

- David, twenty-three, of New York City, asked for a large pot for cooking, *The Assassination of Jesse James* DVD, new running shorts, a gift certificate to Barnes & Noble or Best Buy, and the books *Omnivore's Dilemma* and *Nudge*.

- Isabelle, twenty-five, of San Francisco, is hoping for a MacBook laptop, an iPod adaptor for her car, and mountain boots.

- Her husband, Doug, twenty-seven, asked for Bonobos casual pants, dress pants from Banana Republic, dress shirts from Thomas Pink, and snowshoes.

Gen Yers of all ages and of both genders showcased their knowledge of brands and how important it is that the gift be exactly the right thing (right down to the store from which it's purchased) in these lists. Also apparent is movement away from traditional gender-related product interests. Boys and men are more interested in fashion than in previous generations; girls and women, more interested in technology. These data were supported in our focus groups and survey.

Two giant forces are transforming the role of gender in the kinds of products Gen Yers want and buy: gender convergence, and the central role that appearances and technology play in their lives.

Gender Convergence

Recent research from social scientists shows an ongoing shift toward "gender convergence." Men and women are increasingly similar in how they live, what they want, and who does what. Along with that, marriages begun later in life have made it harder to assume that you can rely on someone of the opposite sex to take care of "those sorts of things." Self-reliance is in, delegation is out. And it's supported by the gender equality of this generation—stereotypes of acceptable male and female hobbies and responsibilities are falling away. There's much more freedom for men to explore formerly female categories like cooking and clothes, and for women to dip into traditionally guy categories like extreme sports and yard care.

Be it through necessity or interest, as guys age their shopping venues expand. Although teenage girls and twenty-something women still shop more at department stores and food stores than guys do, the gap greatly narrows as teens becomes twenty-somethings.

That spells opportunity for the retailers and marketers first in line to meet the needs of the "other" gender. Best Buy is in the process of transforming their stores into a more female-friendly layout and design. There's nothing froufrou about the "sport utility" and "ironman" baby strollers that are a big hit with dads who often prefer to run rather than stroll (and also don't want to look quite so girly) when they're out with their tots. Ace, building on the success of their back-pocket comb, designed a line of men's grooming tools including nail clippers strong enough to cut through gnarly toe nails and ergonomically designed for a man's hand. Barbara K designed a line of home-improvement tools for women that are made for smaller hands; many also have softer grips and come in cute, girly prints. According to her website, Barbara K, who has been featured on the *Today Show* and *Good Morning America*, is all about self-reliance.

Appearances and Technology

The heightened importance of how you look and the essential role of technology in the lives of Gen Yers (not to mention those exacting standards mentioned earlier) have made product knowledge and shopping skills in these categories essential.

Appearance—which translates to clothing, accessories, and personal care products—was once the shopping bailiwick of the gals. Now this sector is capturing more attention from guys—and the older and more independent they get, the more this is true. Technology, the modern-day equivalent of tools, was once the shopping dominion of the guys, but this arena's importance to gals has greatly increased. Gender convergence has elevated the importance of brand and shopping knowledge about tools to women and girls, and brand and shopping knowledge about clothing to men and boys.

That said, what *interests* guys and gals the most hasn't changed quite as much. Guys still like to shop for and purchase "tools"—which include music, electronics, games, and sporting equipment—more than gals do; girls and women still like to shop for clothing, accessories, and home decorations more than guys do. Even for the youngest Gen Yers, the distinction is clear: ten-year-old boys spend more of their own money on video games; girls of the same age spend more on clothing (though candy still tops the list for both).[7]

Both genders, at every age, still like to shop with a representative of the opposite sex when exploring outside of their interest zones. In a mini-survey of college-bound students, 90 percent of the girls we spoke with shopped for computers with their dads and for everything else with their mothers or gal friends. Of the guys we spoke with, nearly all delegated the task of selecting dorm essentials to their moms, shopped for their clothes with friends (frequently female friends) and sometimes their moms, and picked out their electronics themselves. The girls we spoke with were also much more specific in describing their new bedding, clothing, and accessories, and the boys were more specific about their "tools."

The Evolution of the Sexes—at the Mall

Evolutionary psychologists point to a division of labor to explain why girls tend to be more communicative and passionately interested in forming and regulating social groups, whereas boys tend to be more activity-oriented and achieve security through what they do.

Imagine living in tribal times—he needs that focus and fight to kill those beasts and protect the village; she needs a community of others to share tasks, keep the group together, and care for the children and the infirm. We don't need those distinct roles anymore, and they're gradually falling away, but instinct and social training still guide us in those gender-related directions. A bit less so every year, but for now we can still see their influence in the ways that people shop.

The beast that needs slaying today is a great-fitting pair of jeans and the right cell phone plan. Men approach that task pretty similarly to the way they've always gotten the job done: hunt, kill, done—let's eat. The quick search capabilities of online shopping are understandably appealing to men, who spend more money online than women, place a higher value on the speed of the transaction, and also spend less time searching for bargains than women, according to a 2008 article in the *Wall Street Journal*.[8] Meanwhile, women, who have always used the marketplace as a way to learn about and connect with each other, are still doing just that—both online and in stores.

Even our neurology supports this style of shopping: male and female brains are different. The portions of the brain related to emotion and language are more pronounced and react more fluidly in women than in men.[9] The male brain is particularly adept at laser-like focus.

But just as our workday has evolved from running with a spear to running the latest software program, and gender roles and expectations have gone from highly fixed to flexible, gender differences in shopping are also evolving.

Most notably, Gen Y men are more versatile. Oh, they can still knock out a Mother's Day gift selection in twenty seconds, but they can also hang out in a mall all day—especially if it means being with the gals.

Today's more gender-equal, gender-convergent generation is reshaping shopping. Marketers who think this generation of men will be satisfied with a "waiting for my lady" chair at the back of the store will be missing out on a host of opportunities. Target's director of marketing planning, Sally Mueller, says, "Younger guys are shopping more like their sisters. They're going for what's 'on trend.' We're keeping our eyes open to what these opportunities are."

Men's departments have traditionally been afterthoughts in department stores—with little attention to either design or service—because women bought most of the guys' clothes and focused more on the amenities in their own departments. Macy's CEO Terry Lundgren, whose company owns Macy's and Bloomingdale's, says now that more men are buying their own clothing, his stores are focusing more on personal shoppers or at least providing more personal service to cater to these often-rushed customers.

How to Woo a Man

The secret to capturing boys and men at the mall is threefold: keep it simple, give them something to do, and offer them low-key help.

Simple

A big jumble of handbags on a table will attract nearly every woman who walks by. It means "Sale!"—and for most women, sifting through it is a joyful treasure hunt. To men, though, a big jumble of anything looks like chaos, and they'll cut a wide berth to avoid it.

Women want choice, and they're willing to try on way more articles of clothing than men are to find the right thing. A salesperson we spoke with at the upscale young women's jeans department at Neiman Marcus said that she wished dressing rooms could be arranged by clothing size, with one of every possibility in each room. "They bring them all in anyway, then I take them all out until the next one brings them all in again," said the saleswoman. Victoria's Secret does something similar now, offering customers a "Bra Box" with samples of each style in their size.

Men, on the other hand, view lots of choice as overwhelming. Paco Underhill noted in *Why We Buy* that men faced with multiple options will simply leave stores.[10]

Order, clarity, and simplicity are key in attracting guys, who are generally on a mission and more focused on solutions than on options. It gives them a sense of control. Male Gen Yers' love of individuality and the unique makes them more interested in options than older men—and this makes an orderly, predictable approach even more important.

Doing

Tony, twenty-nine, doesn't enjoy shopping because "It's boring; I'd rather be doing something." Tony's brother Dave, thirty-three, chimes in with a groan: "Yeah, it's so passive." For a couple of guys who find "passively" watching football to be anything but boring, something's obviously missing when it comes to retail: action and engagement.

For a visual demonstration of the power of "doing," pop by any Apple store and observe the packs of men and boys playing with the equipment. According to Bertrand Pellegrin, author of *Branding the Man: Why Men Are the Next Frontier in*

Retail, men enjoy shopping more when browsing is an add-on to *doing* something. Mixing in activities, toys, games, food, or sports engages guys; that's why selling clothing to them at sporting events is so successful.[11] Pellegrin also recommends adding events like social mixers, networking, or barbecue nights.

Urban Outfitters is a favorite of our focus group participants—and judging by their success, a lot of Gen Yers feel the same way. Urban Outfitters scatters "toys" among their T-shirts, Chukka boots, and peacoats—like books on how to hide things in public places and 3D anatomy puzzles.

Help—and "Escorts"

There's an old cliché that men won't ask for driving directions. With the popularity of GPS systems, that cliché is about to become extinct—it could be replaced, perhaps with a new one-liner that men won't ask for help in stores. We don't mean that they won't ask for service—they're much more forthright than women in expecting quick checkout service—rather, we mean that they don't like to ask for advice, insight, or different sizes. Especially from men they don't know. Market research informed GPS manufacturers that a woman's voice giving directions will work better with men. The same is true when it comes to getting directions about how to shop or what to buy: it's more effective coming from a woman.

The male Gen Yer's first choice, depending on his age, is a spouse, girlfriend, or female pal, or his mom. Gina, seventeen, of Dallas, loves to shop. Once a month she and her friend Calvin will go shopping. "He likes shopping at some of the same places I do, but he never knows what to get. My other guy friends besides Calvin all have their moms shop for them. I've talked to many of my friends' moms, and they always ask what's in and what they should get their sons. This is how a lot of my guy friends are, because they feel like they're too 'macho' to go shopping."

A few of the married Gen Y women that we spoke with told us they felt like their husbands wanted them to accompany them on shopping trips not only for advice, but so that they wouldn't feel awkward being "a guy in a mall."

In addition to the help that females provide, guys like having them as "escorts" because it makes shopping more socially acceptable. The mall is still considered girl territory, and there's a stigma that shopping is feminine—real men don't shop. Further, most young men think they're not supposed to care about their appearance. An escort's urgings are a good excuse to buy.

Once guys have exhausted their options for help from the women in their lives, it gets sticky. Guys actually like getting help, but they don't want to ask for it, they don't like being told what they should buy, and they don't want help offered before they're ready. What's a retailer to do? Focus on the product and keep it businesslike—unless invited to be more personal. A 2007 Wharton study found that men respond more positively to utilitarian and helpful sales-associate interaction rather than the interpersonal aspects of the experience.[12]

Offering options that meet their requirements (be it the correct size or gigabytes of memory), expediting the process, and showing additional items—without suggesting or requiring a response—works best. Solution-driven exchanges—without offering advice, unless asked—are key. Men are also more likely than women to make decisions based on what's worked for other people. Suggesting that other customers have purchased and loved a product is persuasive to a man in a way that it wouldn't be to a woman. Finally, it's effective to create a connection of service and assistance by emailing or calling when new products have arrived—or when those "doing" events are scheduled.

The Truth About Men and Fashion

Though men and boys have always been aware of the image that's created by the look and style of their clothing (even if it meant wearing the same style of Levis for years), today's young men are more interested in clothes in an overt way. Even guys who *said* they weren't interested later showed us in focus groups that they think a lot about clothes, carefully craft their wardrobes, and are acutely aware of what clothing and appearances say about themselves and others. Though sometimes that means simply trying hard not to look like you're trying hard.

For Tommy, sixteen, of Arlington, Virginia, "Designer is where it's at." He looks like a blond version of Troy from *High School Musical* and dresses at least as well. Still, aside from trips to J. Crew and Polo to buy "plaids and new stuff," he doesn't do much shopping now that "everyone has cars so we can do something else besides saying to my parents that we are going to the mall. The mall is more of a middle school thing," he reports. Still, if they see a movie at the local shopping center, Tommy and his friends often can't resist checking out "new kicks" (shoes) and trying on hats. He buys hats in stores, rather than online, "so I can try it on and make sure I look good in it."

Dressing and fashion is more task-driven for men than it is for women. While women tend to enjoy fashion in its own right, as creative expression and as a social vehicle, men use fashion and dressing in a solution-focused way. When they're younger, fashion is a means of securing their connection with their friends, and they'll purchase according to the norms of their group. Later, they use fashion as a tool to compete in the workforce or as a way to attract women. As guys age, become more confident of their masculinity, and experience greater latitude in the acceptability of a wider variety of styles, their interest in fashion increases.

Our survey results—and the growing emphasis on young men's fashion by retailers—support this. In an increasingly appearance-oriented world, it's no surprise.

"Gen Y guys are far more open to dressing, fashion, and appearance," says *Branding the Man* author Pellegrin. "It's more acceptable and they know it leads to things. It's also more acceptable to be vain—it's not thought of as vanity, more a sense of self or pride. Men are starting to see the potential in self-enhancement."

Pellegrin feels that Gen Y men have gotten more style education through the media than in previous generations.

At the same time Pellegrin notes that fashion for men is still somewhat of a uniform, and for many there's a fear that if they appear overly concerned with their appearance, they'll look "gay." For example, when it comes to working out, guys are more likely to say they're doing it for their health when the real reason is to look good.

Women: It's a Social Thing

Not surprisingly, only 6 percent of our survey respondents thought boys and men liked to shop more than women and girls. In fact, 48 percent of gals said they loved shopping compared with 19 percent of guys. Women and girls also shopped more often—be it online or in stores—and enjoyed shopping for a wider variety of items.

The hunt is where it's at for the majority of women. Which is why women are far more likely than men to be bargain *hunters* and willing to go the extra mile (sometimes literally) for a great deal. It's also why women are far more likely to return things than men are. It's part of the hunt to reassess, reevaluate, reconsider, and often return what they've purchased in favor of something better. Men return fewer than 10 percent of their purchases.

We also found that women enjoyed talking about shopping more, discussing their purchases and considerations, and that they found great emotional rewards in sharing the shopping experience. From back-to-school shopping with their moms, to prom shopping with their friends, to lunch and browsing outings when they're older, and finally shopping for their own kids, shopping is bonding for women.

At every age, the girls and women we spoke with noted a big difference between the way they shop and the way guys shop. Tween girls say that "the boys don't say anything!" and twenty-nine-year-olds say that their boyfriends and husbands "don't have much patience for discussing alternatives."

Gen Y girls and women are twice as likely as guys to say, "Friends help me a lot when deciding what to buy." They're also more likely to say they want their parents and siblings to be involved. The only shopping activity in which Gen Y men are more eager than women to want to collaborate is shopping with their spouses or sweethearts.

Word of Mouth

Men demand, and get, better and faster service when they shop. They complain in stores 50 percent more often than women, according to a 2008 TARP Worldwide study.[13] But even if they're not complaining, many of the focus group respondents we spoke with felt that gender discrimination was alive and kicking in the marketplace. "I don't know if it's because they just look like they need more help or what, but I can be waiting and waiting and a guy comes in and gets taken care of right away," said twenty-six-year-old Anna from Atlanta.

Considering the importance of sales-associate interactions to women, this could spell trouble for the retailer. The Wharton study found that women highly value stores where the sales associates make them feel important, and that women are more likely than men are to be angered by a lack of engagement from sales associates.

And here's the kicker: when women are unhappy with the service they receive in a store, they're far more likely to tell other people about it than men are. They're also more likely to tell other people about good experiences—but as they say, "Hell hath no fury like a woman scorned."

Word of mouth is the most important influence in consumers' apparel and electronics purchases, according to a 2008 study conducted by BIGresearch for the Retail Advertising and Marketing Association.[14]

Sex!

Simone, nineteen, of Tucson, has twelve different Victoria's Secret push-up bras in a spectrum of fabrics ranging from baby pink to leopard print. Her profile on Facebook pays tribute to four of those bras. At a recent party, she and six of her friends posed in a colorful line-up of bras for the guys at the party—and several of those girls later posted a photo of the event on their Facebook profiles. "What's the difference?" Simone says. "It's like a bikini top."

Meanwhile, the seniors in a South Carolina university sorority have an annual tradition of posing for a photo in a no-two-alike array of bras in leopard prints, stripes, polka dots, and colors of the rainbow.

Almost singlehandedly, Gen Y has made lingerie a leading category in women's fashion. Two oddly converging trends have combined to boost the underwear market. Loungewear has become the Millennials' version of the housecoat—something they roll out of bed in and wear to college classes or even to some restaurants. Meanwhile, after decades of women and girls trying everything to hide their bra straps and panties, underwear has become as important as the right purse, displayed in sheer fashions, spaghetti-strapped shirts, and low-riding pants. Colored and wildly patterned bras and underwear are now official elements of the outfit.

From bra obsessions, to thongs, to bare midriffs, not to mention pro expertise with cosmetics, hair care, plucking, and grooming, Gen Y women and girls look hot. And even those who keep their panties and parts covered still seem to look more polished, put-together, and perhaps even more attractive than many members of older generations say they remember girls looking when they were "that age." Add to that the fact that Gen Yers are also more likely to get cosmetic surgery than previous generations did at that age, and to spend buckets more money on clothing, and we have a case for a highly sexed-up, wanton generation. Right?

We beg to differ. Though Gen Y sex is a hot, hot (not that kind of hot) topic in the media and among parents, a good deal of what society worries about has little to do with sex—in that way. Though the courtship and mating rituals of Gen Y are different from those of previous generations (and we'll get to that later in this chapter), their appearance, and society's reaction, are both influenced by these four factors:

1. Projection. The point at which "looking good" becomes "looking sexy" is determined partially by cultural values and partially by a personal assessment. Although Gen Y is clearly pushing cultural boundaries, *sometimes* "sexy" is more in the mind of the person doing the looking—to another person it might just be "looking good." After all, Gen Yers have access to a world of beauty unavailable to most previous generations who had to suffer with panty lines, un-pushed-up anything, frizzy or flat hair, and pimples untreated by prescription acne medicine.

2. "Sexy" doesn't mean the same thing to Gen Yers that it does to others. It comes down to exposure, in more ways than one. Granted, for most, wearing an exposed bra at a party is suggestive. And the Tucson party girls were no doubt hoping to stimulate a little interest from the guys. But to this generation, which has been exposed to so much, the belief that a bra is appropriate for any situation in which you'd wear a bikini top is probably genuine.

3. Each generation is more casual than the last, and "casual" has often been, at first, misconstrued as sexy. Some of what's perceived to be sexual is simply less structured, more casual dress. In the 1950s, women were expected to squeeze it all in (or together) with an industrial-strength girdle that created the famous no-bounce, uni-butt look. Those who didn't were considered to be a bit looser—in more ways than one. The same was true for those who gave up pantyhose in the 1970s and for teenagers who

wore pajama bottoms and Uggs to the mall in the early 2000s.

4. Looking great is more important, even *de rigueur*, in the appearance-oriented, highly visual world of Gen Y. There is tremendous pressure to maximize your appearance—as a statement of self-esteem.

Marketers that know the difference between how Gen Y views "hot" and how older generations view hot-looking Gen Yers are miles ahead when it comes to connecting with them. These consumers can see right through the panderers.

Sex! (Really, This Time)

Beneath society's concern about the sexualized dress of many Gen Yers often lies a concern about their relationships. Courtship isn't what it used to be—but then it wasn't what it used to be when boomers were courting, either.

Gen Y guys and gals are friends—really. Everyone over fifty has heard cautions like "Men only want one thing" or "Men and women can't really be friends; underneath there's bound to be sexual tension." Gen Y has truly tossed out that notion. From childhood friendships, to packs of friends of both sexes hanging out in high school, to adult Gen Yers working together as colleagues and teammates, it's working—most of the time, at least.

Of course that means that dating, mating (or hooking up), and marriage will be different too. We found this to be an area "under construction," and many of the Gen Yers we spoke with expressed a lot of exasperation and confusion. If friendships are easy and clear, pairing off is anything but.

Gen Yers bravely face a considerable challenge as they discover and decide for themselves how to understand gender equality and role convergence when it comes to the profoundly meaningful role that shopping, buying, and money play in courtships and marriages. As is so often the case with this generation, the great benefits of having a world of options and the freedom to choose are accompanied by the burdens of stress, doubt, and misunderstanding.

How to have a relationship isn't the only "option stress" Gen Yers face—they also described to us some angst about how to know when they'd found the right partner. "My parents always told me not to settle—so it kinda hangs over me, if somebody isn't perfect I wonder if I'm settling. I know nobody's perfect, but still," says Jamie, twenty-seven, of Asheville, North Carolina.

The situation is exacerbated when it comes to getting married. Ryan, twenty-eight, of San Francisco, has been living with his girlfriend for the past eight months. "My parents are divorced, so I don't want to make a mistake. I'm not in a hurry, anyway; I'm having fun the way things are." The high self-worth and subsequent high standards instilled by their parents, the social acceptability of living together, a firsthand view of the consequences of divorce, and a generation of guys who often don't feel ready to marry until well into their late twenties have made simply "falling in love and getting married" seem a bit old-fashioned.

Dating Starts at Twenty-Two

For many Gen Yers, friendship trumps traditional romance in high school. Though crushes and pair-ups will never go away (there are those surging hormones, after all), group and mixed-gender friendships and pack-dating have replaced "going steady." No need for an evasive answer to the age-old question, "So, who are you dating?" Today most Gen Y kids can honestly say, "Nobody."

Even proms and dances are often attended by groups of guys and gals rather than couples, and at many high schools single tickets are sold as often as couple tickets. Kids are massively connected to each other through teamwork and technology, and dating collectively seems only natural. Gen Yers say that because guys and girls know each other so well, there's less tension and mystery, which makes dating seems "weird."

Once they're in college, the pattern continues—with a twist. "The hookup has replaced the causal date," says Stanford professor Paula England, who conducted a study of eight thousand undergraduate students across the nation. She defines hooking up as "a situation in which two students, who may or may not know each other, meet at an event and end up doing something sexual; it carries no expectation that either party has an interest in moving toward a relationship." Hooking up, according to our sources, doesn't have to happen at an event; it can happen through craigslist or dating websites, too. According to England, over 75 percent of undergraduate students have had hookups, although many of these encounters do not include sexual intercourse.[15] Although we met many Gen Yers in relationships, there is a notable trend away from traditional dating.

In a *New York Times* "Modern Love" first-person article, "Let's Not Get to Know Each Other Better," twenty-one-year-old Joel Walkowski says, "for my generation, friendship often morphs into a sexual encounter and then reverts back to friendship the next day." He wonders if the hookup is the result of "our plethora of options and utter lack of protocol," a "media obsession that's desensitized and hypersexualized us," and attention spans "measured in nanoseconds."[16]

Social researchers point to several other possible explanations: later marriages make pairing off (or "practice" pairing off) seem less urgent; Gen Yers, who have received more protective parenting, are maturing later—especially the boys, according to Gary Cross, author of *Men to Boys: The Making of Modern Immaturity*[17]; intimacy and the deep, personal communication required by couples has run into a roadblock in the form of technology; and because all groups instinctively resist member pair-offs, Gen Y's orientation toward teams and groups makes forming a couple even harder—at this age, male buddy groups are especially hard to crack.

Whatever the reason, dating isn't as commonplace as it's been for previous generations at this age. And dating is the practice period for the negotiations that all couples will ultimately face in dealing with roles and the meaning of money and purchasing in relationships. Dating really begins when individual Gen Yers are separated from their packs.

We point this out because courtship is such a central theme at this age, and a great many products that Gen Yers buy are related to the search, hunt, and practice period of love. Getting it right and understanding this generation's upheaval of tradition is crucial in connecting with them. Although Gen Yers in their early twenties are still looking for love, they're not necessarily looking for a partner, and they're approaching the hunt in collaboration with their friends.

Can't Buy Me Love

"If I want it to go further, I'll let him pay," says Regina, a twenty-six-year-old journalist in San Francisco, "otherwise I want to split the check. When a guy pays, it's getting serious."

"My boyfriend thinks it's shallow that I like to shop; he says that I should be trying to break that stereotype of nothing better to think about than shopping," says Jen, a twenty-five-year-old graduate student in Los Angeles. "But, really, I do love to shop. I don't know why. Maybe I am shallow!"

"Girls want to know that you have money, and that you will provide, I guess. But most of them make good money so it seems like we should split it. Isn't that what they want? To be equal?" wonders Patrick, twenty-nine, from Chicago.

Rachel, twenty-nine, of San Francisco, says, "My boyfriend makes so much more money than I do, but still it's everything down the middle. I can't keep up, and he gets mad at me instead of just treating me. It's not really the money that bothers me, it's about feeling cared for."

"My husband and I work as a team and have the same values about saving. I guess the only thing that bothers me is that he has no problem spending a big chunk of our money on something like our new TV—which I don't think we really needed—but then he gives me a hard time about buying shoes, which cost a lot less," says Caroline, twenty-nine, from Chicago.

Gen Yers are carving out new territory in their relationships. They're pioneers in a new world of gender and role equality. Considering that the things we buy are often representations of our feelings and the roles we see for ourselves and others, the potential for misunderstandings and hurt feelings in how they spend money and negotiate buying power is huge. The potential for misunderstanding on the part of marketers is also huge: from decision-making authority, to intra-couple discussions about what to buy, to assumptions about male or female types of products, landmines are everywhere.

Watch a movie made in the 1970s or 1980s and you'll see how far we've come in expanding the role expectations of both women and men. For example, now men can adore their wives without being "whipped," and women can be powerful without being threatening. Now it's equally acceptable for men to change diapers and women to do the taxes. And though most enjoy these changes, it also means that in every relationship there's more negotiation. The ease of simply knowing what's expected is replaced by the challenge of assessing and deciding who does what. That's not the hard part, though—often gender expectations are embedded and emotional, and though we may *think* it's unreasonable to expect our partner to be responsible for something like child care or financial security or trash removal, we can still *feel* let down or neglected if those emotional needs aren't met.

Couples conflict occurs over who pays and how to split money at many ages among the Gen Yers, but particularly when Gen Yers settle into relationships. Caring, masculinity, and femininity are all tied up in who buys and pays and what they get each other. And though Gen Yers are sorting through new ways of being a couple, tradition and the relationship modeled by their parents lie beneath the surface.

The result is a generation that's highly conscious of these issues—and therefore sensitive about the marketing messages they receive that communicate underlying expectations of how couples behave. Assumptions about gender roles are kindling for distrust.

Considering the importance of dating and mating as a motivation for shopping, and a host of gender-related social shifts—ranging from men shopping more to gender role convergence—it's essential that marketers get it right. From what they're looking for to where they'll look and with whom they'll shop, old gender-related presumptions won't fly with Gen Y.

6

INFLUENCE: THE FORCE THAT IS GEN Y

Christine's retired father is pretty clueless in the clothing category. "He wears his pants too short. He's just not style-conscious at all," says the nineteen-year-old from Manhattan. "I love my Dad, nerd or not, but I do make fun of him a lot."

She does more than that, though. She convinced him to buy—and wear!—a pair of the popular "Nantucket Red" cotton canvas pants that are popular in the New England beach town where their family spends summers. Since then, she hasn't had much more luck in the fashion arena, but her sway extends far beyond her dad's closet. Her parents added a room above the garage of their Cape Cod home so her thirteen-year-old sister Christine and their friends could—and would—congregate there. The "big room," as the kids call it, has foosball, air hockey, and pool tables, and a big TV and stereo with huge speakers so they can watch movies and listen to music on the big couch or comfy chairs. There's also a small kitchen with a mini-refrigerator that is usually stocked with water and sodas for whoever shows. The girls use it almost every day, demonstrating the brains behind the buying and remodeling trend that has been one of the few areas of growth in the dismal housing market of the last few years: family-friendly homes with rooms or other areas designed to keep the kids and their friends at home rather than out riding around looking for a good time.

The kids have clout.

Behind their influence, Gen Yers have high expectations of their products (and their parents!). We have this generation— their creativity, confidence, love of design, and insistence on innovation—to thank for a host of improvements in shopping that we all enjoy.

Research conducted for the digital marketing agency Resource Interactive in the fall of 2007 shows just how much influence Gen Y has on household purchases in the following categories[1]:

- Clothing/apparel: 90 percent
- Movie videos/DVDs: 85 percent
- Groceries: 85 percent
- Video games/systems: 77 percent
- Cell phones: 71 percent
- Computers: 70 percent
- Sports equipment: 67 percent
- Vacation: 65 percent
- Vehicles: 49 percent

Their impressive purchasing power, their outspokenness about what they like and don't like, their influence over their parents, and their emerging spending power as they move into their adult years combine to make Millennials the most powerful generation in retail. Jim Taylor, Ph.D., vice chairman of the marketing and strategic research consulting firm The Harrison Group, says "they are behaving as directors of the family corporation at a very early age."

How They Put Their Mark on Retail

You have to go back only about five years to see how Gen Y has influenced everything from website navigation to Apple's new product launches. The depth and breadth of change that's taken place in the world of shopping in a very short period of time is largely the result of Gen Y's influence.

Here are some of the ways, further highlighted in Chapter Seven, that Gen Y has influenced retail and shopping:

- Apparel selections in stores now change between six and twenty-four times a year, depending on the retailer and the age of its audience, instead of the old-fashioned turn-of-the-last-century way, with five fashion seasons (winter, spring, summer, fall, and resort).

- Retailers are embracing environmentalism, charities, and other causes. Target gives to education, Walmart Corporation fights hunger, and Sears supports disabled veterans, to name just a few.

- As retailers court young consumers, we've all gotten bigger and better dressing rooms and simply nicer-looking stores that we all might like to linger in a little longer.

- Websites are getting faster, easier to use, more visual and exciting. You don't have to be sixteen to get impatient with a slow page load or a "shopping cart" that's empty after you've added merchandise.

- Shopping has become more mobile, enabled through technology.

- More and better low-end merchandise is partly a response to the economy, but it also stems from the fact that young consumers have made it cool to buy clothes at stores including Target and Kohl's.

- Stores that cater to Gen Y were about the only nondiscounters doing well in the spring of 2009. And BIGresearch's March 2009 Forecast IQ reported that of seven retailers "almost certain" to see an increase in sales heading into the summer, three—Aeropostale, Hot Topic, and The Buckle—targeted young shoppers and the others were all discount chains.[2]

We have young people like Danielle, twenty-four, to thank. This graduate student from Atlanta says, "Fashion is causing a lot of problems in our society. People get focused on status. I think it should be about the design." For her part, she doesn't care who makes her goods, as long as they're well designed. She owns an Apple computer, gives IKEA vases to friends for gifts, and on a typical day mixes finds from Target and Walmart with South American jewelry and a Prada handbag. She got her Prada handbag online last year for a fraction of the retail price (with free shipping and no tax to boot).

Put simply, products have simply gotten better—and certainly more interesting. Whereas their parents might have settled for cookie-cutter cars like the Toyota Camry, Gen Yers, through their comments and their purchases, have convinced automakers to push the envelope in design and customization options.

Their Parental Push

Being their homes' chief technology officers gives these kids unprecedented access to information, which is, of course, power. Teens can get the message out faster and identify new trends and ideas, thanks to their closeness with family and near-constant communication with peers on social networking sites and through text messaging. News about good and bad products spreads far faster in Gen Y's high-tech circles than it does in their parents' often lower-tech ones.

And when it comes time to research a new car, dishwasher, or stereo purchase, it makes the most sense to turn to the household members who are best at culling all the best sources of information on the Web.

The fact that wealthier children also have the money to spend bolsters their influence on household financial decisions. More than half of respondents to a 2008 American Express/Harrison Group study said they "like brands that are preferred by my children."[3] The wealthier children weigh in on every aspect of household life, from "what we do for fun" and planning vacations to buying cars and high-tech products, the study showed. The survey included 1,800 individuals representing the wealthiest 10 percent of U.S. households.

Children in less affluent households still hold considerable sway, as Resource Interactive research and our own focus group research shows. In some of the considerably less affluent homes, the kids often not only have better technological skills but also may be the only ones who use the Internet. For the Gen Yers who are first-generation Americans, they also may well be the only family members fluent in English, making them the *de facto* liaison with the commercial world.

The importance of shopping as a family conversation topic should not be underestimated. Harrison Group's Jim Taylor calls it a "meta-conversation" because it's safe and can help parents glean other insights into their kids. He compares it to talking about driving with teens as a way to talk about maturity.

Of his conversations with his sixteen-year-old daughter, Taylor says, "If I say something directly, it's likely to be seen as an 'old fart' insult, but I *can* talk to her about what to buy."

Mommy Youngest

This growing kid power is a marked change in who's in charge. Moms have dominated shopping in every previous generation; now kids are often more dominant than the mothers. This is due in large part to the new importance and admiration of youth. We are a more visual—some might even say superficial—society. The women's marketing company Frank About Women says about half of baby boomer women believe retailers cater too much to younger shoppers and ignore the needs of older shoppers.

"Our ongoing dialog with women tells us that, for the most part, more than half of women over age forty just don't feel like their clothing needs and sense of style are being addressed in today's retail environment," says Frank About Women managing partner Jennifer Ganshirt. "They don't want to dress like their teenage daughters or their moms, and they're tired of being ignored."

No retailer wants nearly half of its potential client base to be ignored, especially when they have money to spend and will do so when they see something that suits them.

Here's another theory, courtesy of retail consultant Craig Johnson, president of Customer Growth Partners: Women born before 1950 tended to dress like their mothers, but those born after 1950 are far more likely to dress like their daughters, thanks in part to the loosening social and fashion norms that started with Woodstock.

No matter what the reason, there's an unmistakable trend for some middle-aged moms to try to emulate their daughters—or at least their youthful looks and behavior. All across America, girls are sending their moms back upstairs to change. Even when it hurts, parents will take fashion cues from their kids.

Beverley of Pasadena, California, is very candid about how uncomfortable her mother's fashion choices make her. The sixteen-year-old's own funky fashion may be considered "out there" by her friends, but she and her friends have clear views about how their moms should stay within the clear boundaries of trends and good taste.

"No kid wants their mom to wear pants up past her belly button with her shirt tucked in with a belt on," says Beverley. "But we also don't want our moms displaying their saggy boobs to the world."

Laryn, eighteen, of Charleston, South Carolina, is a preppy blonde who wears brightly colored and fairly modest clothing for her age. But she's always been a bit appalled when her mother wants to dress like her, which has been going on for awhile now. "I know that I influence what my mom buys because she is a single mom on the quest to look young, so whatever I bought, she would buy in a different color," Laryn says. "This would proceed to *huge* arguments about it because I'm like, 'Uhhh, hi, I'm sixteen and you're forty-six. Stop taking my stuff!'"

Given their outspokenness about what their moms wear—and their mothers' proclivity to listen—there's far more mother-daughter shopping going on than there was when baby boomers were teenagers. "When *I* grew up, we didn't shop with our moms," says J. C. Penney executive vice president of women's and girls' apparel Liz Sweney, fifty-four.

How Y Moves Marketing and Sales

All of this power gives kids a feeling of freedom to speak up; makes parents far more likely to listen when it comes to clothes, cars, electronics, and most every other line of products; and makes Gen Y a formidable generation for retailers. Gen Y's influence in each area manifests with its own often-quirky qualities.

Department and Discount Stores Take Heed

After J. C. Penney saw research that helped quantify teenagers' purchasing clout with their parents, the retailer decided to redesign its teen departments and refocus on this segment in 2008. The research company TRU, which conducted the teen study for Penney, reported that families are often closer than they were when the parents were kids. In response to the TRU survey, nine out of ten teens said they are "close" with their parents; 75 percent agreed that they "like to do things with their family"; and 59 percent said family dinners are "in." TRU believes the numbers were far lower for members of Gen X (those born from around 1961 to 1979).[4]

Kohl's CEO Kevin Mansell says he often reminds the retailer's analysts and investors that its focus on exclusive brands for teens is directly related to the young shoppers' ability to lure their parents to the store, where they'll spend even more on themselves. Shopping trips become "more productive visits" when Mom gets what she wants too, he says.

Target is always working on new ways to draw these influential young consumers into their stores, in large part because they know they are so key to all other purchases made for their homes, says Sally Mueller, Target's director of marketing planning. Not only have young women decided "It's OK to shop with Mom," Mueller says, but they're also telling Mom what to buy. That's put new pressure on the executives who choose which home goods hit Target's shelves, and they constantly grapple with which products to offer the younger crowd. A recent try: bedding in a bag that doubles as a tote for teens.

For the 2008 back-to-school season, a Facebook application sponsored by Target allowed users to deck out virtual dorm rooms with Target home decor items such as boldly colored art deco couches, hip breakfast bars, and even big-screen TVs and digital photo albums that allow users to directly import pictures of their friends or their favorite YouTube videos into their "rooms." Virtual dorm room designers can even subtly or not-so-subtly advertise their picks to all who view their Facebook profiles. Once users create the college home of their dreams, a thumbnail copy of their room is pasted on their main profile page. More enthusiastic users can choose an option on the virtual dorm room screen that takes snapshots of their pads for more in-depth Facebook photo albums. And of course, you can also simply email them to Mom or Dad.

Likewise, Kohl's 2008 back-to-school campaign included a collaboration with the virtual world Stardoll, where girls can dress up their own and guest avatars—and Avril Lavigne, who is already one of Stardoll's celebrity avatars and has a line of clothing at Kohl's. In the first sixteen days of the campaign Kohl's Stardoll boutique logged 2.2 million visits; 1.8 million virtual items were sold; and 97,000 visitors clicked through to Kohls.com.

"One of the main Internet axioms is to communicate in the avenue [customers] choose," says e-commerce consultant David Fry.

Apparel and Accessories

The Harrison Group's Taylor, coauthor of the book *The New Elite: Inside the Minds of the Truly Wealthy*, says one need only look at Ralph Lauren and Tiffany to see Gen Y's influence. He says young people—especially, but not only, those from affluent households—have been big drivers of the upscale accessories business. Think Chanel and Gucci, brands that this generation's once conservative-spending parents never would have considered.

And the girls have sure got pull when it comes to the rest of their mothers' wardrobes too. Beth Teitell, author of the book *Drinking Problems at the Fountain of Youth* describes this phenomenon as DUI: dressing under the influence—of a teenage daughter, that is.

Young people such as seventeen-year-old Sara, of Murfreesboro, Tennessee, are helping drive the trend, and sometimes they're almost playing the role of the parent.

Sara works long shifts at an ice cream store, even on school nights, to pay for her clothes, which she often buys at Goodwill when they have "ten items for $5" specials on Mondays. But her dad, a manager at a home-improvement store, has more expensive taste, so she helps him choose wisely.

"I pick out my dad's clothes all the time," says Sara, whose parents are divorced. "I go shopping for him with his money. He loves Ralph Lauren. I'm not personally into the name-brand stuff, but he's a manager so he likes to look nice."

Sara's thirty-eight-year-old mother, who doesn't work, often borrows her daughter's clothes and jewelry. "She likes hipper clothing that doesn't make her look like a tied-down mom," says Sara.

The 1980s and 1990s trend toward somewhat conservative attire for adult women helped give a huge boost to women's clothing retailers, including Ann Taylor and Talbots and designers such as Dana Buchman. But a more recent trend toward youthful clothing has also been giving these more classic clothing brands fits in the last couple of years. Many middle-aged women have been deserting their old mainstays for, say, hip new designers at department stores or even Forever 21—or have largely stopped shopping because of the lack of trendy but appropriate options.

In 2008, parent company Liz Claiborne shuttered the Sigrid Olsen brand, which was classic with an *artsy* flair, and demoted Dana Buchman to designing only for Kohl's. That happened as the company's more provocative brand, Juicy Couture, was really taking off, having grown from a $50 million brand when it was acquired in 2003 to about $600 million a year in 2008.

Juicy, founded by two then-thirty-somethings in 1996, has benefited greatly from the trend toward women dressing younger. Mother-daughter shopping is a big part of their business, with both women choosing outfits for themselves.

Still, some kids have their limits with this brand too. Janine, eighteen, of Hunt Valley, Maryland, hid her mother's hot pink Juicy Couture sweat suit because it was, well, just too pink and youthful for her fifty-seven-year-old mother, even if she is a well-toned fitness director. And also because she kept wearing the matching pieces together, a *faux pas* for any true Juicy girl. Megan, seventeen, of Denver, says, "I won't allow my mom to wear my Juicy, thank you. We share, but moms shouldn't cross the line and start dressing like their daughters."

Trouble is, the definition of dowdy—or too young—can be all over the map.

"Talbots? I don't know anything about Talbots," Juicy Couture cofounder Pamela Skaist-Levy said in an interview. "That's what my Nana used to wear."

There must be something in the middle, and Talbots hopes it is starting to find it with the trendier fashions it began to introduce in the fall of 2008—teens may not want to wear these clothes, but they won't try to talk their moms out of wearing them, either. And Talbots' efforts, which were showing some signs of success in early 2009 despite the recession, hold lessons for all retailers who refuse to change with the times. Or who change too much.

Target has long understood and catered to the dynamic with its one-stop shopping for Mom and trendy youthful fashions from a rotating collection of hot designers for daughters (or moms!). Meanwhile, a 2009 TRU study[5] showed more teens continue to name Walmart as their most-shopped store, with Target trailing a distant second. But more teens name Target as their *favorite* mass-merchandise store. TRU spokesman Rob Callender notes that this could change if teens fear a prolonged economic downturn and sense that Target's much-regarded sense of style no longer justifies the prices they charge.

It's not that Wal-Mart, Inc., the world's biggest retailer, hasn't tried: it stumbled in its attempts to lure young people with trendy fashions, but its recession-beater prices helped it build market share as the economy continued its depressing decline in early 2009.

Cars

In the old days—back in, say, the 1990s—car dealers had to remind their salesmen not to ignore women shopping with men in the showroom because not only did they buy a lot of cars, but they also were influencing about half of all purchases. Fast-forward to the 2000s: salesmen are now warned to be careful not to ignore the kids, because now *they're* influencing half of the car sales.

The used-car dealership chain CarMax addressed young people's influence directly in a TV ad in 2008. A mother is making dinner and talking to her son on the phone in the other room while he researches their next car purchase online in the other room. He returns to the kitchen with a sheaf of his research documents.

"Influence from the kids, whether it's for them or for the family, is a common scenario," says Guy Eberhart, general manager of two CarMax dealerships in the Virginia Beach area. Eberhart says he makes sure salespeople realize that the decision making is more shared these days: "We need to educate all of the consumers."

This kid-influence has helped bring back Cadillac, which was never mentioned when talk turned to which brands General Motors should sell in late 2008 or early 2009 to stay afloat.

"We didn't have a lot of success with the baby boom generation," says GM sales and marketing chief Mark LaNeve. "But the ones coming up behind that—X and Y—think Cadillac's cool." There's "absolutely no question," LaNeve says, that young shoppers are responsible for Cadillac's comeback.

"Older people are too busy to know what's cool," says LaNeve, who is forty-eight and has twin teenage boys. "Younger people teach us what's cool."

LaNeve says it was almost a fluke that the Escalade became "kind of the car for the MTV rapper crowd." GM didn't give away cars or pay celebrities to drive them, though they would loan them when asked.

"We didn't want to commercialize their affinity," says LaNeve. "Once we did that, it wasn't cool anymore."

When Ricardo, sixteen, of Murfreesboro, Tennessee, went shopping for a car with his stepfather, he managed to convince him to buy a used Ford Mustang. "I told him, 'We gotta get this car,'" says Ricardo, who moved to Tennessee from Puerto Rico in 2006. They did.

"He's like me and gets along with me. We always play video games," says Ricardo. "We always have our minds on the same thing. I get along with him like a friend."

Tamika, the oldest of five children, influenced her mother's car purchases for the family—and gave them a lesson in a cause that's important to her.

"My mom always has a hectic job schedule, so I help out with the family," says the nineteen-year-old from Long Beach, California. "At one time she wanted to buy this humongous SUV. I thought a family minivan would be better, because of gas. I've always been able to voice those things in my family and to my mom."

Because of high gas prices and environmental concerns, Tamika says she takes special interest in shopping green. "Things I may not otherwise pick up, if I see that it's eco-friendly, it makes them a bit more attractive to me," she said. And because of her clout around the house, green has become a family priority too.

Automakers had only to look as far as the car customization business to see where they were going wrong with young people—and how they could benefit by catering to them. Unable to find what they consider to be distinctive enough cars on showroom floors and in used car lots, Gen Yers are adding new wheels, spoilers, and all manner of accoutrements to their cars. Drivers ages sixteen to twenty-four account for almost 20 percent of the $38-billion car customization industry, said Peter MacGillivray, a vice president at the Specialty Equipment Market Association. And that's just the alterations designed to improve a car's appearance or functionality; the figure doesn't include necessary repairs or replacements.

Stephen, seventeen, would applaud any effort by automakers to make cars more distinctive, reliable, and easily customizable. The Cleveland, Ohio, high school student owns a 2005 Ford F-150 pickup truck, a 1964 Buick Riviera, and a 2008 Kawasaki Ninja ZX-6R street bike. Like his own look—with two pierced ears and clothes that tend towards preppy plaids and "popped" collars—his transportation stands out. He customized his car, truck, and motorcycle to fit his exacting tastes.

MacGillivray says, "As a teenager, the last thing in the world you want to be caught driving is your mom's car, so they started modifying and accessorizing them and created an industry."

Gen Y's favor has also boosted the popularity of some of the new vehicles that are the easiest to make distinctive. In a 2009 study of Gen Yers by Deloitte,[6] their top feature that makes a vehicle "cool" was exterior styling. And about two-thirds or more agreed that a vehicle reflects a person's taste and status and that they consider these factors when making a purchase decision. College students attending a Deloitte conference said their favorite brands included Mini, Jeep, and Scion,[7] which all offer enough options to please any style-conscious car shopper.

Scion, which has the youngest buyers in the car business, lets shoppers build their own Scions online; they can add a custom grille, wheel covers, or a special exhaust pipe. Jeep, like all of the other Chrysler brands, lets buyers choose from a huge assortment of grilles and other parts and accessories through its Mopar division.

Mini goes even further, allowing shoppers to choose from different roofs, dashboard materials, and a host of other special touches. The choices are so appealing to Mini buyers that about 60 percent special order their vehicles—compared with just 6 percent for Chrysler. For about $1,000, you can even design your own roof, and the Mini folks will make it for you, notes Jim McDowell, Mini's sales chief.

McDowell estimates about 25 percent of Mini owners are under thirty, and they are by far the most enthusiastic owners and customizers. "They absolutely love it," McDowell says of Gen Y and his brand. "A lot of young people are back living with their parents, and having the perfect Mini is a way to embrace their individuality."

Ford is taking a more competitive stance with Gen Y drivers through their hybrid Fusion and the new Fiesta, now sold in Europe and coming soon to the United States. Ford Motor CEO Alan Mulally says that the tiny Fiesta is designed to appeal more to young people; he personally declares that "it's awesome."

Technology Officers

The Apple iPhone, with its whiz-bang features and Gen Y–centric marketing campaign, won over the generation, shifted what young people expect from their mobile devices, and, in turn, spawned a series of competitive phones.

"You will see a lot more activity on mobile devices," says Hossein Mousavi, CEO and cofounder of the mobile marketing company mPoria.

Resource Interactive's Nita Rollins points to Apple's App Store and its "army of developers" as a case study in a brand's openness to consumer involvement. With thousands of programs and more than a million downloads since its launch in 2008, "it's a roaring open success," she says. "It is also a prime example of a company tapping primarily Gen Y talent and enthusiasm."

The same is generally true of the social application development community, notes Rollins. The venture capital–backed incubator LaunchBox Digital selected its winning applications, and most had Gen Y developers—such as Satjot Sawhney, a 2008 Columbia University graduate, who developed BuzzHubb for the college student who is "dissatisfied with Facebook's feed and not yet Twittering."

Robert Richardson, CEO of the electronics sales training company Associates Interactive, says, "If the product sales were based on quality or features, Apple would be lucky to be in the top five. However, because they effectively attracted the younger generation, they now set the standard for music players."

Behind the phenomenon is the fact that young people simply have confidence when it comes to electronics. Steve Koenig, director of industry analysis for the Consumer Electronic Association, says CEA has found that 75 percent of teens say they enjoy the challenge of figuring out how to use devices; only 57 percent of adults feel that way.

It's understandable, then, that parents often find it's simply easier to let the kids make the call when it comes to computers or other technology. Teenagers influence much of their parents' shopping patterns when it comes to electronics retail.

"The kids drag the parents in a store to browse, which often is the only reason why the parents ever go to the department or store," says Richardson. "The increase in foot traffic that it creates makes the store 'busy' and therefore more attractive and gives the store an opportunity to market and sell other products to the parents."

After all, the video game kiosks aren't there to convince the kid to buy a game—"They already know every game they want," says Richardson. "[The games] attract the kids and hold them in place for awhile."

Think of it as the equivalent of the ball pit or toy corner in stores such as IKEA or kids' retailers. But then just imagine how far this concept could be taken in retail—beyond the couches and TVs that keep the men happy at Macy's, there are myriad opportunities for stores to add interactive amusements and other items of interest to Gen Yers in stores that want to lure their parents, just as there are ways to make department stores more attractive to kids.

Video games are a category in which "kids" are the primary shoppers and influence a lot of spending as well as how the family TV gets used. But they have helped turn gaming into both a "recession resistant" industry and one that benefitted from the economic downturn, says CEA's economist Shawn DuBravac.

"We've seen the game console move from the basement to the main living room," says DuBravac. "A big part of it is consumers looking for ways to cut back on spending without drastically impacting their quality of life."

His father grew up with arcade games like pong and Pac-Man, which "are nothing like what we deal with today," says sixteen-year-old Kyle of Louisville. That means that, at least in his eyes, his dad doesn't really know what he's doing when he plays. So Kyle says he's in the driver's seat when the two shop for video games, which they do often.

"For people like me, video games, especially stuff like virtual reality, is kind of an escape," says Kyle, who attends LAN (local area network) parties, where video gamers stay up for hours playing with other gamers. "When you're having a rough day you can come home and play a video game and be in a whole different world. People from the '50s, '60s and even '70s don't really know about that." Ahem.

Gen Yers are also bringing their parents around to some of the popular new social networking sites, even though they'd typically just as soon their folks stay off Facebook. Women over fifty-five are the fastest-growing segment on Facebook (though still only 3 percent of users), which pretty much guarantees that young people will be looking for new territory to call their own in short order.

ShopTogether, a site that allows people to instant message each other for advice on online purchases, is growing in popularity with Gen Y parents, thanks to their way-connected kids. John Jackson, CEO of ShopTogether's parent company, says many adult users of ShopTogether were introduced to the site by Gen Y members of their families, often when they go to college and invite family members on virtual shopping trips.

Once customers log on to ShopTogether, they can connect with a friend or family member whose opinion they seek on an item by dropping the item in the chat window. From there, the friend can see the main page of the item and share their own.

"If you want people to buy, you've got to get them where the products are," says Jackson.

Homes

Proximity to children's activities and family friendliness was the *only* home amenity to see an increase between 2007 and 2008. It moved from being the tenth most important attraction in 2007 to third in 2008, according to the American Express/Harrison Group survey.

The National Association of Home Builders hasn't studied the issue of Gen Y influence, but director of economic services Stephen Melman says teenagers' influence is seen in trends including the great room, which can be viewed from the kitchen and becomes an "echo chamber" as the children grow.

Christine, a real estate sales assistant in Georgia, agrees: "Today, when parents choose how they want to live, their teens are given preferential treatment in how they also want to live," she says. "Teens today have more privacy, more choices, and an influential say in what they expect from their own living space."

Christine sees that for herself in her daughter's home a few miles away, where her teenage grandson has three rooms to himself: his bedroom, a full bathroom, and an entertainment, music, and TV room that he can use with his friends, who are also welcome to stay overnight on a futon. His mother made sure that one side of the home's landing was "designated as his area."

This isn't to suggest her grandson is bucking his generation's trend of having close family relations. Sure, he's got all this space, but Christine says that when they are home he prefers watching TV with his parents, with whom he always eats dinner.

With more parents concerned about their kids' safety outside, "children spend much more time indoors than ever before, and this also influences parents' choices," says Christine. "More space indoors is designated for their own use."

Banking

As financial services institutions have begun to offer more sophisticated online services, mobile and text banking options, and anything that's *faster*, Gen Y is first in line and asking for more. People are generally loath to switch banks, but Gen Y's technological demands could change that. Gen Yers jump on innovation in banking—and their acceptance and demands fuel its growth.

Javelin Strategy and Research's Mark Schwanhausser anticipates that it's only a question of time before Gen Yers will expect to be able to do all of their banking from their mobile phone. "Gen Y is more mobile and more virtual; they want their banks to be too," he says.

And it better be fast. In recent research from Javelin, Gen Yers were more likely than others to open an online account because they "thought it would be faster" and also more likely than others to say that the process "took too long."

Whether it's online banking, mobile applications that track finances, using text alerts, or applying for loans—Gen Yers are demanding fast, efficient, technology-enhanced innovation. They want to feel unencumbered by paper, space, or time.

Flip-Flop Phenomenon

College students were behind the concept that flip-flops are acceptable for everyday use, says Brian Curin, president of the Flip Flop Shops franchise. When Northwestern University's women's lacrosse team appeared at the White House in flip-flops in 2005, some were shocked, but it helped accelerate a trend, says Curin.

The now $20-billion-a-year industry, which has outsold athletic shoes in recent years, allows wearers to have a thong sandal for every occasion, from household chores to first dates, Curin says.

"It's the college age group that's really pushing the trend," he says. "There's a lot of influence in that age group. People are still wanting to be young and want to know what's hip, the next hot brand and the next hot style. If young people are wearing it, then it must be cool. That's why you're starting to see members of other generations that are a bit more accepting of flip-flops."

The flip-flop is really part of a larger trend toward more casual dress, and Gen Y men in particular have taken the acceptability of "casual" to new heights. Casual Friday? Why just one day, when every day could be casual? Rob, twenty-seven, of San Francisco, recently completed a high-visibility project for his new job in the IT department of a hospital. "My boss was really happy with it and asked if there was anything I needed; he wanted to make sure I was happy and that I'd stay. I asked him if I could wear shorts to work. When I started I wore shorts once and was told to go home and change. Maybe now that they see that I'm good at what I do I'll be able to wear shorts. I mean, who cares?" Rob still can't wear shorts to the office, by the way, but he did get a better computer (his second choice).

The Gen Y Clerk Conundrum

Gen X, baby boomers, and other more senior shoppers expect a higher level of personalized service than Gen Yers do, says retail strategist Katherine Toll of the global consulting firm Kurt Salmon Associates.

"When you get a [teen] shopper in, that's someone who wants more of an informal interaction," says Toll, whose clients include Hot Topic and Tween Brands. "They're looking for loud music and to see themselves in the person working there."

This creates a problem for retailers; because members of Gen Y have lower service expectations as clerks, they often miss the point of the kind of service required to satisfy older shoppers.

For example, when they're selling consumer electronics, Gen Y salespeople are often the most knowledgeable in the store about the products. And about three-quarters of the salespeople at consumer electronics stores are members of Gen Y, Robert Richardson estimates. Young people, he notes, "gravitate to what interests them." But although older salespeople may not be as facile with the products, he says, they are typically much better at "engaging consumers in conversations about a shopping and product experience."

It's the *talking* about the products to customers that poses a big challenge to Gen Y much of the time.

"They talk like they text. They express themselves in short bursts that are abbreviated in all senses of the word," says Richardson. "And they expect the person on the other end to understand that short form of communication."

That can be true whether you're talking about a fashion-savvy twenty-something female clerk or a teen guy selling video games. They figure everyone spends as much time as they do talking and texting about the merchandise. And if they don't perform impeccably at sales, the usual incentive—*keeping* your job—doesn't resonate like it once did.

Teens and twenty-somethings don't have the fear of being fired that older workers do, nor are they burdened by the feeling that they need to stick around very long. A January 2009 study by Deloitte found only 8.5 percent of nineteen- to twenty-seven-year-olds are seeking "job security" even in the dismal economy.

"The assumption is they'll be able to do well and better" no matter where they go, says Jenny Floren, CEO of the recruiting firm Experience.

It's hard to get members of Gen Y to truly feel they are part of a retail team, says Richardson. One day in the spring of 2008, he was scheduled to be at a store—part of one of the five largest retail chains, he says—when he learned that every associate in the electronics department had quit. When he does the secret shopping missions at electronics retailers, he's amazed how many different "uniforms" he can see in one store. Even though salespeople are all supposed to dress the same way, he'll often see seven different variations on the company uniform—something that makes the already difficult task of finding a sales clerk all the more difficult these days.

The clerks will tell Richardson, "I don't see how [a uniform] makes me part of the group," he says. "If you talk to the associates wearing the off color, they usually haven't been there long and will say, 'It's close enough and I'm still being me.'"

Although they may not make the best salespeople, Gen Yers also don't expect or demand as much of store employees, which tempers the trend's downside. Young shoppers also love connecting with other Gen Yers and are more likely to form a bond with a salesperson closer to their own age.

"They're less attuned to whether the service they get is good," says Richardson. So his job is to convince Gen Y employees that people who are spending more than $100 on a product expect some education and service to be part of the process, even if they don't expect that themselves. In our survey of two thousand consumers, the most commonly cited complaint about shopping was either unknowledgeable or discourteous sales personnel. The most innovative retailers and manufacturers are working hard to find new ways to satisfy and engage younger workers and to retain baby boomers as part-time employees.

Along with the career path and opportunities, Floren says location is key to Gen Y, as is whether the company has a purpose or mission that's ethical. They also often say they want to make a difference.

The Y Factor

Whether they're shopping, selling, or helping their parents make a purchase, Gen Yers are the ones to watch in today's marketplace. Though they may not hold the purse strings, they hold the attention of those who do. And shortly their spending power will top that of all other generations. Equally important is the influence they have in transforming the way we all shop and buy. Think you have more to learn? Read on for strategies and tips from successful retailers.

7

WHAT WORKS WITH GEN Y

Chelsea, thirteen, and her sixteen-year-old brother, Brady, would not be caught dead in a department store. Anything but a loud, parents-free specialty store is just so not them. The Kansas siblings prefer only name brands and only want to go to Hollister, American Eagle, or Abercrombie & Fitch, though Chelsea also favors Victoria's Secret's Pink line. They're so enamored with the almost overpowering smell of their favorite retailers that they opened their 2008 Christmas presents from the stores "and started inhaling," says their mom, Leslie. When Leslie found what she thought was the perfect pantsuit for Chelsea to wear to a school band concert, her daughter refused to even walk inside Dillard's (where she once got most of her clothes) to see it. Given the economy, Leslie refused to get Chelsea a $200 pair of Ugg boots for Christmas until her daughter agreed to pay half, which she happily did from her babysitting stash. Chelsea goes to the mall about every other weekend, crowds into the specialty store dressing rooms with four to six friends, and always returns with something. But it's Brady who is the real fashion plate: he must have "awesome shoes, the right jeans, and some sort of cool hat," says Leslie. "It's insane." Teenagers everywhere crave places they can call their own, and price—even sometimes when they're paying with their own money—still often equals prestige. That's put pressure on department stores and discounters to find ways to lure the young with hip environments and must-have fashions, all without turning off their cash-strapped parents, who are often still paying.

From sexy, parentless playgrounds like Abercrombie, to the sleek movie-set-like home store CB2, to iMovie lessons at Apple, retailers and marketers are desperately seeking ways to get Gen Yers to buy from *them*. Their future depends on it. The quest to get Gen Yers in their doors (or onto their sites) ranges from the obvious—investing millions in their websites—to the subliminal, such as mood-scenting their stores.

A summer afternoon at Westfield's Annapolis mall with retail brand and design expert Steve McGowan drove home the point in living color—not to mention scent. The fifteen tween and teen stores at this upscale mall were, in many respects, a study in sameness, with several appearing interchangeable in their design and merchandise: black patterned T-shirts and jeans. Was that Garage or Urban Behavior? The retailers apparently had all decided what works with kids and were sticking with the formula.

But walk into Abercrombie & Fitch and sister store Hollister and, like it or not, you're truly transported into another world of shopping. As McGowan noted, "We've totally left the mall." At Hollister, which had only recently started selling body products, the uninitiated (read: adults) are nearly bowled over by the thick cloud of cologne in the air. It burns the eyes and lingers in the throat. But that's hardly the only indication that this is a young-people-only haunt. The cavernous clothier is also nightclub-dark, and overstuffed chairs and couches form a lounge by the checkout, which is lined with magazines and CDs for sale, including the latest music by teen sensation Colbie Caillat. The water nearest to this Maryland store is the Chesapeake Bay, but as in Des Moines, Louisville, and anywhere else there is a Hollister, there was a real-time camera showing the waves crashing at Huntington Beach, with California time ticking along at the bottom of the screen. No matter that no one's surfing round there; the preppy beach scene, surfboard behind the counter, and ads with barely clothed beautiful people help create an image for the brand that many young people would like for themselves.

And that, the thinking goes, makes them more likely to buy, say, nine-inch-long skirts and several layers of spaghetti-strap shirts.

In this chapter, we'll survey the landscape of what's been successful with Gen Yers in the retail arena and, more important, why it's worked. As you'll see, it's often the subtle, emotional differences that make the biggest impact—most of which are invisible to the untrained eye. We'll pull apart what works from retailers like Urban Outfitters, who create intoxicating treasure hunts in their stores; Zara, where impulsive purchases are irresistible; and upstart websites Karmaloop and Threadless, who win by helping Gen Yers get that custom look they crave.

The Emotional

Truly skillful marketers find ways to connect with consumers that are often imperceptible. Indeed, it's often hard to tell you're being pitched to these days. For marketers, especially those catering to this manipulation-leery generation, that's often the sign of a successful campaign. But we all benefit if we know why we're doing what we're doing when we're shopping. And when the strategies are successful, marketers should take note—and notes.

Sets and Scenes for the Senses

Shoppers don't consciously notice the vanilla scent that makes them feel right at home in—and kind of warmly toward—*that* particular home furnishings retailer. Not any more than a fashion-conscious young woman understands the real reason why she just seems to shop longer in departments with lots of mirrored surfaces. And though a teenage skater may not know that the heavily researched music and the perfect lighting have something to do with it, he finds he's always drawn to *that* store. No matter how few shoppers are at *that* particular mall, it always seems convivial, even exciting—that's because of a layout that suggests movement and, in fact, does get those who are there moving around.

The sets and scenes created in shopping environments have been proven to create moods that inspire purchases. They encourage shoppers to feel a lifestyle that can be theirs for but a few dollars; they transport shoppers into a nostalgic past, or they amp up the adrenaline, which generates a feeling often mistaken for excitement—the result of which is, frequently enough, a purchase.

Because retailers can control every touch point in their stores—unlike in the real-world environments where their advertisements are seen or read—all of these aspects of the retail environment have become part of the new focus on experiential retailing. "It's retail theatre," says McGowan, who once worked in theatre design. "It should ignite all the senses."

The rhythmic thumping of the music played in many teen and tween retail environments is known to get the heart pumping. Add to that a DJ who knows how to read and play a crowd, make it nice and loud, and you've notched up the heartbeat a little more. Now mix in either vivid colors and creative design or sensual lighting and photography and the heart takes yet another jump. And that's the point. When the adrenaline flows, all we know is that we're, well, stimulated. Our brain then surveys the environment to figure out why. It's a mysterious little disconnect we all share. Physical arousal doesn't come with a mental explanation. Now you know why scary movies work so well to get couples, ahem, connected. A person feeling scared by a movie may mistake that to be attraction for her date. Similarly, when a shopper's heart is pumping a bit more than usual and she spots a cute top, it's easy for her to feel like she likes the top more than she actually does.

Even without the adrenaline, music creates emotion—specific emotions. Can you imagine a romantic movie or a thriller without music? Retailers also know that music can make people feel more comfortable, linger longer, and become less anxious about lines and crowds.

Now add in smell. Though not yet a common technique, more and more retailers are considering scent as a way to emotionally connect with their shoppers. Most of the retailers that use scents do so to add an emotional brand note to their environment. Sony Style stores have a vanilla and mandarin orange scent that was specially formulated for them and is supposed to relax shoppers and make them feel more comfortable in the store. Thomas Pink, the U.K. shirt store, has long been known for the crisp-shirt smell of their shops, and Tommy Bahama for the beach scent that's misted around the shop doors so that passersby get a "sense" of vacation as they walk by. Other retailers are considering the power of scent to inspire emotion. This is more complicated—and it's also becoming big business. Casinos started the movement, and some believe they've found a scent that actually gets people to linger longer and gamble more. Even if it's the teensiest bit successful, it could mean millions in gambling revenues. Stores have scented baby sections with lavender to get folks in the nurturing mood and misted pine scent in Christmas departments. Those make sense—but what about lingerie departments or men's stores? The problem lies in our brain's unconscious interpretation of scents. Turns out that "cinnamon bun" is a sexually arousing scent to men—but a store scented like a bakery might accidentally send shoppers out for a snack. Stay tuned; without a doubt, retailers will continue to explore scent as a way to get emotionally close to their consumers.

Retailers have long used lighting to lure people in, help guide them through their stores, enable them to see the merchandise clearly, and, of course, seal the deal. The bigger the ticket, the better and less, well, obnoxious the lighting. Warehouse clubs and discounters go heavy on lighting that creates a "discount" look, while higher-end stores use very low ambient lighting to provide a more relaxed atmosphere, according to design experts. Stores are increasingly adding colored lights to attract consumers' attention, but ironically, it's the most natural light of all that may increase sales most. Some studies have linked daylight streaming through skylights to higher sales.

One of the hot new trends in lighting is the idea of pace. Lighting is used to create "highs and lows," says retail branding and design expert Christian Davies of FRCH Design Worldwide. After all, if the entire store were brightly lit, "you'd be exhausted," Davies says. About a decade ago, stores would bathe the aisles in lights and keep the level lower on the merchandise. Now store designers keep the light on the product—so you don't have to go to a window to get a good look—and the aisles have lower light to make the experience more soothing.

Retailers, especially those trying to lure Gen Y, know they need to keep both their merchandise and the store looking new, as shoppers want to keep coming back to what feels like a different experience—an adventure, even—each time they show up. Forever 21 and H&M stores have managed to "stay relevant" for their customers, says Steve McGowan, because they have designed their stores in a way that can be changed regularly—appealing to their young customers' short attention spans. Forever 21 changes the color of their stores about every three months. Urban Outfitters practically rebuilds their stores every few months. And H&M has almost-billboard-sized graphics in the store that change regularly.

All of these facets have to work together to communicate … something, says Davies. And few in retail do it better than the nearly universally adored Apple. If you took all of the Apple products and signage out of an Apple store and replaced it with Dell merchandise and signs, Davies notes, everyone would still think of it as an Apple store because of the distinctive design.

Cutting Supply to Increase Demand

All retailers are trying to pare their inventories so they don't have to resort to too many markdowns, which cut deeply into profits. But retailers ranging from Zara to Nike to J. Crew go a step further by deliberately limiting the availability of hot-ticket merchandise in order to cultivate a fear of missing out, to create buzz and thereby increase the stature of an item, and, most important (at least for retailers), to give shoppers that very necessary reason to buy *now*.

"Hard to get" doesn't work only in dating. Hard-to-get retail items skyrocket in value and interest, and the harder they are to get, the higher their value. Scarcity tugs on the brain in one of two ways: through a herd mentality or through a fear of missing out. You know you're in the grip of the herd mentality when you start to think, "If everyone wants one, it must be great!" T.M.X. Elmo, anyone? Something universally desirable, hard to get, and in your hands also elevates your stature with the crowd. The other way herd mentality works is by ensuring a great value. That would look something like the dozens of heads bowed around the circular bins marked with cup sizes at the Victoria's Secret clearance sales. There's a reason why retailers jumble products together to signify a price reduction—they gather crowds, and crowds gather more crowds. It's human nature.

Closely related to this is the second way that hard to get works—through the fear of missing out. For younger Gen Yers, that "in" item often feels very, very necessary. And for older Gen Yers, that unique and distinctively "me" item is all the more irresistible if they know it won't be there tomorrow. Our research shows that the fear of missing the chance to buy a limited-time-only item is one of the biggest whys behind Gen Y buys. It's also part of the reason for the success of H&M and Zara.

To a certain extent, all sales (especially limited-time sales like twenty-four-hour sales or midnight madness sales) work by creating a fear of missing out on both the item and its great price as supply decreases. But some retailers have taken the concept to new heights.

Nike, a master at this, often comes out with new designs that everyone knows will be in short supply, which further fuels the already explosive popularity of sneakers with young men.

That was the case when Nike was preparing to release just two hundred pairs of its limited-edition, $150 "Lobster Dunk" sneakers in Boston. Some young men had been living on the street for *three days* waiting for the red sneakers to go on sale. As marketing executive Phil Johnson wrote in *Advertising Age* in June 2008, at least one of the kids was planning to resell the sneaks on eBay for more than four times what he paid. But the furor also said something about the power of passion when it comes to kids and their clothes. "The Lobster Dunks opened my eyes to the mystery of why we like what we like, and how far we will go to pursue what we desire," wrote Johnson.[1]

When Target started its GO International limited-time-only designer program in 2006, for the first year the retailer changed designers every three months. The following year Target made the change every two months. In 2008, it was down to a forty-five-day designer rotation, says spokesman Joshua Thomas. That's because young customers in particular want to see new clothes most every time they visit stores. And this helps create that get-it-while-it's-there mentality that boosts sales for the discounter. The teens and twenty-somethings who gravitate to Target's cutting-edge fashion-for-less, offered by designers that have included Luella Bartley and Jonathan Saunders, often log onto Target.com to keep up with the fashion comings and goings. The site provides information about the designers, interactive features of models wearing the clothes, and, of course, a way to buy them before the store moves on to the next designer.

"We're trying to be trend right [and] create a sense of urgency and excitement," says Target vice president of apparel design and development Michael Alexin.

Gen Y–focused websites such as Karmaloop and Threadless appeal to this get-it-now philosophy in different ways. Threadless, which specializes in T-shirts designed by its customers, says it keeps very limited quantities of shirts in stock so the shirts become "limited edition" and so it can focus on introducing new shirts "rather than restocking old designs." Karmaloop, an urban streetwear site, touts on its site that it gets new merchandise in daily—thereby encouraging frequent log-ins. CEO Greg Selkoe says he stops selling any brands once the merchandise is sold in the mass market, unless the manufacturer agrees to sell special limited editions to his site. After all, he says, the site's young clientele wants to be on the cutting edge. He stopped selling the Le Tigre and Members Only brands after they became too mainstream.

Being sold at Target, he says, "would be the kiss of death" for a brand on his site.

The Hangout

The concept might seem anathema to many older shoppers— Yikes! A pack of teens!—but one of the biggest Gen Y–focused efforts in retail now is trying to get as many young people as possible to linger in their stores. It communicates that a store is cool—or hot, or sick, or whatever the complimentary term of the day is—to young people who would rather use the voice and presence of the crowd than advertising to figure that out. Spencer's CEO Steven Silverstein says his chain eschews the movement toward open-air lifestyle centers because enclosed malls are where his customers hang out. "We open our arms to these kids," says Silverstein, who says the chain's in-store events have been hugely successful.

Says Steve McGowan: "It's the 'mall rat' reinvented."

The popularity of the Apple store as a place to congregate around cool products has proven the brilliance of Apple's move to position the store in this way—and has spawned many followers. Sony Style stores are designed to make consumers want to linger and touch everything from the silk wallpaper to the maple wood cabinets to the etched glass counters. The products are displayed as if they are works of art but, unlike at a museum, the stores actually encourage touching and testing because the company figures that makes you more likely to buy. The concept for the

G by Guess stores is basically a club where shoppers can chill. There are even "pre preparties" on some Friday nights—making the store literally little different from a nightclub, except for the fact that what's being sold is to wear rather than to drink. A late 2008 website promotion invited customers to hit the stores from 5:00 to 9:00 P.M. and "enjoy special promotions and get down to G by Guess beats while getting into a new outfit."

Many stores, including Neiman Marcus's Cusp, Puma, and even Lord & Taylor, have regular disc jockeys to help get people in the mood—for spending. And it's not just clothing stores that are trying to create this feeling. Whole Foods works on creating a nightclubby atmosphere with actual happy hours that can be for charity or "networking events," or simply to try out different beers during Oktoberfest.

Considering that the experience people have with your brand *is* your brand, events hold great sway. Events that engage shoppers are not only a draw when people are shopping less, but they also tell customers that they matter. Tarot card readings, theme parties, hot dog stands, and photo sessions are only the beginning.

Stores will often use the tried-and-true practice of featuring celebrities at in-store events to try to lure more young people. Of course, the very definition of celebrity has broadened considerably in the Internet age. Hot Topic has featured online gossip blogger Perez Hilton, and J. C. Penney highlights its Fabulosity line by model-turned-designer Kimora Lee Simmons. Simply being a store that celebrities shop at—such as the out-of-the-way L.A. boutique Intuition—is enough to put a retailer on the map for tourists, who show up hoping to catch a glimpse of, say, the *Desperate Housewives*.

In case young people run out of things to say—or text—to each other, savvy retailers are trying to entertain them in ways that go beyond music. Roman Tsunder, president of the marketing firm Access 360 Media, develops in-store television networks that are the stores' own version of MTV, with almost nonstop product placement. The programming is exclusive but mirrors MTV, with teen-favorite artists, their videos, extreme action sports, and bloopers. Tsunder, whose clients include Journeys shoes and Fye entertainment, says sales of Journeys sneakers or board shorts can increase by up to 50 percent while the videos are playing—something he proved by comparing sales at Journeys stores with the network running and without. When asked if they'd go to Journeys to watch the TV even if they didn't have anything to buy, 85 percent of customers polled agreed. (Of course, they only *thought* they had nothing to buy.)

"They don't just buy products." says Tsunder. "The young adult consumer needs to be entertained."

Indeed, Gen Y does want shopping to be fun. Which is just what Urban Outfitters is—a really good time. The store is particularly appealing to guys, who enjoy playing with the merchandise as much as considering it for purchase. Urban Outfitters mixes in clothes, toys, sometimes racy books, and even housewares in a sporadic, ever-changing display that feels like an adventure to shoppers. Many of our focus group subjects described it as a place to just hang out when there's nothing else to do, because "you never know what you're going to find" and "if you're with your friends you can always find something funny [to play with or share]." It's social, it's engaging, and oh, by the way, it's also selling merchandise. In 2008, as many of its competitors were seeing double-digit monthly sales declines, Urban Outfitters was watching its sales soar in the other direction—with double-digit quarterly sales *increases*. Though sales were down a bit in early 2009, Urban Outfitters stores were still seeing sales increases, and analysts were predicting that the company's earnings would grow at an average annual rate of 20 percent for the next five years.

Speeding Up Design

For many generations, "traditional," "heritage," and "time-tested" are selling points that work. For Gen Y, "new" is much more powerful. This generation has seen gigantic leaps in the functionality of the latest computer, cell phone, or iPod; consequently they have a strong belief in the power of the new. Couple this with shorter attention spans and the fact they are easily bored, and the message is clear: to make it with this crowd, retailers need to update their technology and selections constantly and shorten the time it takes to bring products to market.

That goes without saying in the electronics industry, but even in areas such as the cosmetics industry, our belief in technology, science, and the power of "new" means that Gen Yers won't be satisfied with, say, simply moisturizing. From cookware to cars, products that describe new means of scientifically delivering customizable benefits may not have been believed by previous generations—but they're insisted upon by Gen Y.

The faster retailers can mimic what's on the runways or the backs of celebrities, the more current and on-trend their merchandise will be. Not long ago, trend spotting often had to be done a year in advance—for next summer's seasons, say, even before a current summer's merchandise had been sold. Penney and other retailers were forced to make "educated guesses," as Penney's president Ken Hicks calls them, based more on speculation than on hard data.

Now, thanks to advanced software and computer systems, months have been shaved off the time needed to take a design from a concept to the sales floor. Stores can closely monitor what styles are selling, at what rate, and in which sizes, then adjust inventories accordingly. That means department stores and the larger specialty chains can better compete with boutiques. They're also better positioned to take on such retailers as H&M, Zara, and Forever 21, which specialize in moving the latest styles into—and out of—stores with sizzling speed and are among the most popular with the teen and twenty-something set.

One of the secrets behind Zara's ability to speed designs from concept to sales floor in about two weeks is that its store managers, not designers, often call the shots on what gets made, according to Kerry Capell in an October 2008 article in *BusinessWeek*.[2]

Zara store managers track what's selling and what customers say they want but can't find; these managers then send orders to the designers at parent company Inditex. Up to 70 percent of Zara managers' salaries comes from commission, Capell writes, so they have plenty of incentive to "get it right." This Spanish company also has fine-tuned its supply chain so that it saves time and money on shipping by producing its apparel at home or in neighboring countries, not in Asia, and can get new merchandise to the United States in forty-eight hours.

Many stores were still using the phone and fax machine to place big orders until quite recently, says Joe Skorupa, editor of the retail publication *RIS News*—and some still do. "It was done in a very manual, very slow, error-prone process," he says.

Software allows designers, buyers, and manufacturers to view the same fabric swatch or color at the same time, ending the need to fly designers around the globe or to send overnight packages. That helps get Fergie's latest fashion into, say, Forever 21, at Gen Y speed. Retailers using some of the new software can also make smaller, more frequent orders, which lets them adjust orders more easily once certain styles or sizes fail to sell. This is especially critical if you want Gen Y in your store.

Pushing the Envelope

From American Apparel's hollow-eyed, scantily clad models to the fashion G by Guess touts online as "sexy," there's plenty of evidence that sex is used to sell apparel—and the stores' popularity shows that it often works.

But the tactic can prove to be a delicate balancing act when retailers are targeting young shoppers but need to avoid alienating their parents. One such parent—Jeanette, of Olney, Maryland—recalls a trip to Hollister with her then-fourteen-year-old daughter and finding the suggestive in-store graphics, music, and lighting almost unbearable. Another mother in the store shouted that if the store manager would lower the music and raise the lights for twenty minutes, she'd "make it worth your while." When the manager went along, all the other moms in the store breathed a sigh of relief.

The role of sex, loud music, dim lighting, or whatever else parents find intimidating or offensive (skull and crossbones, the $250 price tag on jeans with "hand frayed edges," snarky sales people) is precisely that: to intimidate or offend parents. This serves two purposes: it helps make the store feel more like a place for kids (not parents) and therefore cool, and it feels exciting and rebellious.

That's even more true at Spencer's, which was a favored haunt for many baby boomers when they were teens seeking lava lamps. ("We're the lava lamp capital of the world!" exclaims CEO Silverstein, who shopped at the store for black lights and posters when he was a kid.) Now his customers rely on the chain for gauges to stretch their ear lobes, memorabilia for the extreme fighting league known as the UFC, and sex aids or "romantic products," as Silverstein calls them.

"We've always occupied that sense of cool—with an element of irreverence," says Silverstein. But he acknowledges, "Things now have gotten more extreme."

Indeed. Once it was Farrah Fawcett posters; now Spencer's eighteen- to twenty-four-year-old customers drool over posters of Los Angeles tattoo artist and former reality TV star Kat Von D in suggestive poses.

From the gauges and other "body jewelry" to the "places they will pierce," Silverstein says his customers are simply "expressing their independence" much as "we did in our day by growing our hair. There's a shock value that we perceive because we are older."

Talk about shocking. Many Gen Yers consider American Apparel the best place to shop for basic T-shirts. But it's so much more. Their CEO, Dov Charney, has faced at least three sexual harassment suits in recent years and acknowledged to *Portfolio* magazine that along with being the creative director at a company that often features near-nude models in advertising, he's a fitting model.[3] A video on YouTube shows Charney parading around a factory during working hours in a pair of the chain's underwear briefs and a tank-style T-shirt that says "Delightfully tacky yet unrefined." "It's f—— great, eh?" he says to plant workers. He told *Portfolio* it was done as a spoof to entertain workers.

The chain embraces both controversy and interactivity on its website and in ads on adult-themed sites. That provided a cushion during the 2008 economic meltdown.

For Halloween 2008, *American Apparel* posted pictures of shoppers with the best costumes. The winners included a "Girls Gone Wild" imitator, wearing a narrow black bandeau across her chest with the word "Censored" written on it.

"We know people like to talk about our ads," wrote one company employee and blogger.[4] "More often, it's tongues clucking and fingers wagging in disapproval, but this time, we seem to have some blogs taking to our defense about our first nude ads for the web." (One such blogger writes solely about sex, and her site counts American Apparel as one of its two home page advertisers.)

Its physical stores can be intimidating to some, and the "Living Dead" dolls and skull and crossbones bras could give even the goth set pause. But Hot Topic's website and blog in November 2008 were bubbling with glee over the recent release of the vampire-and-werewolf movie *Twilight*.[5] It also advertised the movie cast's tour to malls around the country. The store put blog posts on MySpace to stir up more excitement and count down the days until its *Twilight* merchandise was in stores. The chain had reason to cheer: the *Twilight* link was helping propel the once-shining retail star back into the limelight with soaring sales just as the economy was formally declared to be in a recession.

"The new provocative *is* vampires," says Ken Nisch, chairman of the brand and design firm JGA. "Vampires are kind of a secret handshake where you fall into the world of fantasy and graphic novels."

Abercrombie often does the very same thing—pushing the envelope and dropping the zipper a few more notches with each successive advertising campaign. Abercrombie's Gilly Hicks underwear brand and stores actually feature nude male models on their website. Such sites often require people to attest that they are over eighteen before entering—though Gilly Hicks doesn't. Rightly or wrongly, what could make a site *more* enticing to many young people? Especially the under-eighteen set?

Abercrombie is "sort of like an aging adult video star," says Nisch. "You have to continue to take more off and be more outrageous to maintain your audience. There are ways to be provocative under the guise of sophistication without being so sleazy," he says, and he suggests leaning more toward a rebellion theme than one of provocation based on sex.

How to Do Everything

If life's all about connecting—which it most certainly is for these young people—why not link up with their favorite stores too? One of the best ways for retailers to facilitate this connection is to listen to Gen Yers, provide a forum for them to inform other consumers, and when those consumers seek it out, teach them too. It's a collaboration that benefits both sides.

Apple, already many Gen Yers' favorite hangout, offers classes on how to use Apple's professional creative applications, including digital photography and video editing. Some stores even host free "summer camps" for young people on topics including how to make movies and create websites.

While many baby boomers may want to hire Best Buy's Geek Squad to come set up their computers or plasma TVs, many Gen Y would rather learn how to do it themselves. Enter online tutorials—a growing trend among electronics retailers, who feature video explainers on how to use their products. Best Buy even has a "community forum" where company experts and other consumers help you find out everything from what software updates you need to what you need to know for the 2009 digital TV conversion, along with a place to "swap stories" with other GPS users.

Even Betty Crocker—a favorite baking brand for baby boomers and *their* mothers—is into viral video marketing, with online explainers available whether you're longing to make a Barbie cake or a butterfly cake. The company believes the move makes it both more relevant to its core (read: old) customers, while it gets the chance to reach more digitally savvy younger ones.

Tween and teen girls want help figuring out fashion so they can feel more self-confident in their choices. But it can't be help in any heavy-handed sort of way. And frankly, they'd rather hear from their friends—or at least their contemporaries.

After Wet Seal started offering young women the opportunity to put outfits together on their site in 2008, the outfits their customers were designing were outselling some of the ones their buyers posted. Fablicious, a website for young women, goes a step further. The site, which attracted 170 retailers in its first week in business in late 2008, offers commissions on sales to those who design outfits using apparel featured on the site.

In stores, retailers are using bold, frequently changing visuals of models showing their fashions in a variety of styles, as well as salespeople who do far more than tell customers something looks good on them.

The displays at the Dots fashion chain, which caters to an often-ethnic clientele of eighteen- to twenty-four-year-olds, became more like three-dimensional magazines, full of style tips and life-sized photos of girls wearing the stores' styles. Dots management and FRCH Design Worldwide also decided to reemphasize the close relationship customers felt they had with the sales staff. The store's customers already viewed the clerks as close friends, so FRCH recommended a new emphasis on customer service to give the staff an even closer connection to shoppers.

Magazines have always been a major source of inspiration for young people. But now, with online magazines, videos, and the ability to rate merchandise and interact with other consumers, you've got a world of young people—on retailers' staffs or not—helping each other figure it all out.

Talking Technology

Technology is like a secret handshake to Gen Y; those who know it and use it well are in the club, those who don't are—well, too old to listen to. Technology means "new," "quality," and "cool." Which is exactly who Gen Y wants to do business with. From mobile applications to websites to social networking to in-store digital application, if you want to play with Gen Y, you better come with technology.

Kelly Mooney, president of the digital marketing agency Resource Interactive, says Gen Y doesn't distinguish between stores and websites: "It's one brand."

That means retail websites have to be state-of-the-art and offer a chance to connect. Amazon was first, but now most multibrand retailers are featuring product reviews and product suggestions based on previous purchases, and many are offering the chance for consumers to somehow participate. The options include Anthropologie's use of Flickr to allow people to post their pics at the store's site (without actually going on Flickr) or Gap allowing site visitors to remix *Jingle Bells* using the celebrities featured on their site during the 2008 holiday season.

Outreach to consumers can be casual; in fact, that often makes it more appealing, as it translates as "real" for phoniness-phobic Gen Yers. But they want to know that the retailer respects them and wants their business, which sites do by giving them some control and anointing them with status by singling them out on the site or offering them rewards for their purchases or participation.

Cashmere Marketing's thirty-one-year-old president, Ted Chung, combines grassroots "street teams"—young people who hand out promotional items—with text campaigns and website promotions for clients including Disney. A mobile promotion campaign doesn't mean marketers are only using texting and cell phones, says Chung. They're also trying to drive young consumers back to websites where there may be a movie being promoted or a new series of ringtones offered.

Chung's street team members often graduate to online handouts, "viral video seeding" of content that YouTube and other sites will run for free and to help garner online "word of mouth." Teams of kids who "have relationships with social websites" will help get clients' marketing messages into blogs and out to their networks of "friends." As to whether this is transparent enough for advertising-leery young consumers, Chung says, "Obviously someone has to be paid to do it. What it is that you're doing is enriching their experience and connecting in the right venue—terrestrially or online."

The key, says Chung, is finding the "communicators in their culture and lifestyles"—that is, the up-and-coming Snoop Dogs of the world—and getting them to "organically and proactively promote" products.

In other words, by influencing the influencers. The most effective way to do this is to be where they are and to let them "own" your product. Influencers should be invited to know more, get more—like product samples and peeks at new offerings—and give more feedback. In other words, they should be allowed to become part of and a spokesperson for the brand.

It's Social, It's Networking, and It Works

Gen Yers appreciate and value their relationships with brands and retailers, and that's precisely why they're less interested in advertising—which feels like simply being told what to do, like, or buy—and more interested in collaborations and interactions that feel genuine. The same is true whether you're talking about tweens or twenty-somethings: things like invitations to create ads on YouTube, applications to send to friends on Facebook, and online reviews are effective because they're more of a collaborative relationship. Not to mention more fun and active than passively consuming information.

"If you've got a new product and want to get buzz, sending an email is a great way to do it, but Facebook allows retailers to create a more viral experience," says Dave Hendricks, executive vice president of operations at Datran Media, which provides the technology for retailers and other businesses to target consumers through social media and email.

The company, which used to specialize only in email marketing, now develops Facebook pages for retailers. Unlike email, Facebook "influencers" share what they're doing and watching with their friendship groups, expanding the marketing messages' reach, says Hendricks.

Companies should use websites, social networks, blogs, and virtual worlds—everything that is part of the Web 2.0 world—to get consumers more involved with their brands and to become part of marketing activities, concludes a December 2008 "special report" in the *Wall Street Journal*.[6] After all, it's a lot cheaper and faster way for companies to keep abreast of what their customers are thinking than using focus groups or surveys. The report's other conclusions include giving consumers a reason to participate, such as free products; listening to and taking part in conversations on blogs; resisting "the temptation to sell, sell, sell"; and embracing experimentation, such as trying out life in virtual worlds.

Samsung drew attention to their LED televisions in March 2009 through an astonishing YouTube video, "Extreme Sheep." In the video, sheep are strapped with lights and herded across a field to enact a giant Pong game, fireworks displays, and a recreation of the Mona Lisa. Within a week of its posting, the video had been viewed over four million times. Aside from the obvious—that "Extreme Sheep" put Samsung in the minds of millions—this viral campaign was also effective for the subconscious emotional boost Samsung received. Only the most stoic could watch the video without feeling astonished, even delighted; these emotions become linked to Samsung. And the state-of-the-art sheepherders—clever, highly competent, and creative—become a mirror to the values of Samsung—not necessarily consciously, more through association.

Social networking shopping sites including Kaboodle and Stylehive are also increasingly getting attention from retailers, who see them as a step toward more collaborative product development with young consumers.

When retailers engage in a dialogue by responding to negative consumer reviews with apologies or explanations, that's taking it to a higher level. This is truly a unique and powerful opportunity for marketers—consumers are hungry for information, to have an exchange, and to feel they're part of the process. From Twitters updates so that devotees know they're insiders, to humble apologies that quell a rancorous review, being part of the dialogue through social networking or brand websites is a technique in its infancy. The possibilities are limitless—consider that a million people a day sign up to be part of Facebook. In terms of media dollars, social networking is far less expensive than traditional advertising, although the time requirements for managing the process are significant.

Facebook, MySpace, and other social network users are a medium in themselves. The exponential power of connectivity can create users that have the reach of a prime-time television ad—carrying messages that are potentially more influential than any television ad, because they're perceived to be more genuine.

Though it's a marketing communication vehicle in its infancy, and the idea of relinquishing control of your message to others is scary, to stay out of the game is to render yourself irrelevant to this generation. Using social media effectively requires humility and a genuine desire to add value to the lives of your customers—both good characteristics to demonstrate when marketing to Gen Y, no matter what your medium.

Marketing Mobility

When mobile technology became mainstream, it must have felt to Gen Yers as if they could finally breathe. To Gen Y, a mobile phone is like life's remote control. Almost all of them have one, after all. Just as younger consumers could never understand how a store wouldn't also have a website, Gen Yers will soon find it impossible to believe that all commerce and information wouldn't be available on that mobile device otherwise known as the Gen Yer's third hand or auxiliary brain.

Teens and twenty-somethings are twice as likely as their elders to use mobile devices for tasks other than talking. Gen Yers are also far more likely to opt in for text promotions, mobile coupons, and mobile search services. That stands to reason, as they're far more likely to eschew landlines in favor of mobile phones, and email in favor of text messages.

When Harris Interactive asked cell phone users about their preferred type of advertising in 2008, about two-thirds of adults and teens cited text messages.[7] Yet teens were more likely than adults to accept advertising images (47 percent, versus 35 percent of adults) and were more interested in viewing mobile ads with incentives (56 percent, versus 37 percent of adults). Teens were also twice as likely as adults to want entertainment or music downloads in return for responding to mobile ads.

Gen Y wants information about their favorite brands and retailers, but they want to be in control, and they won't be passive about it. Gen Yers are willing—even eager—to hear marketing messages, but these have to be either insider information that's important to them, such as information about a new release, or a way to save money on something they like; or they need to feel compensated for their time by, again, a coupon or something like free phone minutes or music. Companies that honor this exchange are richly rewarded. Penguin books, for example, ran a campaign to launch Nick Hornby's novel *Slam* on a "free" mobile network in Europe that exchanges advertising for minutes. They achieved a 67-percent response rate to the campaign, which included a ninety-second audio preview to the book.

"Any retailer going after teenagers, who are the early adopters, has to connect with them on their most used media device," says Access 360 Media's Roman Tsunder.

Tsunder says his company has done mobile campaigns for many youth-oriented retailers and has gotten promotion redemption rates of up to 30 percent. A 20-percent-off text promotion for G by Guess in the fall of 2008 generated a 14-percent redemption rate; compare this with email coupons, which often have only a 1-percent to 2-percent response rate.

Stores are also rapidly making it possible for consumers to search, and sometimes buy from, their inventories while using handheld devices.

Gen Yers use technology to shop far more often than their parents do. Hossein Mousavi, CEO and cofounder of the mobile service mPoria, says that in late 2007 the mobile commerce company was guessing who their users were, but assuming they skewed pretty young. Now he knows that not only are they members of Gen Y, but there is heavy use among urban youth, which he says could be related to a lack of access to a computer at home. He estimates that at least two-thirds of mPoria's users—who can buy from retailers ranging from Gamestop to buy.com on handheld devices—are teens and twenty-somethings.

Peter, seventeen, of Rockville, Maryland, used his cell phone to do a lot of his 2007 Christmas shopping using mPoria, at one point when he was in the back of a theatre during a boring movie. He ordered his sister a camera, his girlfriend a picture frame, and his father a Tommy Hilfiger sweater.

"You usually don't have the computer in front of you," Peter says, explaining the appeal of palmtop shopping. "I have it in my room, but I'm not usually home."

Apple's iPhone app, the Find, locates the nearest store carrying an item you're shopping for and then runs a price comparison with online shopping sites. Similarly, shoppers using wireless devices can also use the mall-search service NearbyNow to check store inventories.

Companies in Asia have been doing so-called QR (for quick response) for years, but Ralph Lauren was the first retailer here to offer QR codes in its advertising. These codes allow camera phone users to scan bar codes in advertising and be linked to a website—in this case, RL's—where they can buy the merchandise. The systems can also show which stores are in the seeker's area or send promotional codes.

GPS-enabled cell phones have made "location awareness" the big focus in mobile marketing, says Resource Interactive futurist Nita Rollins. Retailers can fine-tune and target, say, text message promotions by sending them only to shoppers in their immediate geographic area or even those in the mall. That's something NearbyNow used—until especially popular promotions caused near stampedes at stores and created safety problems in the malls.

Charmin's been providing free public restrooms in heavily trafficked areas, such as at state fairs, for nearly a decade. In the spring of 2009 they began sponsoring a mobile phone application that directs users to the nearest restroom when they're out and about. Now that's what we call getting close to your customers!

Virtual Worlds and Gaming

Video games are just about ubiquitous—studies show nearly all young adults play video games, especially the guys. The world of gaming got a huge boost with the introduction of the Wii and the Xbox 360; now this phenomenon extends to the far reaches of the Internet and its many "virtual worlds."

At least a hundred million people "inhabit" these virtual worlds, most of them teens, and they're spending $1.5 billion a year on clothing, pets, and accessories. And we're talking

1.5 billion real dollars, not virtual dollars. Target, Walmart, Walgreens, and other retailers sell prepaid gift cards for use in more than twenty-five different virtual worlds.

If there was ever any doubt that shopping and buying are related to emotional and communicative needs, this lays it to rest once and for all. We all shop and buy to tell others what we think of them, to show who we are, to fortify ourselves, and for dozens of other expressive and esthetic needs—and it's no different when you shop till you drop in a virtual world.

"Probably the most powerful way that virtual objects create real value is through self-expression," says Susan Wu, a principal with Charles River Ventures, in a post on the *TechCrunch* website. "RockYou[.com] is now serving 150 million+ widgets a day—widgets that people put on their Facebook profiles to differentiate themselves, much as they do in the real world with accessories and bling."

In August 2008, as its sales in the real world were falling, Sears "built" a two-story boutique in the virtual world Zwinktopia, which sold more than 850,000 items in its first sixteen days. The retailer also hosted a fashion show, allowing members, known as "Zwinkies," to get more immersed in the brand and products.

Not surprisingly, the sites also offer the opportunity to click through and buy the real thing for the girl in the terrestrial world.

Buoyed by their success, in the fall of 2008, Zwinktopia launched "Zwinky cuties" for girls aged six to twelve, because the website noticed it had to turn away droves of prospective users each month because they did not meet the required age of thirteen. Cuties can still earn ZBucks by playing Zwinktopia games, but the younger site will also offer monthly subscriptions of $5.95 a month for a VIP-like membership in the Zwinky Cuties world. These Zwinky "Jet Setters" can spend their virtual bucks on pets, furniture, avatar accessories, games, and a virtual passport that shows badges and awards from Zwinky activities. In late 2008, the company was considering opening retail stores in the "real" world, to help connect real products to girls' Zwinky experiences, just as Webkinz allows owners to connect physical toys to online communities and activities.

Though most of the virtual worlds seem to lean toward the feminine, girls have actually come later to the gaming party—in the largest numbers when Nintendo's Wii offered sporting and music interactive games.

Vector City Racers is a video game and virtual world that could have hundreds or even thousands of kids playing at the same time. The Vector MMO—for massively multiplayer online game—is targeting young boys from about ages six to twelve with an automotive theme.

Vector City Racers is described as a large virtual world split into different cities that have games and a variety of other entertainment options. Users play hide and seek or tag with friends in their cars or simply "drive" around. Recognizing that even the youngest Gen Yers want to put their stamp on things, the site lets them customize and personalize their cars and also work on them in a virtual garage. As users play through the game and participate in activities, they can earn rewards and upgrade their cars on a performance-level.

Preliminary studies suggest that gamers are actually more willing to join in marketing efforts than most other consumers. Even *Advertising Age* Marketer of the Year Barack Obama took out ads on the Xbox 360 version of the high-speed driving video game Burnout Paradise. Those playing the game who are connected to the Internet are also connected to an in-game system that allows real-world sponsors to place ads on billboards and elsewhere in its digital world.

The growth in gaming is staggering[8]:

- The video game software category grew 62 percent between 2002 and 2007 (at 2007 prices).
- Console/handheld games sales grew 57 percent between 2002 and 2007, to $8.6 billion—thanks in large part to the release of hot games such as Wii Sports and Halo 3. Sales are expected to reach $11.7 billion in 2012.

- Online games sales grew 554 percent between 2002 and 2007—to $1.4 billion—and are forecast to more than double by 2012. The neck-snapping success of World of Warcraft, which had over 2.5 million subscribers in the United States and 10 million worldwide in late 2008, was a big driver update.

- Mobile phone game revenues increased from $67 million in 2002 to $641 million in 2007. Mobile gaming is no longer restricted to games in the phone; new generations of phones can accept game downloads and are more suit-able for game play.

Video games or consoles top the wish lists for many teen boys, helping to make the industry "recession resistant if not recession proof," says the Consumer Electronics Association's economist and research director Shawn DuBravac. He attributes this to the fact that with the economy falling into recession, many families, like his own, have found gaming consoles and games cheaper than most trips and many outside activities.

Associations, or "If You Like This, You'll *Love* Our Product!"

As we've discussed, young people can't *stand* being hit over the head with an advertising message. Enter what could be called "association marketing"—whereby you attract Gen Y through their favorite causes, celebrities, or other brands. This creates an often subliminal link that resonates with the speedy teen and twenty-something brain. Association works like a metaphor—and it's even more powerful because it's nonverbal and therefore bypasses the logical parts of our brain. Associating a product or brand with another brand is equally effective—the characteristics of each rub off on the other, and if it's a good match the relationship can work like dynamite—blasting each into a new realm of "coolness." More powerful brands can also carry along newcomers in the same way; consider the benefits to Jawbone when Apple began carrying it in their stores.

Just as their parents might decide which brands are "good" by the fact that they are sold at higher-end department stores, these younger consumers figure it must be okay if Fergie or Apple says it is. So it helps Gen Yers make the kind of snap judgment that passes for decision making these days—and who are we to say it's in any way inferior to the old-fashioned way?

Licensing, Product Placement, and Other Brand Links

From Honda's co-branding efforts with Disney for the big-screen release of *High School Musical 3* to Virgin America's association with the HBO series *Entourage*, this form of marketing by association takes products people either don't know or simply aren't using and ties them to something with a more widespread acceptance in hopes of piggybacking onto it.

In September 2008, Virgin America co-branded planes on the New York–to–Las Vegas route with the popular HBO series. In a stunt that publicized both the new route and the show's new season, jets on the route were wrapped in *Entourage* signage, the first episode of the fifth season was screened, and high-rolling first-class flyers were offered the option of "Entourage Class," which included cashmere blankets to use on the flight and Godiva chocolates.[9]

Nike's consumer satisfaction even got a boost thanks to its partnership with iPod to market "sports kits," which let runners track their progress on their iPod nano while listening to tunes. Along with the music, you get feedback of time, distance, calories burned, and pace through the headphones. According to the University of Michigan's customer satisfaction index, in the third quarter of 2008, Nike's rating jumped 4 percent, in large part because of the deal. And the higher score put Nike on a par with Adidas, which had typically been ranked much higher.[10]

Why not start the somewhat subliminal marketing even younger? Just in time for preschool in 2008, New Balance rolled out a Sesame Street collection of infant and children's sneakers featuring celebrity endorsers of a different sort, namely Elmo and the Cookie Monster.

That followed the debut of Reebok kids' sneaks featuring Iron Man and the Incredible Hulk and sold only at Kids' Footlocker. As Reebok's Neil Hernberg explained to the *Boston Globe's* Jenn Abelson, "For the most part, the mother is still making the buying decision, but she's more influenced by her children than ever before."[11]

You can't help but notice the huge red cups of Coca-Cola that Simon, Paula, Randy, and Kara sip from when they're judging on *American Idol.* Those cups are part of the 4,636 product placement occurrences on *American Idol* between January and June 2008. According to the Nielsen Company, there were 204,919 brand occurrences on broadcast and cable networks during those six months.[12] And no wonder: clothing worn by a character (wardrobe placements account for 28 percent of all placements) is a bit like an endorsement, and less disruptive than advertising.

Cash-strapped communities are more open to sponsored assistance from brands. It's an opportunity for marketers to get closer to consumers and break through the clutter of a crowded media marketplace. In April 2009, KFC paid for road repairs in Louisville, Kentucky, in exchange for the ability to "stamp" their repairs with a "Re-Freshed by KFC" message that'll last until it rains. In addition to contributing to KFC's image by showcasing the brand as imaginative and fun, KFC's contribution and participation in the community create goodwill.

Cause Marketing

Charity tie-ins work in much the same way as other co-branding efforts. Marketers hope that a connection to breast cancer or education—to cite two causes popular with retailers—will put their product in a positive light if a portion of the price (or the company's revenue) goes to the charity. And this can be especially effective for those targeting teens or twenty-somethings.

It's not that Gen Yers are more charitable than older folks. As you may recall from Chapter Four, getting involved with causes (even if it's just buying one T-shirt over another) helps young people feel a sense of purpose in life, and being seen by others as charitable contributes to a positive self-identity. Likewise retailers, sportswear, and even sodas get an image lift with consumers when they are linked to philanthropy.

Also, though many Gen Yers may love to shop and buy, they also know that greed really isn't good. So what better way to assuage any guilt, than to give while getting?

MAC cosmetics' funding of AIDS programs includes 100 percent of the proceeds of sales of its Viva Glam lipstick line. That helps make the product MAC's best seller. Nancy Mahon, executive director of the MAC AIDS Fund, says Gen Yers in particular are attracted to retailers' efforts to connect with causes. MAC reminds consumers that the cost of one tube of Viva Glam can provide seven hot meals to homebound AIDS patients.

Even Barbie, who had been going rather Hollywood in recent years (see Bling Bling Barbie), came with "eco-friendly accessories" for Earth Day 2008. The Barbie "Bcause collection" was made out of excess fabric and trimmings from other Barbie doll clothes and products that would have otherwise been thrown away.

Indeed, going green is another way to reach younger consumers who long to feel "connected" to brands. Green, after all, isn't just about the health of our planet—it's about feeling like they are part of a cause that is important. We're all looking for purpose and meaning in life, and some retailers have done a great job of forging a connection with consumers through the emotional gratification those consumers receive by feeling part of the green movement.

Cause Celeb

Because celebrities are so appealing to many members of Gen Y, brands and products that are endorsed or used by the athletes, politicians, actors, and activists that Gen Y holds in high regard are often catapulted into "cool" through association. It had been about a decade since the Totes Isotoner Company teamed up with a celebrity endorser—in its mid-1990s relationship with former NFL quarterback Dan Marino. But when teen singer Rihanna sang the song "Umbrella" in 2007, it really hit the right note at headquarters. Not only did the song become a Grammy-winning hit, but the line of glitzy Rihanna umbrellas became big hits too—and with a much younger audience than the company had ever reached before, according to a June 2008 *New York Times* article.[13]

Smart retailers seed the market by "placing" their fashions in the hands of celebrities. B-list celebrities sometimes deliberately wear an A-lister's outfits in the hopes of showing up on *People* magazine's "Who Wore It Best" online competition.

Juicy Couture's high-priced track suits never truly took off until the company sent one to Madonna—with "Madge" embroidered on the jacket—and she started wearing it in public in 2001. Victoria's Secret didn't have any idea how big its Pink sleepwear line could become when Jessica Simpson wore a pair of the sweatpants on her reality show in 2005. Young women went crazy trying to find the sweat suits. Within three years, sales increased from about $300 million a year to $1 billion, thanks in part to the jumpstart Simpson's rear-end advertising gave the brand.[14]

Celebrities, to put it simply, are an official stamp of approval that make shoppers of all ages—but Gen Y especially—feel more confident in their choices. They also have the visual pull necessary to draw attention to a product that might otherwise be overlooked in today's crowded marketplace. Gen Yers have a lot to choose from and a lot of latitude in creating their own special looks—and celebrities, who strive for originality, provide ideas and inspiration. Though most Gen Yers, and certainly older consumers, will *say* they're not influenced by celebrities, their purchasing behavior proves otherwise.

When any doubt creeps in for twenty-year-old Charlotte about how an outfit looks, the Avon, Connecticut, native channels her source of style inspiration: *Sex and the City*'s main character Carrie Bradshaw. "Whenever I'm wearing something I feel is weird, she's like my style icon," Chelsea said of Sarah Jessica Parker's former TV role. "I know she's a fictional character, but so many women love Carrie and just wish they had the balls to dress like her. I just think, 'Carrie would wear this—she'd totally rock this. I might as well wear it.'"

When MAC signed musical star Fergie to become spokeswoman for the Viva Glam brand in February 2008, John Demsey, Group President for parent company Estée Lauder, says he had no idea how popular the then-thirty-two-year-old star was with young people. Shortly afterward, he says, a *Woman's Wear Daily* survey declared that Fergie, out of *all* celebrities, had resonated the most with teenagers.

"Pop culture and teen culture converge at some point," says Demsey.

But even shoppers in their twenties and older are drawn by the celebrity stamp of approval.

"It crosses the ages," says Jaye Hersh, who owns the L.A. boutique Intuition. "They can pretend they have a piece of some shiny life and feel like theirs is a little more exciting."

Truth, Action, and Collaboration: How to Research and Reach Gen Y

It's not that Gen Yers are opposed to advertising and marketing— it's that they want it to be honest and transparent. And of course, they want it on their terms and in terms they might use. Still, they are less likely to believe what they hear in advertising and will act more on what they experience than what they are told. That's one of the reasons they love samples—a way to force marketers to "prove it!" (and also a way to get sales: more than a third of customers who tried a sample in an Arbitron survey bought the product that very day). They're also more likely to trust product reviews from total strangers than what companies tell them about products. And they love anything that includes them in their favorite brand's inner circle.

Victoria's Secret used street teams and flyers put into shopping bags at its store in Manhattan to promote a giant pajama party it hosted in the summer of 2006 on New York City's Pier 54. The Victoria's Secret Pink Pajama Party drew close to three thousand people, all dressed for sleeping, according to an article in *Brandweek*.[15] Most were college girls, which fit the plan to target eighteen- to twenty-four-year-olds perfectly. When Pink hosted "Pinkapalooza" on the Santa Monica Pier two years later, ten thousand young people showed up.

When interactive marketing expert Kathy Sharpe, forty-nine, adapted her technology to facilitate video sharing for her client, Fujifilm, she wondered, "How far can we push language?" The technology, by the way, is called "Videothang," so she was already working outside the typical grammatical toolbox. Working with a largely Gen Y staff, she knew there were all sorts of attempts to change and shorten words for use in text messaging. For the name of Fuji's video-sharing site, they settled on "offzhook," a takeoff on "you're just off the hook," a counterintuitive compliment among Gen Yers. "I happen to like words, and I was an English major," says Sharpe. But such "deconstruction of words" is something marketers will have to buy into if they want to reach text-oriented teens and twenty-somethings, she says.

Manufacturers and marketers are learning that a key to attracting young shoppers is investing in their lifestyles, says Cashmere Marketing's Ted Chung. He says the Toyota Scion brand's sponsorship of music festivals and other events helped popularize the quirky cars with a young audience.

"You need to rethink the model completely," says Sharpe. She agrees with Chung: "Go into their communities. Be there and let them get engaged with you."

Author Don Tapscott concluded in his book, *Grown Up Digital: How the Net Generation Is Changing Retail and Marketing*, that "simple promotion of products and services is no longer as relevant as engaging customers." The brand, he says, is becoming a "more complicated construct." Instead of being determined by what the company says it is, it is now more a product of a consumer's relationship with the brand.[16]

Gen Yers, says Chung, are "all screaming to identify themselves. If you invest in a lifestyle community, by purchasing your brand they are telling peers what they're all about."

Product Repping

By now you're as convinced as we are that Gen Y *wants* to be involved with the brands that matter to them. What better way than by asking them to be your ambassadors?

Urban streetwear website Karmaloop offers its customers the chance to become "reps" for the merchandise, giving them cards with 20-percent-off discounts they can pass on to those who say, "Hey, love your jacket!" and everyone else they meet while out and about. Those who get the discount cards are asked to enter the rep's special code so he or she gets money or merchandise if they're able to "sell" the merchandise. These new customers also get 10 percent off every time they return to the site. The pitch on the website reads, "Karmaloop is looking for a few street wear culture fanatics to help us spread the word and crush McFashion." Top-selling reps are featured on the website—some have more than one hundred thousand points, which can be earned on a dollar-per-point basis or if they upload pictures of themselves selling or their own-style flyers or other promotional materials, especially if they get a Karmaloop banner on another site.[17]

Levi Strauss's limited-edition 23/501 jeans and shoes sold out in *fifty seconds* because of an inventive social networking campaign that featured a widget loaded with unreleased hip-hop tracks from big-name performers. The widget also included product information and photos, a countdown clock to launch time, and the locations where the product would be available. Fans downloaded the widget, posted it or sent it to friends, and voila! Shoppers were lined up and ready to buy.

Threadless, the T-shirt site, sells mostly those designed by its customers and a few by outside designers. By becoming a member of Threadless, you are automatically a member of the "StreetTeam," which means you earn points any time you link to Threadless from other sites, send a photo of yourself in a Threadless T-shirt, or sell a shirt through a referral. At least one "top earner" had amassed more than forty thousand points.[18]

Trend Spotting and Brain Picking

Before they start asking teenage consumers to simply become their buyers (which may not be too far off if they're already designing, selling, and getting paid for it!), retailers must continue to make educated guesses about what's going to be hot in the coming months and years.

One way or another, retailers and manufacturers have to work harder than ever to stay ahead of the curve. Trend watching has become an art—informed, in fact, *by* art, and by cultural shifts around the world.

Gen Yers' relationship with the Internet means that their interests are on display through their searches. Besides browsing the "viewed," "sent," "commented," or "reviewed" numbers posted on websites, free (at least as of this writing) services such as Google Analytics and Google Zeitgist will track down the latest yearly or even hourly trends and website usage figures.

To stay ahead of the fashion curve, Target sends young designers to apparel shows, color conventions, and even music festivals around the globe to see what's "young and hip," says Target's Michael Alexin. "We need to predict what will influence what our guests will want," says Alexin.

Technology has also turned customers into trend spotters. Karmaloop, which has one store in Boston along with its popular website, may follow a few trends, but it helps start them too. CEO Selkoe gives out his cell phone number to customers and designers alike, preferring to hear straight from the sources what they want or are selling that may be the Next Big Thing. In the fall of 2008, he even started selling "boat shoes" to oblige the sector of the street wear–types who were making a mock-preppy statement.

"These kids are more fashion conscious," says Selkoe, wearing a sweatshirt that says "Superlative Conspiracy." "They want things that are more unique."

And top retailers are starting to make it their business to get out of the office and closer to their consumers—and not just in their stores. Many also use Gen Yers on their staffs. Macy's CEO Terry Lundgren meets regularly with groups of twenty-something employees to pick their brains. He figures one of them may take his place someday, so he needs to "make sure I spend enough time with them answering their questions." But he also wants to learn why, despite a hefty company discount at the company's Macy's and Bloomingdale's stores, the young executives often choose to shop at specialty stores instead.

"I want them to buy more from us," says Lundgren. "I want them to buy from us because it's the cool place to shop."

Lundgren learned that young professionals found a void in stores like Macy's, which had hip juniors departments with casual clothing and party dresses and then misses departments that veered toward a more conservative style than many wanted to wear to work. Boutiques and specialty shops were more successfully catering to this crowd. These conversations with employees lead to the creation of the BCBG Generation line of career clothing for young working women now in Macy's stores.

The company used a five-story new Bloomie's in New York's trendy Soho region to test strategies. Although 95 percent of the merchandise in Soho is also sold at the more staid 59th Street store, the apparel and accessories were "edited" to appeal to twenty- and thirty-year-old customers, with a heavy emphasis on brands such as Theory, Vince, and Tory Burch. The plan proved so successful it's being used to develop two new Bloomingdale's stores: one that's slated to open in 2010 in Santa Monica and one expected in 2011 in Washington, D.C.'s Georgetown.

These younger shoppers, says Lundgren, are a "totally different customer."

Considering the costs (and sometimes sketchy findings) of focus groups and surveys, it's a wonder every company doesn't utilize a volunteer advisory board. Provided that applicants are vetted (to screen out competitors and to ensure participation), engaged enthusiasts are potentially more knowledgeable about things like how products are used, pet peeves, and what they wish retailers offered than the marketers of those products. Though not necessarily representative of *potential* markets, enthusiasts are also a great source of inspiration for new ideas. Even better, because they're engaged and appreciated, they're likely to become active advocates.

In Conclusion: Our Top Four Tips for Marketing to Gen Y

1. Get close. Really close. This is not the same as simply studying Gen Y trends and the hots and nots, nor is it the same as simply knowing their opinions, demographics, or purchase behavior. It's the kind of closeness that comes only from empathy. By that we mean understanding and caring why they have those opinions and why

they do what they do. It requires suspending judgment and (corny as it may sound) caring about them.

Gen Yers have been loved, cared for, and courted their whole lives, and though this makes them sometimes stunningly optimistic and certainly more confident, it also means they're more demanding. Getting close requires an investment of yourself by engaging your heart as well as your brain. It's not enough to sit in an office and analyze data. You have to feel what it's like to be in their shoes.

2. Engage and inspire your Gen Y customers. Make them part of the process, from design to delivery. Campaigns and brands that honor and involve Gen Yers can work what seems like magic: they sell out jeans in fifty seconds, create recession-proof products, and even elect presidents. Gen Yers want to be part of it all, not passive recipients—and they certainly don't want to be told what to buy. They'd rather tell you what to make, and then tell their friends to buy it. Technology is the enabler; the powerful passion and creativity of Gen Y is the fuel. Of course, the ultimate is to hire and involve Gen Yers in your workplace— you'll get better answers (and the right questions) and more loyal employees too. Not to mention that young people connect more readily with other young people than with "company representatives."

3. Get real. Humility, honesty, and smarts go a long way with this generation. Part of getting close to and involving Gen Y is having the right attitude. They admire strength, not power, and honesty trumps hype any day. Humanness, humor, and the inspiration of great ideas and innovation are what it takes to earn Gen Y's respect.

4. Technology is currency, and you need to have it. It's not only Gen Y's enabler—it's yours too. Putting technology to work the right way means using an array of media and constantly revising your strategy to capitalize on the

"latest." If you do, the opportunities are limitless. At no other time in history have consumers *wanted* to read "25 Things About You," clamored to make their own ads for your company, or eagerly sold your products to their friends just for recognition. Using technology well with this generation also means that everything you do has to be faster, more responsive, more visual, more emotional, and intuitively designed.

Gen Yers are not only the taste-makers, influencers, and most enthusiastic buyers of today; they're also the mature, high-income purchasers of the future. And they herald the way that everyone will shop, connect, and buy as they champion the technology and tastes that in short order become mainstream. As we say, you've got to know Gen BuY—and we hope this book has helped you get there.

8

ADAPTING TO GEN Y'S SHOPPING PREFERENCES AND POWER

Views from Our Experts

In the process of researching this book, we interviewed dozens of experts. Along the way we met some people who stood out as truly understanding Gen Y—and who had cultivated impressive ideas about how to reach them. So we asked them to contribute some words of wisdom to pass along. Our experts summarize and apply much of what we presented in this book and offer insights unique to their expertise. Here are some of the best deep thinkers when it comes to Gen Y and retail, branding, consumer marketing, and research—now, and with an eye toward the future.

Be True to Your "Cool"

By Kenneth Nisch

"Cool job [*I'd like to work there*], cool clothes [*the latest and hottest*], cool friends [*where we want to hang out*], way cool brands [*what they say about me*] . . ." For this consumer, it is not just about good looks, or the way the garment, the CD, or the book fits, but how it "fits" into the consumer's view of life. Today's "fit" for Gen Y involves ethics, social-networking, community involvement, and—a highly influential and deal-breaking issue—the retailer's creating a sense of place.

Place can exist as an online presence or in the store environment; through the sales associates, editorial, or in-store marketing. It also lives through the brand's "touch" points: taste, scent, and sound; and its "feel" points: relevance, honesty, and personality.

Shopping for Gen Y is about:

- *Creating customer-generated marketing, product, and design*: Contributing their creative power
- *Being available anytime and anywhere*: Accessing when and how it suits them
- *Being where they are*: Reaching them by cell phone, computer, at school, in the movies
- *Respecting their values*: Gaining, securing, and honoring their trust.

Brand culture and the environment exist beyond the store's four walls. Brand teams, event sponsorships, sourcing, labor practices, charities, and expected vendor standards are important to the Gen Y consumer's sense of being. Yet it is not all so serious, because ironically, these customers—whose values need to be understood and respected—take pleasure in the escape of retail during these "best years of their lives" with the fewest responsibilities, the most freedom, and enviable disposable income.

Gen Y consumers are looking for opportunities to partner with the retailer: designing their own athletic shoes with Vans or customizing their own accessories with Startiste; becoming a pseudo-rock star through the magic of Guitar Hero and fail-safe karaoke with LeadSinger; or, as in the case of LittleMissMatched, breaking the rules by mismatching their clothing. These are all companies that recognize this consumer's need to be heard.

The ongoing success of retailers focused on this consumer segment is only as great as their level of passion to stay in touch, listen, share, and, in some cases, seek forgiveness. Without these commitments, the brand is likely to be relegated to the lowest level of brand hell. Staying relevant in all touch points as a place they want to work, a brand to wear, a place to meet friends and do business is the key to reaching these target consumers.

Nisch is an architect and chairman of JGA, Inc., a retail design and brand strategy firm in Southfield, Michigan. JGA's clients include Metropark, Spencer's, The North Face, Hershey's, Borders, Hot Topic, and Torrid.

How Retailers Can Reel Gen Y In

By Jennifer Black

The driving mantra for the Gen Y shopper is that there are no rules. Retailers will have to up the ante if they want a piece of this consumer's dollar. It used to be that great product drove purchases. Times have changed. This customer is savvy in a multidimensional way. The Internet has changed the world of retailing.

Retailers must have a special niche in the market and must sell into multiple channels of distribution. Retailers cannot simply lease space and sell merchandise. For example, Nordstrom and the Buckle are renowned for the level of service provided. These companies have brick-and-mortar stores yet have also developed a strong Internet marketing presence.

Because of the Internet, retailers have an incredible amount of personal information about their customers—how they shop, where they shop, what they shop, even why they shop. Smart companies will utilize this data to become intimate with their potential customers. American Eagle and others have already been spotted targeting specific categories of shoppers on Facebook pages. Websites will continue to showcase the latest in technology, becoming a destination in their own right.

The store environment will be a major factor in drawing this generation in and enticing them to buy. Today's Gen Y expects an entertaining environment—eclectic and theme driven. The store must stand for something and connect with the young shopper. Urban Outfitters is a good example. From right at the entrance, the store's ambience engages the Gen Y customer both visually and mentally. The atmosphere encourages browsers to stay and shop around, and the longer they stay, the more likely they are to buy. J. Crew has remodeled a landmark New York store into "The Liquor Bar," a high-end shopping experience for guys. Tomorrow's merchants will also focus their efforts toward a friendly, casual, "green" experience, as well as the tech experience that is a given in this consumer's life. It may include a virtual world where merchandise can be put on your body via computer imagery. The more technically inclined the retailer, the more apt this consumer is to make purchases.

The shopping experience must be easy. Gen Y is accustomed to instant gratification and has no time for hassles. Therefore they will also shop at stores that are consistent in merchandise offerings, whether it is apparel, shoes, or accessories.

This group is cash conscious and savvy about competitive pricing. They understand the price/value relationship. This generation is not encumbered with strict codes of fashion. The retailers that realize this and execute on it most effectively, as well as think outside the box, will succeed. Thus these winners of tomorrow will reap the rewards of customer loyalty and affinity.

Black is a retail stock analyst and has been president of Jennifer Black & Associates in Lake Oswego, Oregon, since 2003. She follows apparel retailers including Nordstrom, Hot Topic, PacSun, and Gap.

Activate the Store—and Make It "More than a Store"

By Bertrand Pellegrin

The store of the future is within our grasp. Where once a store was merely a dispensary of goods, it is now a place that can offer a sense of discovery, aspiration, and community. The faster, better retail environment uses technology to enhance how the customer connects to the brand—and vice versa.

But it takes more than that to connect to the Gen Y customer. This is a customer who is keenly sensitive to what's "real": an environment that feels authentic and doesn't demand a purchase but instead invites the customer to participate in the process of discovery and an enhanced personal profile. It's the idea of being an active customer as opposed to a passive one. In a world where many of the common public meeting places are either contrived or barren of significance—take the town square of so many cities and towns—the store has the potential to offer a unique combination of community and authenticity.

The most successful and authentic brand experience for the Gen Y customer is one that feels organic and appears to be activated by the individual. Far from being blatantly orchestrated (think theme restaurants), a great store does not aim to simply sell the product, but rather to establish an emotional significance that resonates with an individual's sense of self and desire to believe in something more inspiring than the objects he or she came to buy. It's like a thrift store, where so many of this generation enjoy searching and discovering, experimenting with the old and the new, and in the end, creating a look—thanks to vintage clothes—that is distinctly unique. Urban Outfitters has had enormous success with this formula, blending cultures, eras, and pop culture references with merchandise that acts as interlocutor for customers connecting and belonging with their peers.

Increasingly, a store that brings together a target customer, be it Gen Y or the boomer, must offer an array of value-added features that makes the purchase a deeply personal experience. Starbucks maximized this in turning the humble coffee shop into the "third place" or satellite destination outside of the home (first place) and office or school (second place). REI, Inc., is another example of what happens when a store offers a gathering place that communicates its brand message to a captive audience through an engaging and interactive in-store experience. They recently developed a forty-two-thousand-square-foot flagship experience in Boulder, Colorado, that features a community zone where workshops, demonstrations, and other activities encourage interaction and create an animated atmosphere of learning and discovery.

Pellegrin is a global retail and brand development consultant. His portfolio includes projects for Louis Vuitton (LVMH), Lane Crawford Hong Kong, Ltd., Lotte Korea, Microsoft, Bank of America, and the Las Vegas Sands Corporation. He is the author of Branding the Man: Why Men Are the Next Frontier in Fashion Retail.

Create Communication Communities

By Phil Rist

Gen Y is more influenced by what they hear from others than by any other form of advertisement. Out of twenty-three different media, word of mouth ranked number one in seven of the eight merchandise categories available in BIGresearch's June 2008 Simultaneous Media Usage (SIMM) survey, lagging behind only coupons in the grocery category.

The way in which Gen Y likes to communicate and the media they use are vastly different from the methods of older generations. Although they prefer face-to-face communication most of all, they are much more likely to use their cell phone, instant messaging, text messaging, blogging, and online communities such as MySpace or Facebook to discuss services, products, or brand after searching online.

Gen Y is also more likely to regularly use many new media, including iPods, blogging, and instant messaging. They are 197 percent more likely than older generations to use text messaging, creating a forum for advertisers to reach out to Gen Y and invite them into their community.

An example of the effectiveness of new media in marketing is President Barack Obama's 2008 victory over John McCain. Obama garnered 66 percent of the youth (eighteen to twenty-nine) vote, according to cnn.com. A key component to Obama's campaign was reaching out to voters through new media; he announced his vice presidential choice of Senator Joe Biden through a text message to supporters. His remarkable online presence (he had close to three million supporters on Facebook and four times as many friends as Senator John McCain on MySpace.com) aided Obama in his victory, helping him to capture the attention and influence of Gen Y. According to BIGresearch's May 2008 American Pulse Survey, 47.4 percent of Gen Y planned to use the Internet to get information on the candidates, a medium dominated by then-Senator Obama. Retailers and product marketers should capitalize on the fact that Gen Y is more immersed in technology than any generation before them, and they are using these tools to become more educated about products and talk with each other about what to buy. Creating a community for Gen Yers to communicate with each other should be a major part of any advertiser's marketing program.

Rist is vice president of strategy at the consumer intelligence firm BIGresearch. He is also cofounder of Prosper Business Development Corporation, the parent company of BIGresearch, and coauthor of the books When Customers Talk *and* Media Generations.

Reaching Gen Y Through Technology and Experience Design

By David Hogue, Ph.D.

Traditional websites attempt to control the customer experience by keeping the customer on the site, and success is often measured by the depth and duration of visits. The boundaries of the traditional website are being removed as customers take more information and interactivity with them to personal pages and social networks. For Gen Y, the customer experience extends far beyond the website, and if retailers are to reach this audience they must go where they spend their time rather than relying on customers coming to them. Portable experiences go with the customer in the form of widgets, gadgets, and applications that can be placed on personal pages and shared through social networks. Do not measure success by the number and duration of visits to a website; instead, measure the reach of the brand, content, and functionality beyond the website and the frequency with which people use and share it.

Gen Yers use the Internet as a repository of their lives; nearly all of their important information is stored and available to them online. As companies gather, analyze, and utilize this information, customer experiences online will become more personalized. Privacy will always be an important issue, but where previous generations expect total control and near secrecy of their personal information, Gen Y assumes that if the information has been given and access has been granted, then that information can, will, and should be used to create personalized experiences. Websites and applications will become smarter as customers' individual behavior, history, and preferences will be used to generate experiences and products designed for the person rather than a broad target market segment. Gen Y expects the experiences created for them by websites to be just as personalized as the experiences they build for themselves.

Social interactions are central to Gen Y's activity on the Internet, and barriers to quick and simple communication are not acceptable. Web services and applications connecting customers' profiles, histories, and social networks with their online activity will allow people to share more information quickly and easily, with fewer hurdles and much less effort.

Gen Y will redefine the way we interact and communicate with one another, how we share information, and how we construct our social, political, and economic relationships. Our challenge may be not how to reach them with technology and experience design, but rather how to follow their lead and better understand the world they are creating ahead of us.

Hogue is director of information design and usability at Fluid, a San Francisco–based web design and development agency focusing on e-commerce and rich Internet applications. He specializes in human computer interaction, applied psychology, and interaction and experience design for websites and applications. Fluid's clients include Reebok, Timberland, The North Face, Charles Schwab, Wells Fargo, Microsoft, and Sears.

Reaching Gen Y Customers by Engaging Gen Y Employees

By Leah Reynolds

Retailers who need to attract Gen Yers as consumers will first have to figure out how to engage them as employees. This may be harder than it sounds. Many retailers are managed by members of older generations who don't understand what Gen Y values at work.

Worker needs and expectations have shifted dramatically over the past twenty years, but the majority of employers have not. Across all industries, employers have yet to redesign their work environments, management styles, approaches to rewards and recognition, and methods of communication to keep pace with the demands of their new workforce.

What, exactly, needs to change in order for retailers to engage Gen Y employees? Retail management must embrace young talent as a valuable source of information and connection to their Gen Y customer. By involving Gen Y employees in strategic product and customer service decisions—and tapping them as a fertile source of ideas on how best to reach their peers in the marketplace—employers will foster a culture of respect that extends to all employees, regardless of age or level in the organization.

Retailers need to examine the career development and mentoring opportunities offered to younger employees. Gen Yers are motivated by challenge. They are anxious to learn, to grow, to have chances to achieve meaningful goals. Retail employers must rethink performance management and rewards systems to encourage rapid development of young talent and create new ways for seasoned workers to gain recognition through mentoring and knowledge sharing.

In addition, investments need to be made to retool the technological infrastructure and approaches that many employers use to communicate and train within the workplace. For example, retailers who have not adapted for social media technologies are losing opportunities to gain valuable customer and employee input and to foster brand recognition and loyalty. Gen Y employees can lead the way to this new world of Web 2.0, in which mastery of networking applications allows for sophisticated forms of influence, persuasion, and community building.

The first step is to build the business case for workplace transformation. Answer these questions: What's at risk if we don't make the necessary changes to engage Gen Y workers? What will happen if one of our competitors successfully adapts before we do? What's the upside potential if we fully engage Gen Y as consumers? The great news is that the efforts retailers make to rethink and recreate the workplace will be appreciated by each of the generations in their workforce. A savvy retailer has the opportunity to win with all the generations in their workplace and succeed in capturing the often elusive Gen Y consumer.

Reynolds is the national lead for "Generational Talent Strategies" at Deloitte Consulting LLP, where she works with organizations during talent and human resource redesigns, mergers, acquisitions, and shifts in corporate culture. Reynolds previously worked for her own and other human resource consulting firms, including Towers Perrin, where she was a practice leader.

Interactive, Not Reactive

By Michael Dart and Monica Tang

Gen Y's formative experiences have been shaped by an overabundance of material possessions and access to the most technologically advanced products in history. What does this mean to retailers? These forces are creating a new generation of consumers that has retail executives scratching their heads.

Gen Yers respond positively to retailers and designers who provide products, selling environments, and services that represent and fuel their lifestyle. Successful retailers will be those who create more interactive retail formats, have more expertise about the products and services they sell, become increasingly involved in the design and creation of the products they sell, and broadly deploy technology to increase consumer interactions.

Marketers will have to venture even further beyond the four walls of the store, pushing the consumer experience into another dimension. Wii gives us the ability to play tennis, skateboard a halfpipe, and channel a rock star right at home. Could Wii shopping be next, with Gen Y consumers making purchases within a 3-D e-commerce environment? Gen Yers are reshaping retailing and consumer goods right now, but this is just the beginning.

As retailers, you should expect the landscape to change dramatically over the coming months and years as brands try to keep up with Gen Y:

- Think pop-up stores (temporary stores that retailers unexpectedly open for a short period of time), but instead of real merchandise, there is only virtual merchandise. This merchandise is sold via an interactive environment that provides a multidimensional shopping experience without the use of physical product.

- Gen Yers spend innumerable hours on social networking sites, such as MySpace and Facebook. Picture how these sites may be leveraged to support a retail environment. In a Facebook news feed, you are provided updates on all your friends, telling you what they're doing, what events they are participating in, what music they're listening to. Envision a news feed that says, "John just bought board shorts from O'Neill. Click here to see what John bought and to buy similar products."

- Environmental consciousness is no longer just a trend; especially among Gen Y, it is a lifestyle that affects decisions they make every day. Given the green mantra of buying local and consideration of carbon footprints and offsets, how are retailers going to respond in a way that addresses Gen Y's passion to save the earth? Will carbon offsets be the new gift-with-purchase or the impulse item purchased at the cash wrap as stocking stuffers?

Successful retailers will captivate Gen Yers by getting inside their heads and planting the seeds, while allowing Gen Y to think it is calling the shots.

Dart leads the strategy and private equity practice at the global consulting firm Kurt Salmon Associates, where he helps private equity funds and global retailers understand the changing retail and consumer landscape as they consider which retailers to invest in. Tang is a retail strategist and futurist at Kurt Salmon, where she works with specialty retailers around the world.

The Future of Market Research

By Kathleen Kusek

Now that we are solidly into the millennium, there is clear consensus among marketers that consumer understanding is no longer simply "nice to have," but rather critical to business success. Quite fortunately, never before have we had access to so many tools and techniques to effectively mine our consumers' hearts and minds.

In the future, savvy marketers will use an "all of the above" approach to mining the consumer insight in order to win. Those tools include traditional market research like quantitative analysis of product sales, product usage, and demographic profiles, layered with innovative qualitative research.

The future will combine analysis from brand managers, who have been trained to understand and know their consumer as well as their best friend, and "consumer scientists" (lab coats optional), who can identify not only what consumers say and do but also what they really deeply want and emotionally need. Our consumer scientists of the future will share true insights based on their superior understanding of things like neuropsychology, the stress created by the delta between ideals and reality, and other aspects of psychology that aren't taught in top business schools.

Executing this "swarm" research, we'll enlist all possible channels to learn about those precious consumers—purchase scanning data, third-party research, online chat rooms and surveys, in-home interviews, store intercepts. Wherever our consumers are, we need to be there too.

Oh, and the focus group? Wasn't it Einstein that said a problem well defined is half solved? He was no dummy. The focus groups of the future will have fewer people for shorter amounts of time. We won't have seven to ten respondents for an hour and a half to two hours anymore. In too many cases, the meaning of "focus" has been lost in our focus groups. Instead, they've become a catchall for every wild hare that the extended marketing team may have—a faster (though not necessarily cheaper or better) way to answer important questions that can and should be addressed quantitatively. If we are just looking for an unanalyzed response from an appropriately screened respondent, we can easily get the answer online for a fraction of the time and cost, never ever requiring a middle seat on the redeye for the marketers.

Marketers, however, will ultimately be the ones on the hook to translate those insights into motivating messaging, innovation, and product improvement—arguably the hard part.

Kusek is the principal of Firehouse Marketing Services, a consumer research and brand strategy consultancy. She's had nearly twenty years of experience in advertising, consumer research and brand strategy for companies including Kellogg, Clorox, Del Monte, Hershey's, IAC, TiVo, Pioneer Electronics, PG&E Corp., Constellation Brands, and the Four Seasons Hotels.

Reaching Their "Mirror Worlds"

By Nita Rollins, Ph.D.

Digital Millennials are the first real post-PC generation; their smart phones are not only their primary digital device but, some would say, their primary means of discovering what it means to be a social being. For brands, Millennials' perpetual connectedness via mobile phones and social networking profiles has been their most salient trait for about five years. Facilitating and being part of this perpetual connectedness was a brand's route to relevance. But another millennial trait is about to usurp simple connectedness: their collective location awareness—and the importance they ascribe to *place* as a marker of self (yes, just as brands endeavor to be).

Mobile phones once again are the technological driver of this generational trait, but only those that are *location-aware* (thanks to cell tower triangulation and GPS). These phones and their geo-applications, along with cyber cartography—the constitution of information-rich, up-to-the-minute digital maps of astounding physical accuracy—mean that brands have to put themselves on the map, literally. Why? Because the more accurate and personally useful digital maps become—with the help of anyone willing to geotag their photo or geo-annotate a place—the more people expect them to constitute a complete "mirror world," as the gamers call it.

Brands must recognize that there are consequences to being left out of this mirror world. As web surfing gives way to world surfing, brands have to be at the right places at the right time. Most important, they have to be part of the *Fourth Place*. After home (first), work or school (second), coffee shop/athletic club/church (third), the Fourth Place is a fusion of virtual and real, a spontaneous hot spot created by people oscillating between digital coexistence in a geo-annotated space and the heightened possibility of suddenly meeting up—at a store, nightclub, park—in the real world.

Rollins is the futurist at digital market agency Resource Interactive, where she specializes in trend spotting and "blending" in technology, culture, and consumerism. Rollins is the author of Cinaesthetic Wondering: The Beautiful, the Ugly, the Sublime, and the Kitsch in Post-Metaphysical Film, *and coauthor (with Resource Interactive President Kelly Mooney) of* The Open Brand: When Push Comes to Pull in a Web-Made World.

The World of Commerce in Their Hands

By Mark Schwanhausser

Gen Y will be the first generation of Americans to embrace the idea that their cell phones and mobile devices will become an irreplaceable banking tool—a mobile wallet—that will keep them in touch with their finances around the clock and around the globe. They'll set limits and prohibitions on their accounts so that their banks must first alert them to approve suspect transactions or verify large withdrawals in real time. Kids will text their parents that they need cash, then watch as a deposit posts seconds later. As they walk around the store, they'll scan a product's bar code, read online how consumers rate it, then instantly search the Web to determine whether a nearby store or an e-tailer is selling the item for less. When they step to the cash register—which will increasingly be an anachronism, because the register will be used for cash transactions less and less—they'll "tap" their phone rather than swipe a plastic card.

In fact, gone will be the day when consumers swipe anything. They will no longer carry wallets and purses stuffed with credit cards, debit cards, prepaid cards, rewards cards, merchant cards, frequent-user cards, payroll cards, and so forth. Instead, all their accounts will be registered in their mobile devices. At first, consumers will just scroll down a phone menu to select the card to use at the register and trigger a coupon or discount. In time, though, software inside the mobile device will determine how much money is available in their checking and savings accounts, analyze their upcoming bills and cash flow, and size up whether it's wiser to draw the money from their bank accounts or charge it. If it's the latter, it will identify the card with the best reward or the heftiest discount for a given purchase.

Shoppers will simply tap their phones against a store ad or poster as they walk in, and the store's computers will recognize them and load their phones with special offers based on their past purchases and what's in inventory that day. Setting an item in the grocery cart or scanning it into a mobile device will trigger additional store discounts or promotional offers. At some stores, payments will automatically clear as customers step past sensors at the doorway.

The enormity of this challenging vision can't be underestimated. It will require unprecedented cooperation among banks, technology providers, telecommunications carriers, and even the corner merchant. Nonetheless, there are so many benefits that a generation of consumers will likely one day take it for granted that they hold the key to their finances in their hands.

Schwanhausser is a research analyst at Javelin Strategy & Research, which provides quantitative and qualitative research on financial services topics. Schwanhausser specializes in helping banks and credit unions understand how and why consumers use online and mobile banking.

Roadblocks on Easy Street

By Marian Salzman

The young consumers of Gen Y have grown up in a paradise of endless expansion. Yet now they're finding that their hyperconnectivity means 24/7 exposure to global economic apocalypse. For most members of Gen Y, the recession of the early 1990s is ancient history, and the dot-com crash of the early 2000s barely crossed their radar. As recently as 2007, we were heaping praise on these plugged-in kids for their rabid self-confidence. Though we were a little thrown by their demand for a more laid-back, good-time workplace, we were envious of their seeming ability to prioritize the experience of life ahead of business, or at least to blend the two into an entirely new ethic that seemed to be successful. So what happens to them now that Easy Street is suddenly riddled with roadblocks?

The most likely scenario is that they will rise to the challenge. Because of all they have been afforded in life, they constantly push the envelope and don't take no for an answer. And despite their apparent self-centeredness, they have an earnest streak. They want to make their world better, and they are sure to announce just how they'll do it.

Going forward, Gen Yers will be thinking a lot more about "value" and "values." During much of their formative years, value increasingly came to mean lots more for the price—bigger, faster, more power, more convenience. Now, the greedy rise of "more" has hit a ceiling. Real value means meeting needs and having a sense of money well spent, not wasted. Listen for vocal Gen Y consumers: "I'm not paying for all those extra features; I just need the basics."

As for the bigger issue of values, until the economic crisis that began in 2008, having more, doing more, and being more were the goals to reach. Now, as people scale back the greed and feel empowered by new leadership, watch for consensus building around values such as stability, sustainability, cooperation, and peace of mind. Young consumers will be less about quantity of product and much more about the quality of experience a brand delivers and the ethics the brand lives. They will look to support positive change via their purchases, increasingly responding to cause-related products and marketing.

And with the economic downturn likely to dominate life for a while to come, Gen Yers will feel more connected than ever with the online space, where they can gain access to the things they need in a cost-effective, timely way: information, connections, entertainment, distractions. And where they can get as near to or far from reality as they choose.

Salzman, an acclaimed trendspotter, is partner and chief marketing officer at the public relations company Porter Novelli. She is credited with popularizing the term "metrosexuality" and is the author of fifteen books, including Next Now: Trends for the Future *and* The Future of Men.

Notes

Introduction

1. *Retailing Today*, "Survey: 73% of People Shop for Fun," June 15, 2006, www.retailingtoday.com.
2. Laurel Kennedy and Kathy Mancini, "Why Ask Y? Meet the Millennials: Generation Why?" May 2008, http://nielsen.com/consumer_insight/ci_story1.html.
3. Pew Research Center for the People and the Press Surveys, *Generations Online in 2009*, 2009, http://people-press.org/reports.
4. C. A. Martin and L. W. Turley, "Malls and Consumption Motivation: An Exploratory Examination of Older Generation Y Consumers," *International Journal of Retail & Distribution*, 32(10) (2004).
5. Resource Interactive, proprietary research, 2007.

Chapter One

1. Pew Research Center for the People and the Press Surveys, *Internet & American Life Project*, 2009, http://people-press.org/reports.
2. Harrison Group, *Teens in the Marketplace Report*, 2007.
3. EPM Communications, Inc., "Marketing to Teens and Tweens," *Youth Markets Alert*, 1(4) (2007).
4. M. Learmouth, "Sarah Palin *SNL* Online Clips Soon to Eclipse TV," *Advertising Age*, October 23, 2008.

5. Karl Fisch, "Did You Know," newly revised edition created by Karl Fisch and modified by Scott McLeod, November 7, 2008, http://www.btang.net/.

6. Pew Research Center for People and the Press Surveys, *How Young People View Their Lives, Futures, and Politics: A Portrait of Generation Next*, 2007, http://people-press.org/reports.

7. Deloitte, *State of the Media Democracy*, 3rd ed., 2009.

8. Pew Research Center, 2007.

9. Harris Interactive survey conducted for Charles Schwab and Age Wave, 2008, as reported August 20, 2008, HealthNewsDigest.com.

10. Consumer Electronics Association (CEA), *CEA's Teens and Technology Study*, 2008.

11. Fisch, "Did You Know," 2008.

12. Caroline McCarthy, "Nielsen: Twitter's Growing Really, Really, Really, Really Fast," *All Things Digital*, March 20, 2009, http://voices.allthingsd.com/20090320/nielsen-twitters-growing-really-really-really-really-fast/.

13. "Number of New Blogs Per Day," *Internet Business*, May 30, 2008, http://www.internet-business.com/number-of-new-blogs-per-day/.

14. Kansas State University, Digital Ethnography, March 17, 2008.

15. Stars for Kidz, "Surfin' on Mom's Turf Poll," May 2007, www.starsforkidz.com.

16. Deloitte Consulting LLP, as reported in YMA *Datafile*, 1(4) (May 9, 2007).

17. Research Brief from MediaPost, January 2, 2007.

18. M. Learmouth and R. Parekh, "How Twittering Critics Brought Down Motrin Mom Campaign," *Advertising Age*, November 17, 2008.

19. B. Teitell, *Drinking Problems at the Fountain of Youth* (HarperCollins, 2008).

20. Horatio Alger Association of Distinguished Americans, Inc., *The State of Our Nation's Youth*, 2008.

21. Fisch, "Did You Know," 2008.

22. Anderson Analytics, *2009 U.S. College Student Report*, 2008.

23. National Center for Education Statistics, U.S. Department of Education, Student Effort and Educational Progress, Degrees Earned by Women, Indicator 27 (2008).

24. WeMedia/Zogby Interactive, *The State of the News Media 2008*, as reported in research brief, *Two Thirds of Americans Dissatisfied with the Quality of Journalism*, March 2008.

Chapter Two

1. Teen Research Unlimited, as reported in Jones Lang LaSalle, "Gen Y and the Future of Mall Retailing," 2002, http://www.jllretail.com/NR/rdonlyres/4420B744-4281-422E-978C-0D8F1AF547E8/16026/GenY_longfinal.pdf.

2. National Association of Home Builders.

3. U.S. Bureau of the Census, Estimated Median Age at First Marriage, by Sex: 1890 to Present.

4. http://en.wikipedia.org/wiki/Recession.

5. The College Board, Trends in College Pricing, 2008, http://professionals.collegeboard.com/profdownload/trends-in-college-pricing-2008.pdf.

6. Aberdeen Group, "The Performance of Web Applications: Customers Are Won or Lost in One Second," 2008.

7. Mark Brohan, "Survey: More Than a Pretty Face," *Internet Retailer*, January 2009.

8. Brad Stone, "Is Facebook Growing Up Too Fast?" *New York Times*, March 28, 2009.

9. Eric Sass, "Tweeters Use Twitter for Business," *MediaPost News*, Online Media Daily, February 26, 2009.

10. Brian Morrissey, "Forrester Finds That Marketers Still Relegate Efforts to the Sidelines," March 16, 2009, Adweek.com.

11. Keller Fay Group, as reported in *Colloquy*, 15(3), 2007, http://www.loyalty.com/BaseComponents/FileHandler.ashx?id=43d95de8-af4c-4b8f-b236-548281144586.

12. M. J. Weiss, "To Be About to Be," *American Demographics*, 25(7) (September 2003).

13. P. Feld, "What Obama Can Teach You About Millennial Marketing," *Advertising Week*, August 11, 2008.

14. The National Retail Federation and BIGresearch Holiday Consumer Intentions and Actions Survey, October 27, 2008.

15. Yahoo! News, "Britney Spears Is Queen of Yahoo! Searches," December 1, 2008.

16. D. Browne, "Blogs to Riches: Perez Hilton Migrates into Cosmetics, Fashion, and Music," *Wired Magazine*, September 16, 2008.

17. Colin St. John, "Data Mine: Teens and Fame," *Psychology Today*, January/February 2006.

18. J. O'Donnell, "Fashion Buyers, Sellers Look to the Stars of TV, Film," *USA Today*, May 29, 2008.

Chapter Three

1. Alessandra Galloni, "Fashion Journal: Prada vs. Prada: Overcoming Fashion Phobia," *Wall Street Journal*, January 18, 2007, p. D.1.

2. National Retail Federation, Consumer Intentions and Actions Survey conducted by BIGresearch, July 2008.

3. J. Neff, "Scientists Prove The 'Axe Effect' Is Real. Sort Of," *Advertising Age*, January 7, 2009.

4. J. Cook and J. Fermino, "Proms Can Be 'Grand' Nights," *New York Post*, May 7, 2007.

5. F. Eltman, "Cancel the Tux and Turn the Limo Around: Long Island Principal Nixes Senior Prom at Parochial School," Associated Press, October 16, 2005.

6. EPM Communications, "Cautious Consumerism: Americans Try to Save Money, But Still Spend on Necessities And 'Feel Good' Items," *Research Alert*, 27(3) (February 6, 2009).

7. Lisa Jacobson, *Encyclopedia of Children and Childhood in History and Society, Allowances* (2003); Sarah Mahoney, "Teens: Recessions Are For Grown-Ups," *Marketing Daily*, February 27, 2009, http://www.mediapost.com/publications/?fa=Articles.showArticle&art_aid=101179.

8. NPD Group, *Kids' Share of the Wallet*, as reported in *Women's Wear Daily*, 2008.

9. Mark Dolliver, "Mark Dolliver's Takes: Mixed Blessings," March 12, 2007, Adweek.com.

10. Bridal Association of America, U.S. Wedding Statistics, http://www.bridalassociationofamerica.com/Wedding_Statistics/.

11. American Student Statistics, Student Debt Assistance, http://www.amsa.com/policy/resources/stats.cfm.

12. Schwab's 2007 Teens & Money Survey, conducted by StrategyOne, http://www.schwabmoneywise.com/views/survey/teensAndMoney.php.

13. M. J. Dotson and E. M. Hyatt, "Major Influence Factors in Children's Consumer Socialization," *Journal of Consumer Marketing*, 22(1) (2005): 35–43.

14. Harrison Group, General Population Study, fielded in September 2007.

15. J. Zaslow, "Blame It on Mr. Rogers: Why Young Adults Feel So Entitled," *Wall Street Journal*, July 5, 2007.

16. Fidelity Investments, Research on Gen X/Y, as reported in "Fidelity Research on Generation X/Y Shows That Financial Intentions and Actions Are Often in Conflict," 2008, http://www.globeinvestor.com /servlet/story/BWIRE.20080828.20080828005442/GIStory/.

17. Junior Achievement, 2008 teen holiday spending poll, as reported in "Teenagers Save the Holiday Shopping Season," http:// retaildesigndiva.blogs.com/retail_design_diva/2008/11/teenagers-save .html (accessed November 17, 2008).

18. BIGresearch, *Consumer Intentions and Actions Survey*, special data run received by email, January 28, 2009.

19. M. Sires, "The Power of Positive Thinking: How Gen Y Will Get Through the Recession," *Ypulse*, November 2008, http://www.ypulse .com/the-power-of-positive-thinking-how-gen-y-will-get-through- the-recession (accessed November 18, 2008).

Chapter Four

1. Marguerite Reardon, "Teens View Cell Phone as Essential," CNET .com, September 15, 2008, http://news.cnet.com/8301-1035_3- 10041377-94.html.

2. Fisch, "Did You Know," 2008 (see Chapter One, note 5).

3. *Youth Markets Alert Datafile*, 3(10) (March 11, 2009).

4. Y-Pulse, "Y-Pulse Mashup East: Engaging Viewers Through Multiple Screens," posted by Meredith, 2008, http://www.ypulse.com/ypulse- marketing-mashup-east-engaging-viewers-through-multiple-screens.

5. ExactTarget, 2008 Channel Preference Survey, May 22, 2008.

6. Consumer Electronics Association, CEA Teens and Technology Study, 2008.

7. S. Vedantam, "Social Isolation Growing in U.S., Study Says; The Number of People Who Say They Have No One to Confide In Has Risen," *Washington Post*, June 23, 2006.

8. Rochsester Institute of Technology, Survey of Internet and At-risk Behaviors, June 18, 2008.

9. OTX and The Intelligence Group, "Teens' Online Behavior," as reported in research brief: *Teens Online Buy Stuff, Prefer Reality Over Virtual Sometimes, and Have Concerns*, July 23, 2008.

10. BIGresearch, American Pulse Survey, November, 2008.

11. Mindset Media, "Mindset Media Profile of Mac Users," as reported in "Mac owners Are Just Like, Well, the Mac Guy," *Advertising Age*, 2008, www.adage.com (accessed January 28, 2008).

12. 2007 retail study by *CosmoGirl* and General Growth Properties, *The Consumer You Can't Afford to Lose*, released June 12, 2007.

13. *Internet Retailer*, "Top 500 Retailers Are Taking Up Residence on Social Networking Sites," January 14, 2009, http://www.internetretailer.com/dailyNews.asp?id=29060.

14. Fisch, "Did You Know," 2008.

15. N. Carr, "Is Google Making Us Stupid?" *The articleTitleantic*, July/August 2008.

16. G. Small, *iBrain: Surviving the Technological Alteration of the Modern Mind* (HarperCollins, 2008).

17. MacArthur Foundation, Living and Learning with New Media: Summary of Findings from the Digital Youth Project, November 2008, www.digitallearning.macfound.org.

18. D. Tapscott, *Grown Up Digital: How the Net Generation Is Changing Your World* (Columbus, Ohio: McGraw-Hill, 2008).

19. Viacom Brand Solutions International, "Golden Age of Youth," as reported in research brief: *Youth Is Not an Age*, 2008, https://www.mediapost.com/?fa=Articles.showArticle&art_aid=93951 (accessed November 10, 2008).

20. P. Underhill, *Why We Buy: The Science of Shopping* (New York: Simon & Schuster, 1999).

21. BIGresearch and Survey Sampling International, August 2008 American Pulse survey.

22. American Psychological Association, Task Force on the Sexualization of Girls, Report of the APA Task Force on the Sexualization of Girls. Washington, D.C.: American Psychological Association, 2007, www.apa.org/pi/wpo/sexualization.html.

23. Sarah Mahoney, "Teens Prefer to Shop the Mall Instead of Online," *MediaPost*, November 16, 2007.

24. Center for Media Research, "The Fractured Web Community Impacts Marketing Focus," research brief, November 6, 2008, mediapost.com.

Chapter Five

1. Bryant Ott, "Gender Lines Blurring at Retail Stores," Gallup Poll News Service, December 13, 2005.

2. Ray Smith, "Counting on Guys to Buy," *Wall Street Journal*, November 29, 2008.

3. J. Neff, "The Battle of the Brands: Old Spice vs. Axe," *Advertising Age*, November 17, 2008, http://adage.com/article?article_id=132559 (accessed November 17, 2008).

4. NPD Group, "Insight into the Youth Beauty Market," as reported in "The Tween Beauty Queen," 2008, http://www.npd.com/press /releases/press_080515.html (accessed November 5, 2008).

5. Vanessa O'Connell, "Bubble Gum at Bergdorf's," *Wall Street Journal*, February 15, 2007.

6. "Kids, The Economy and Christmas," Reuters, November 25, 2008, http://www.reuters.com/article/pressRelease/idUS37619+26-Nov-2008 +PRN20081126.

7. Experian Consumer Research, Simmons Kids Fall 2007 Full Years Study, as reported in "89% of Kids Are Computer Savvy," 2007, http://www.marketingvox.com/89-of-kids-are-computer-savvy-041983/ (accessed on November 18, 2008).

8. Ray Smith, "Fashion Online: Retailers Tackle the Gender Gap," *Wall Street Journal*, March 13, 2008.

9. L. Brizendine, *The Female Brain* (Bantam Books, 2007).

10. Underhill, *Why We Buy* (see Chapter Four, note 20).

11. B. Pellegrin, *Branding the Man: Why Men Are the Next Frontier in Retail* (Allsworth Press, 2009).

12. Wharton School of the University of Pennsylvania, Jay H. Baker Retail Initiative and the Verde Group, "Men Buy, Women Shop," as reported in "Men Buy, Women Shop: The Sexes Have Different Priorities When Walking Down the Aisles," http://knowledge.wharton .upenn.edu/article.cfm?articleid=1848 (accessed November 25, 2008).

13. TARP Worldwide, Word of Mouth poll, as reported in "Consumer Word of Mouth Changes Buying Habits 60% of the Time," 2008.

14. Retail Advertising and Marketing Association (RAMA)/BIGresearch, "Shoppers Say Word of Mouth Is Biggest Influence on Purchase of Electronics, Apparel Items," November 21, 2008, http://www.nrf.com /modules.php?name=News&op=viewlive&sp_id=606.

15. P. England, E. Fitzgibbons Shafer, and A.C.K. Fogarty, "Hooking Up and Forming Romantic Relationships on Today's College Campuses," in *The Gendered Society Reader*, ed. M. Kimmel (Oxford: Oxford University Press, 2007).

16. J. Walkowski, "Let's Not Get to Know Each Other Better," *New York Times*, June 8, 2008.

17. G. Cross, *Men to Boys: The Making Of Modern Immaturity* (Columbia University Press, 2008).

Chapter Six

1. Resource Interactive, proprietary research, 2007.

2. BIGresearch, ForecastIQ analysis, Prosper Technologies, LLC, March 20, 2009.

3. American Express Publishing and Harrison Group, *The Annual Survey of Affluence and Wealth in America*, 2008.

4. TRU-Insight, study conducted on behalf of J. C. Penney, 2008.

5. TRU Study of U.S. Teens, 2009.

6. Deloitte, The Deloitte Automotive Gen Y Survey, January 10, 2009.

7. S. Carty, "Automakers Are Listening to What Gen Y Wants," *USA Today*, January 16, 2009.

Chapter Seven

1. P. Johnson, "What Lobster Dunks Can Teach Us About Marketing to Emotions," *Advertising Age*, June 3, 2008.

2. K. Capell, "Zara Thrives by Breaking All the Rules," *Business Week*, October 9, 2008.

3. C. Hoffman, "American Apparel Exposed," *Conde Nast Portfolio*, November 2008.

4. Nip/Tuck blog, *American Apparel*, http://www.americanapparel.net /presscenter/dailyupdate/dailyUp.asp?d=30&t=1454 (accessed January 25, 2009).

5. BIGresearch, ForecastIQ analysis, Prosper Technologies, LLC, March 20, 2009.

6. S. Parise, P. Guinan, and B. Weinberg, "The Secrets of Marketing in a Web 2.0 World," *Wall Street Journal*, December 15, 2008.

7. Harris Interactive, *Consumer Acceptance of Mobile Advertising* study, May 28, 2008.

8. Mintel, *Video Games – US* study, July 2008.

9. A. Hampp, "HBO's *Entourage* Plays Wingman for Virgin America," *Advertising Age*, September 4, 2008.

10. University of Michigan, "American Customer Satisfaction Index, Q3 Scores and Commentary," November 18, 2008.

11. J. Abelson, "Sneaker Wars Are Shifting to the Smaller Sizes," *Boston Globe*, June 18, 2008.

12. Nielsen Company, "Product Placements Decline 15% in First Half," press release, September 15, 2008, http://www.nielsen.com/media/2008/pr_080915_download.pdf.

13. J. Creswell, "Nothing Sells Like Celebrity," *New York Times*, June 22, 2008.

14. B. Cummings, "Tickled Pink," *Brandweek*, September 7, 2008.

15. Ibid.

16. Tapscott, *Grown Up Digital* (see Chapter Four, note 18).

17. Karmaloop website, http://www.karmaloop.com/krp/index.asp.

18. Threadless website, http://www.threadless.com/streetteam.

Acknowledgments

We'd like to acknowledge and thank some of the many who helped us along the way.

We thank our agents, Jim Levine and Lindsay Edgecombe, who provided invaluable guidance from proposal to promotion, which included Jim's sage advice and Lindsay's important Gen Y eye. Thanks to the wonderful folks at Jossey-Bass, including our editors—Rebecca Hopkins, Genoveva Llosa, Mark Karmendy, and Kristi Hein—who were tremendously supportive throughout. Thanks to our Gen Y research assistants, especially Erin Kutz, who started with us after a USA Today internship and was working for a big-deal news service as we went to press. And a big thanks as well to Iris Stone, our über high school researcher, who was full of her own insights and is now headed off to college and, we just know, bigger things.

Kit would like to thank her colleagues at Golden Gate University for their generous support, especially Dan Angel, Janice Carter, Barbara Karlin, Terry Connelly, Paul Fouts, Tasia Neeve, Cassandra Dilosa, Frances Sadaya, and Marianne Koch. She is also grateful to her incredible students, who are a source of inspiration every single day. Most important, Kit is deeply grateful to her husband, Russ, who is the reason why she calls herself the "world's luckiest girl," and to Diana and Douglas Dykstra, Laura Faller, and Karen Berardi.

Jayne would like to thank the editors who added retail to her beat at *USA Today* and made it possible for her to take some time off to work on this book. They include Jim Henderson, Geri Tucker, Rodney Brooks, Judi Austin, and Fred Monyak. Speaking of time to write, Jayne would also like to thank her husband, Richard Willing, and her daughter, Cate, for giving her time to work as well as a lot of material to work with. And many thanks, as well, to Jack, Karen, Maggie, Hank and Jake O'Donnell; Jackie Watson; and Haley Waggener.

Many professional experts, friends, and other contacts who are not quoted by name in the book also provided invaluable insight and access. They include Ellen Davis, Scott Krugman, Kathy Grannis, Casey Chroust, Brian Dodge, Holly Davis, Scott Silverman, Chrissy Wissinger, Beth Souther, Kena Frank, Helen Clark, Marcia Smolens, Richard Rubin, Michelle Bogan, Greg Berardi, Michael Finney, Anastasia Goodstein, Tom Vacar, Jacqueline Lane, Rebecca Winter, Marcy Goldstein, Jim Sluzewski, Susan Giesen, Lena Michaud, Kevin Dugan, Vicki Shamion, Joe and Laura LaRocca, Rochelle La Rue, Alicia Nieva-Woodgate, Pam Goodfellow, Maribeth Harper, Tamara Mlynarczyk, Lisa Barrow, Mark Winter, Kevin Sterneckert, Joyce Payne, Mary Ann Milo, Christine Yarrow, Kathleen Horrigan, Carla White, Jonathan Adkins, Laura Bojanowski, Constance DeCherney, Liz Jaeger, Debi DeFrank, Catherine Mesner, Annette Haines, Maura Dolan, Todd and Peg Allen, Pete and Lauren Mitchell, Susan Buchanan, Bill Fanning, Barry Petersen, Diana Mey, Paula and Bobby Donlan, Crystal Gromer, Liz Solomon, Lisa Whitmer, Keli Twyman, Karey Quarton, Jessica Delmar, Mary Placido, Brianne Pins, Dana Harville, and Dawn Miedler.

We are grateful to the hundreds of Gen Yers and parents who opened their lives and hearts to us and made this book come alive with their stories and insights. Some didn't want their names used, so within the book they got pseudonyms, and many got pseudo-cities too. The ages stayed the same as they were when we interviewed them (if only ours could as well). Here we thank many of them, with their real names: Lowell Perry; Susan, Gordy, and Lily Heil; Caroline Regan; Anna and Ally Kraus; Leslie, Abbey, and Emily Fox; Denise, Jessica, and Theresa Fay; Sam Morley; Richard McLean; Emma Zaretsky; Alma and Josh Gill; Sinead Daly; Kristen Kroflich; Mallory and Loren Mueller; Joua Xious; Trey Dixon; Jordan Matthews; Chris Hammond; Robbie Squibb; Stacia Shewmaker; Elizabeth Godown; Maria, Janelle, and Christopher Pierson; Paul Morichetti; Kara Shaw; Eliza McKendree; Allison and Taylor Saffer; Carolyn Birkmeier; Taylor Whitsett; Ben Stevens; Michael Huber; Lee Bennett; Kate Reid; Nick Stone; Rachel Thomas; Kayleigh Burnip; Brooke Sach; Erin Reid; Ella Farahvashi; Donna Pease; Rachel, Molly, and Sara Rogers; Milynn Armistead; Tim and Mary Hurd; Wendy, Shelby, and Brody Queal; Maggie Simons; Jamie Kirsch; Sara Morgan; Jenny Gough; Geoff Kaump, Greg Clifford; Thomas Leaf; A'Jene Waters; Christopher Padgett; Jamie Seff; Rebecca Peterson; Richard Hatfield; Bobby Groves; Morgan Lipscomb; Brennan Milligan; Chris Hornick; Elizabeth Warner; Stevie Ondra; Greer Martin; Hannah Turner; Stephanie Schmitt; Austin Smith; Charlotte Guyett; Allison Buggirello; Claire Fama; Helena Kalman; Gwen Ledford; Sarah Mitchell; Ally Beran; Jessica Gibson; Sharon Schmidt; Ashlee Ferlito; Lindsay Keach; Brandon Beckerman; Kevin Hein; Ansley Whipple; Laura Heinlein; Xaiowan Chen; Julia Forrester; Isabelle Heiner; Mary Liebman; Geoff Kaump; Greg Clifford; Christina and Nick Berardi; Ben Mitchell; and Thomas Leaf.

About the Authors

Kit Yarrow is an award-winning consumer research psychologist and a professor of both psychology and marketing at Golden Gate University in San Francisco. She's taught consumer behavior at universities around the world, from Slovenia to Malaysia, including the Helsinki School of Economics and U.C. Berkeley. As a recognized consumer expert, Kit's made frequent appearances on *ABC World News*, *Good Morning America*, *CNN*, and *Marketplace*, and she's often quoted in publications such as the *New York Times*, the *Wall Street Journal*, and *U.S. News & World Report*. Her consulting clients have included General Electric, Del Monte, and Nokia. Kit lives in San Francisco with Russ, her husband and favorite golf partner.

Jayne O'Donnell is a retail and automotive reporter for *USA Today*, where she's written about subjects as diverse as the fashion challenges facing baby boomer women and teen driving risks. She has been a columnist for *Woman's Day* and has been published in a wide range of magazines including *Parents*, *Good Housekeeping*, and *CosmoGirl*. She has appeared often on TV as a shopping or car expert, including on *Good Morning America*, Fox Business Network, CNN, MSNBC, and *Live with Regis and Kelly*. Jayne has won both public service and journalism awards for her work alerting the public to auto safety hazards. She lives in McLean, Virginia, with her fiscally conservative husband, Richard Willing, and their shop-happy daughter Cate, who is nine.

Index